ISLAM'S POLITICAL CULTURE

❋ *Islam's Political Culture* ❋

RELIGION AND POLITICS IN PREDIVIDED PAKISTAN

BY NASIM A. JAWED

University of Texas Press
Austin

Requests for permission to reproduce material from this work should be sent to
Permissions, University of Texas Press, P.O. Box 7819, Austin, TX 78713-7819.

♾ The paper used in this book meets the minimum requirements of ANSI/NISO
Z39.48-1992 (R1997) (Permanence of Paper).

LIBRARY OF CONGRESS CATALOGING-IN-PUBLICATION DATA

Jawed, Nasim A., 1940–
    Islam's political culture : Religion and politics in predivided
Pakistan / by Nasim A. Jawed. — 1st ed.
        p.   cm.
    Includes bibliographical references and index.
    ISBN 0-292-74079-4 (cl : alk. paper). —
    ISBN 0-292-74080-8 (pbk : alk. paper)
    1. Islam and state—Pakistan.   2. Islam and politics—Pakistan.
3. Pakistan—Politics and government.   4. Religion and state—
Pakistan.   I. Title.
BP173.6.J38   1999
320.5'5'09549—dc21   98-53899

For my wife, NILOFUR,
and my children, FERHAAN, SHEEREEN, ISMAH, *and* MOHSIN

Contents

List of Tables

Preface

This book examines Islamic views of some major political issues and investigates the political ideological dimension of Islam. As a historical case study, it deals mainly with predivided Pakistan (1947–1971).

The character of the study is defined by its two attributes. First, it employs, simultaneously, a social scientific approach, as well as a humanistic perspective. Departing somewhat from the standard practice of examining mainly the published writings of Muslim intellectuals, this work includes the findings of a survey I conducted in Pakistan in 1969. It studies the survey's empirical findings vis-à-vis Muslim political ideas reflected in Islamic texts, both traditional and contemporary. Second, despite its relative brevity, the work aims to provide answers to most major political ideological questions. It probes pointedly, yet broadly, the major Islamic positions on critical issues.

The discussion is organized around three major topics: the attitudes toward national identity, the polity, and the economy. Following a brief introduction, chapter 2 discusses the first major topic. It describes the three types of "nationalistic" orientations—Islamic, secular, and "Islamic-cum-patriotic"—that the survey indicated and discusses their association with the sociocultural background of the respondents as well as with the recent historical experience of Pakistan and Bangladesh. Chapter 3 discusses the contemporary Muslim understanding of the purpose of the state, the form of government, the process of legislation, and the relation between Islam and democracy. Chapter 4 assesses the relative popularity of the three types of economy (free, socialist, and mixed), describes their various Muslim conceptualizations, and explores the cultural and historical reasons for the appeals of socialistic and free economies. Chapter 5 highlights normative pluralism in contemporary Islam and concludes the study with a review of some notable approaches in the current literature concerning issues treated in this work.

Acknowledgments

Part of chapter 4, including some findings of the survey conducted for this work, appeared originally in my article "Islamic Socialism: An Ideological Trend in Pakistan in the 1960's," in the journal *Muslim World*. I thank Hartford Seminary Foundation for permission to use the material contained in the article.

I would also like to thank the Asia Foundation of San Francisco for providing a travel and research grant that made possible a year's fieldwork in Pakistan. Needless to say, the positions taken in this work are this writer's alone.

Several of my colleagues at California State University, Chico, read part or all of the manuscript. I am grateful to Joanna Cowden, Carl Peterson, Larry Bryant, Robert Cottrell, and Laird Easton for their valuable suggestions and comments. I am also grateful to Provost Scott McNall for his interest in the work.

Nancy Riley, retired secretary of the History Department at Chico State, more than proofread the manuscript. Sharon Casteel and Lois Rankin at the University of Texas Press supervised the book's publication. Mary M. Hill did the copyediting. I am thankful to all for their professional advice and gracious assistance.

Over the long years of my interest in Islamic, Middle Eastern, and South Asian studies, I have learned from many teachers, friends, and associates. I would like to acknowledge my academic and personal indebtedness especially to those with whom I worked at the University of California, Los Angeles, and at the University of Chicago: Fazlur Rahman, Gustave von Grunebaum, Georges Sabbagh, Stanley Wolpert, Leonard Binder, Nikki Keddie, and Speros Vryonis, Jr.

Last, but not least, I am grateful to my wife, Nilofur, and my children, Ferhaan, Sheereen, Ismah, and Mohsin. Their inspiration and help made the completion of this work possible. The book is lovingly dedicated to them.

A Note on Transliteration

A simplified version of the standard transliteration method is employed in the text for spelling Arabic, Persian, and Urdu terms. The objective is to maintain a middle ground between simplicity and technical precision, to render foreign terms more or less exactly without compromising readability of the printed text. The following practices are employed to achieve this objective:

1. No diacritical marks are employed in personal and institutional names.

2. For transliteration of terms, diacritical marks are used somewhat sparingly:

    a. The diacritical underdot—used in formal texts for such Arabic letters as the guttural h and velar s, d, t, and z—is dispensed with altogether.

    b. The macron (ˉ) is employed consistently for the long vowels ā, ū, and ī.

    c. The symbols for *ain* (ʻ) and *hamza* (ʼ) are included when they occur in the middle of a word, excluded when the sounds they represent occur at the beginning or the end of a word (for example, *sharīʻa;* but *ulamā,* not *ʻulamāʼ*).

ISLAM'S POLITICAL CULTURE

1 ✴ *Introduction*

ISLAM AND POLITICAL ISSUES

"In Islam," said Sir Muhammad Iqbal, the poet-philosopher of Islam (d. 1938),

> it is the same reality which appears as the church from one point of view and the State from another. . . . The essence of *tawhīd* [mono-theism] as a working idea is equality, solidarity and freedom. The State from the Islamic standpoint is an endeavor to transform these ideal principles into space-time forces, an aspiration to realize them into a definite human organization.[1]

Other Muslims, as well as Western scholars of Islam, have noted the ideal of the so-called unity of church and state in Islam. Commenting on the classical Muslim understanding of Islamic political values, Bernard Lewis writes:

> For Muslims, the state was God's state, the army God's army, and, of course, the enemy was God's enemy. Of more practical importance, the law was God's law, and in principle there could be no other. The question of separating the church and state did not arise, since there was no Church, as an autonomous institution, to be separated. Church and state were one and the same.[2]

The reality of premodern Muslim politics—of caliphate and sultanate, of dynastic monarchy and tribal solidarity, of the *millet* system (the communal organization of society along religious boundaries) and the communal law—changed long ago in many Muslim lands; and the medieval Muslim sciences, literature, and education that sustained traditional Islam have by and large fallen into disuse, at least among the modernized sections of

Muslim society, which long ago replaced the traditional secretaries, administrators, and generals who along with the higher *ulamā* (scholars of traditional Islamic sciences) once played the role of elites in the Muslim societies.

Yet, during the past quarter century, numerous political developments across the Muslim world have dramatically pointed to a reassertion of Islam's political culture. The success and resilience of the Islamic revolution in Iran; the fierce, long, Afghan military resistance conducted as *jihād* against the Russian-controlled government in Afghanistan; the devastating strife between the secular military government and the Islamic popular opposition in Algeria; as well as progressive revival of some traditional Islamic laws in Pakistan, Egypt, and Malaysia are testimonials to the resilience of Islamic political sentiment and the resurgence of its traditional political values in these modern times. The current resurgence of Islam, however, is far from monolithic. It has theological, cultural, as well as political dimensions, and the political ideas and values associated with it are themselves enormously diverse.[3]

In the popular media most Islamic sociopolitical developments are frequently attributed to a vaguely defined "Islamic fundamentalism." In many journalistic writings, the term is ill-defined, its use often indiscriminate. The reckless use of the term in the popular media usually presents a simplistic view of contemporary Islamic ideas and movements and masks the important diversity in values and attitudes among contemporary Muslims. More seriously, in some political commentaries such an indiscriminate use of the word does not just obstruct a correct understanding of contemporary Islam, it leads to a distortion of reality and reinforces sensationalism.[4] The term has, therefore, lost whatever value it initially had in identifying a particular orientation within Islamic religion.

The fact is that even without its current popular misuse, the term "fundamentalism" is an unhappy choice for labeling what one seeks to identify in the Islamic context. Originally borrowed from studies of modern Christianity, the term could be reasonably employed to designate only a parallel development in Islamic religion. However, the ideas associated with the term "fundamentalism" in Western Christianity are mainly theological: the nature of God, the virgin birth, the physical resurrection of Christ and his physical second coming, the infallibility of the Scriptures, the substitutional atonement.[5] By contrast, what divides the so-called Islamic fundamentalists from liberal Muslims is mainly their understanding of Islam's social and political values. Disagreement on theological matters—such as the nature of God, the nature of prophecy, and the Qur'ān as the revealed message of God—is rare. Indeed, even the discussion of theological issues is minimal in the serious writings of twentieth-century Muslims. The two major pre-occupations of Muslims in the twentieth century—first the struggle for independence from European colonialism, then confronting the problems of nation building—have directed their intellectual energies mostly into political and ideological, rather than theological, matters.

The political and ideological debates among contemporary Muslims are mainly a quest to understand and resolve the sociopolitical problems that the Muslim societies have been facing. These debates point to a Muslim reaffirmation of some traditional elements of Islam's political culture; at the same time, these debates have produced some Islamic political ideas that are essentially new. The task of understanding the contemporary Muslim ideas is made doubly difficult by the fact that contemporary Muslims some-times employ traditional Islamic terms for new, untraditional ideas; con-versely, they sometimes use modern terms for traditional Islamic concepts. Iqbal's statement quoted above is in itself an example of assigning new meanings to old terms.

Clearly, then, if one seeks to understand Islamic political ideas and atti-tudes of contemporary Muslims, one must empirically learn their exact na-ture and character before associating them with any conventional political orientation, compare the observed attitudes with classical Islamic political ideas for clarity and perspective, and measure quantitatively the extent of their popularity among contemporary Muslims.

This work is offered as a contribution to such an empirical and analyti-cal study of contemporary Islamic political culture. As a case study, it deals mainly with Islamic political attitudes in predivided Pakistan (1947–1971). The main concern of this study is only those attitudes and values for which Islamic support is claimed. Occasionally, however, it does take notice of secular attitudes, essentially for the benefit of a perspective in which the Islamic political attitudes might be placed. The attitudes studied here are related to three major topics: national self-identity, political system, and economic order.

The main goal of each search is to discover the ideas and values held by contemporary Muslims in the land of the study's concern and to learn the

Islamic justification claimed for them by their holders. Two aspects of the attitudes are discussed here. From a qualitative perspective, the discovered attitudes are described and elaborated on; usually they are also compared with premodern traditional Islamic attitudes on the subject in order to register any departures from traditional Islamic forms. From a quantitative perspective, the relative popularity of the attitudes among the *ulamā* and a section of the modern educated "new middle class" is explored.

Besides describing the individual attitudes toward various political issues, the study also seeks to discover any clusters of attitudes and values that may be upheld by individual Muslims. Whenever appropriate, it presents the discovered attitudes in relation to the main orientations in each of the three major areas of its inquiry: national identification, political system, and economic order.

What this work does *not* deal with may also be noted here. It neither deals with historical political events per se nor seeks to study the attitudes in their strict chronological order. It does, however, trace historical development of some attitudes. Islamic political institutions and organizations are not, as such, the subject matter of this study. Finally, although this study quotes political views and ideas of several contemporary Muslim intellectuals who tend to lead certain contemporary Islamic schools of thought, it does not seek an exhaustive description of the thought of any such intellectual. Once an attitude or an orientation is adequately elaborated and illustrated in the following chapters, no further attempt is made to comprehensively describe the position of every single intellectual.

As a study of Islamic attitudes in predivided Pakistan, this work provides the ideological backdrop that partially explains two major political developments that took place in that country.

The first of these political developments was the dismemberment of Pakistan itself. In December 1971 Pakistan was divided. A new Muslim country—the contemporary Bangladesh—emerged in what was formerly East Pakistan. The survey conducted for this study two years prior to the division found secular political ideas substantially more popular in what became Bangladesh than in the former West Pakistan. This study outlines the extent of the disagreement between the middle-class professionals in the two regions on specific Islamic political issues—a disagreement that, although not the main cause of Pakistan's breakup, nonetheless played its role in widening the mutual alienation of the two regions that finally resulted in dismemberment of the original Pakistan.

The other major historical development is even more directly related to Islamic political values. Since the mid-1970s Pakistan has been enhancing its formal political commitment to "Islamic ideology." It has been incrementally changing its laws in an effort to make them consistent with Islamic norms and values and has created formal judicial institutions to examine and evaluate any laws that are challenged as repugnant to Islamic injunctions. It now implements Islamic laws concerning intoxicants and some crimes and collects part of the Islamic welfare tax, *zakāt*, through governmental agencies.[6] This process of "Islamization"—most vigorous under the rule of General Mohammad Zia-ul-Haq (r. 1977–1988)—has been interpreted by some observers as politically motivated: partly a shrewd effort to legitimize the military control of the country under the late General Zia, partly a pragmatic political strategy to buttress the nation-state.[7] Undoubtedly, such political considerations have played their role in the move toward "Islamization" and continue to do so. Yet most of these observers grant that the legal and institutional Islamization took place not in a vacuum but in the milieu of some Islamic political ideas. Indeed, the recurring, almost persistent willingness of governments in power, as well as of many political parties in opposition, in Pakistan to project themselves as supporters of Islamic ideals itself attests to the wide appeal of Islamic political culture among the general populace in Pakistan. As Anita Weiss notes: "Islamization programs and political motivations are interwoven throughout the Muslim world. In many areas, the reaffirmation of Islamic laws and values into the state infrastructure is seen as a way of defining national identity in the postcolonial world."[8] This work defines and highlights the ideological backdrop of legal and institutional "Islamization" in Pakistan.

Since this study deals mainly with predivided Pakistan, the nomenclatures of its two former provinces, West Pakistan (for postdivided Pakistan) and East Pakistan (for contemporary Bangladesh) have been frequently used here. Occasionally, East Pakistan's current name, Bangladesh, is appropriate in some contexts.

Despite its regional and historical focus, however, the subject matter of this study encompasses several important topics related to Islamic political attitudes as they become prominent in many Muslim countries around the globe. Statistical distributions of Islamic political ideas across social classes doubtless differ from country to country, but the issues, the positions, and the reasonings are often similar across the Muslim world. Theoretically, only empirical studies, conducted periodically in different Muslim societies,

can determine reliably the exact popular understanding of specific ideas—
as well as the precise range of popularity of such ideas—across various
strata in those societies. Such empirical studies, based on field surveys,
are, however, extremely difficult to conduct. The subject is sensitive, the
concept of survey research unfamiliar, and the governmental regulations
inhibitive. Together they often create circumstances in which even the best-
intended scholarly efforts become suspect. It is, therefore, not surprising
that despite a large number of works on contemporary Islamic resurgence,
survey-based studies of the subject are extremely rare. In view of the serious dearth of such studies, therefore, the findings of this empirical study
can contribute—in appropriate cases—to our general understanding of
Islam's political culture in the contemporary Muslim world at large.

The issues discussed here are indeed part of larger contemporary debates. The positions, the attitudes, the arguments, the perspectives represented here come from the actual discourse of Muslims recorded during a
moment of great political importance. These arguments and statements, as
well as the hopes and the apprehensions they reflect, illuminate the typical
problems experienced by Muslims in constructing modern states. They
illuminate further the common, though mutually divergent, Muslim reac-
tions to democratic values and modern governmental institutions, as well
as to some important economic practices and institutions.

SOURCES AND METHODOLOGY OF THE STUDY

This study is based on two types of sources: one, those tracts, articles,
and essays written by Muslims that are expressive of their beliefs, views,
and values concerning matters political and Islamic. The majority of such
writings from which the study quotes were published during the thirty-
four-year existence of predivided Pakistan (1947–1971), with which this
study mainly deals; however, in a few cases, when it was felt that a prevalent contemporary attitude would be best illustrated by the statement of
Dr. Muhammad Iqbal (d. 1938), who seems to have immensely influenced
the contemporary Muslim attitudes in Pakistan, his statements in years
prior to the creation of Pakistan are quoted. In some relevant instances,
documents published after 1971 have also been quoted here.

The second major source on which this work is based is the data collected through a survey that this writer conducted in undivided Pakistan
from January to July 1969. A sample of 163 persons was selected from four

occupational categories according to the method described below. The occupational categories belonged to two social classes: practicing lawyers, university teachers, and journalists from the modern educated "new middle class"; and the *ulamā* from the traditional religious leadership. For the purpose of this study, "*ulamā*" as a social category are defined as those scholars of Islam who have received a mainly traditional Islamic education in traditional Islamic schools (*madāris*) and who are either teaching in such schools or hold positions of *imāms* (leaders of congregational prayers) in mosques. Conversely, the new middle class is seen as consisting of those who have received a mainly nontraditional education in modern colleges and universities and who hold occupations associated with the nontraditional sector of the economy. These categories were chosen because they represented the most vocal and influential sectors of their classes in matters ideological.

The interviews obtained from these 163 individuals have been used here for quantitative analysis. An additional thirty-one persons were selected more purposefully for special interviews. The responses of these thirty-one individuals have not been included in quantitative analyses and statistical descriptions presented in the following chapters. It must be stated at the outset that even the 163 persons whose responses are quantitatively analyzed here did not strictly constitute a true probability sample. The distribution pattern described in this study, and the generalizations based on them, should be viewed in the light of this limitation. A probability sample was very much desirable, but in view of the lack of all relevant information on the population strata of this survey—*ulamā,* lawyers, university professors, and journalists—it was an ideal extremely difficult to achieve. Furthermore, the practical problems of unavailability or unwillingness of the selected elements would have greatly taxed the time and resources of the researcher. Considerations of economy along with serious limitations of survey research in such a country as Pakistan almost dictated the terms. However, familiarity with the conditions and behavior of the population strata was used to the advantage of the study as much as possible. The selection of respondents was made in the following manner.

For *ulamā,* four major mosques each in Lahore and Karachi (Pakistan) and Dacca (now part of Bangladesh) were selected, their *imāms* approached and interviewed. If the *imām* of a chosen mosque was not available, that of another major mosque was approached. In every one of the three cities, two major *madāris* (traditional religious schools) were visited and one or more of their senior instructors interviewed. "Major" mosques were considered to be those that stood out in every one of the three cities for their size and attendance as well as the centrality of their location. These three criteria usually tended to conjoin in the three cities. (The obvious exception to this rule, however, was the historic mosque whose big size was not necessarily paralleled by either big attendance or central location.) "Major" *madāris*, too, were taken to be those that were bigger in size in student attendance than others in the same city. A total of twenty-nine *ulamā* respondents were interviewed: twelve in Dacca, eleven in Lahore, and six in Karachi.

As for lawyers, it is a common practice among them in Pakistan to wait in halls adjacent to the courts between hearings. This was found to be the best place to approach lawyers practicing at district courts and high courts of Karachi, Lahore, and Dacca and to make appointments with them for subsequent interviews. Of the total of forty-five lawyers, ten were interviewed in Karachi, twelve in Lahore, and twenty-three in Dacca.

For professors, the universities of Karachi and Dacca as well as two colleges in Karachi, one in Dacca, and three in Lahore were visited. Of these, one college in Karachi and one in Lahore were exclusively for women, and they also had a predominantly female faculty. In Pakistan most colleges do not have individual offices for their faculty. The common faculty halls, where the faculty waited between their lectures, therefore provided the meeting ground. Of the total of forty-seven professors, ten came from Karachi, eighteen from Dacca, and nineteen from Lahore. Within each city the numbers were roughly equally distributed among the educational institutions visited there.

For the journalists, three leading dailies each in Karachi, Lahore, and Dacca were selected and their offices visited. Of these, one newspaper in Lahore and one in Dacca were published in English; the rest were published in Urdu in Karachi and Lahore and in Bengali in Dacca. At each office, one senior editor, two subeditors, and, whenever available, two reporters were interviewed. Of the total of forty-two journalists, fourteen were from Karachi, nine from Lahore, and nineteen from Dacca.

Of these 134 professionals, then, 60 were interviewed in Dacca, 40 in Lahore, and 34 in Karachi.

Apart from these regular respondents, eight politicians, ten Islamically oriented intellectuals, eight civil servants, and five members of the religio-political group Jamaat-i-Islami were also interviewed. Their responses have occasionally been quoted here to illustrate some attitudes, but since these respondents were purposefully selected, their responses were neither quantified nor treated the same way as the sample of the regular 163 respondents who were chosen according to the above-described method.

The following politicians and intellectuals were interviewed: Shaikh Mujibur Rahman and Dr. Kamal Husain, who later became the first prime minister and the first foreign minister of the newly independent Bangladesh, respectively; Muhammad Hanif Ramey and Mian Mumtaz Daulatana, who served as chief ministers of the Punjab province at different times. Among the intellectuals were Dr. Fazlur Rahman, the former director of the Islamic Research Institute, Pakistan; S. A. Rahman, a former chief justice of Pakistan; Abul Hashim, the director of the Islamic Academy, Dacca; Mawlana Zafar Ahmad Ansari, former secretary of the board of Talimat-i-Islamiyya, Pakistan, who later chaired a national commission for making recommendations to the government of General Zia-ul-Haq for a new constitution for Pakistan (1977–1988); Inamullah Khan, secretary of Mutamar al-Alam al-Islami, Karachi; Shaikh Muhammad Ikram, director of the Institute of Islamic Culture, Lahore; Allama Allauddin Siddiqi, chairman of the Islamic Advisory Council of Pakistan; and three other members of the council, one of whom, Dr. Halepota, later became the director of the Islamic Research Institute, Islamabad. Among those civil servants who were interviewed were the director of the Civil Service Academy, Lahore; the directors of the Bureau of National Reconstruction and the Department of Awqāf of Punjab; and the deputy director of the Bureau of National Reconstruction, East Pakistan. Members of the Jamaat-i-Islami were all from Karachi and included a former head (*amir*) of the Karachi branch. Briefer, informal interviews were also conducted with the founder and the late president of the Jamaat, Mawlana Abul Ala Mawdudi, as well as with Professor Khurshid Ahmad, then a member of the Jamaat's Advisory Council. All but one of these special interviews were conducted by the author. Of the 163 regular interviews, twelve were conducted by three graduate students, the rest by the author.

The interviews were fully structured in the case of the regular 163 respondents and nearly so in case of most of the rest. A written schedule (later referred to in this work as the "questionnaire") was used from which the interviewer read to the respondents. The questionnaire included 100 substantial questions on various Islamic and political issues; some questions were open-ended, others were closed. Of the total of 100 questions, responses to only forty-six questions have been analyzed here. Others — most of which dealt with subjects such as the conceptions of the "East" and the "West," as well as an understanding of Islamic morality — are not included in this study. An additional 29 questions sought to determine various social properties of the respondents. The reduced questionnaire is reproduced in Appendix A.

The interviews usually lasted from one and a half to two and a half hours, and some were taken in two installments. Abbreviated notes were taken by the interviewer along with checking the appropriate boxes on the answer sheet which he kept on hand. Except for those respondents who expressly permitted identifying their statements by their names, the responses have not been identified in the following chapters.

The reduced questionnaire sought to discover attitudes related to five major topics: national self-identity, the polity, the law and legislation, economic relations, and morality. The major questions in all of the first four areas were: What public goals, institutions, policies, regulations, or arrangements did the respondents desire? How did they see those desired elements vis-à-vis their own understanding of Islamic demands and teachings? How did such elements compare with a traditional, that is, premodern, understanding of Islam?

The questions on "national" identity explored specifically how the respondents conceived of their "nation": what they considered its bases, which groups were the objects of their loyalty and how were such loyalties ranked by them, in what sense was the concept *umma* (Islamic "nation") understood, and what were respondents' views toward any sort of world Muslim unity.

The questions on the polity sought to discover the perceived necessity, functions, and ultimate goals of the state. The questions explored respondents' understanding of the Islamic political system, investigating specifically what were considered to be the characteristic features of an Islamic state; to which western political system was the Islamic political order considered close in spirit; how was the latter seen to differ from, or resemble, democracy. Questions on law and legislation sought to ascertain respondents' understanding of Islamic character of the law in predivided Pakistan, their views on the desirability of Islamizing the law, and their choice of the method in accordance with which the law could be Islamized as well as their choice of the agency to which such Islamization could be entrusted.

The questions on economic matters explored the perceived elements of the Islamic economic system as well as the characteristics of the economic orders desired by respondents, especially with reference to ownership and the production and distribution of wealth. The questions examined further respondents' views toward Islamic socialism, *zakāt* ("poor tax"), and bank interest.

The questions on morality solicited respondents' feelings about the religious (or nonreligious) character of their motive for what they considered moral behavior, their sentiment toward supporting some aspects of religious morality with legal sanction, and their understanding of the demands of religious morality and civic virtue in certain matters.

The last section of the questionnaire dealt with personal and social background. It noted such social properties of respondents as income, marital status, mother tongue, and the types of communities in which they grew up. One set of questions sought to assess the extent of social and cultural traditionality/modernity of respondents, and another set the amount of social change they underwent in two generations.

Because of the variety and complexity of responses that were received for many questions, as well as to facilitate computer-aided data analysis, many questions were divided to yield several variables each; other, simpler questions were translated into single variables. All variables were assigned names and captions for identification. Appendix B indicates which of these (primary) variables are related to which questions of the questionnaire. The specific responses covered by every one of these variables, too, are identified by names and short captions. After the specific answers (i.e., raw data) received in response to specific questions were rendered into primary variables and their values, additional composite variables were then constructed on the basis of primary variables in order to explore major aspects of this study. These new composite variables, too, were assigned names and captions. The composite variables were often achieved by collating and combining the raw data.

Most of the tables included in the following chapters present distributions or demonstrate correlations of these composite variables, rather than distribution of the raw data. The raw data themselves are presented mostly in the form of repository tables in Appendix C.

2 ❋ *Islam and National Identification*

In view of the many definitions of the term "nationalism," a discussion that makes use of it must begin with an explanation of what the writer means to convey by it. For the purposes of this chapter, nationalism may be defined as essentially consisting of two elements: one, a feeling of identity with a group of people; two, a desire to achieve or maintain the political independence of the group with which one identifies and, thus, to draw and secure the boundaries of the sovereign state where that group lives.[1] However, a departure from this use of the term in this chapter may occur when it is used with an adjective, for example, Islamic national identity, or when it is used within quotation marks. In these instances "national" is equated with "collective."

For nationalists, securing and maintaining their nation-state constitutes a categorical imperative. For them it is an inner command that must be followed. Thus, nationalists give their loyalty to their nation-state simply for the sake of their nation, and they give it unconditionally.

It is often said that Islam is in itself a sort of nationalism, in which *umma Muhammadiyya* (the Muslim community) occupies the place of the nation. According to the traditional, widely accepted theory, Islam requires of the Muslim community that at least some persons from amongst the community actively seek to create a state and secure its boundaries. And Islam, too, demands from its followers political loyalty to this state. However, between Islam and modern nationalism there are two major differences. First, *umma Muhammadiyya* is considered by the Muslims to be a community of faith, that is, of rational choice, while a nation is considered by the nationalist to be a natural community to which one belongs merely by virtue of being born in it. Second—and this is more important than the first difference—traditional Islam demands that a state fulfill the practical needs of the *umma.* The prevalent Sunnī tradition in medieval Islam saw the state merely as an expedient, a necessary means to secure conditions in which each Muslim could work for his own individual salvation. Traditionally, a Muslim gave his loyalty to the state either for this reason or for the law and order that the state provided and that he needed to protect his life and property so that he would be able to engage in social and economic pursuits. Such utilitarian reasons appear secondary to true nationalists.

Despite these differences, the demands of nationalism and Islam are similar enough to make them rivals. The two are rivals, first, because both demand the primary loyalty of their followers. Although it is probable that in certain conditions the interests of both Islam and nationalism converge, there remains a theoretical possibility of their mutual conflict. Second, both Islam and nationalism offer to their followers objects for self-identification. And here, again, although it is possible that in rare times the boundaries of the national community coincide with boundaries of the Islamic community, in actual circumstances one is usually wider than the other.

Discussing the historical expansion of nationalism across the globe, Benedict Anderson asserts: "Nation-ness is the most universally legitimate value in the political life of our time." He argues that "nation-ness" or nationality is "capable of being transplanted to varying degrees of self-consciousness to a great variety of social terrains, to merge and be merged with a correspondingly wide variety of political and ideological constellations."[2] Anderson's work provides an important analysis of the history of nationalism in Europe and includes many cogent arguments in support of the secularization theory. However, unless one takes "nation-ness" in a very general sense of "communal solidarity," it does not appear to be the most universally accepted legitimate value in the Islamic world. There is unquestioned, universal support in the Islamic world neither for nationalistic reasoning nor for nationalistic sentiment. Obviously, a majority of contemporary Muslim governments, as well as many Muslim individuals in the contemporary Muslim world, accept the basic principles of nationalism. Many other Muslims living in the same contemporary Muslim societies, however, reject the nationalist notions emphatically. Still others support various syncretic ideas that represent, indeed, a "merging"—in one sense or another—of the old and the new, the religious and the secular, the ideological and the territorial criteria of nationhood.

This chapter seeks first to assess how much real (i.e., modern secular) nationalism existed among the Muslims in undivided Pakistan and to what extent rival political loyalties—old or new, Islamic or secular—occupied the minds of its peoples. Second, it analyzes the theories that the Pakistanis and their Muslim predecessors in British India developed in an effort to reconcile the conflict they may have felt between national and Islamic loyalties. Finally, it examines the social and historical factors that may have given rise to these various conceptions of collective identity. The following discussion of these issues includes findings of the survey that the author conducted in predivided Pakistan. (The survey is described in Chapter 1; the questionnaire employed in the survey is reproduced in Appendix A.)

THREE TYPES OF NATIONALISTS

The survey findings, as well as an analysis of Muslim writings in contemporary Pakistan and Bangladesh, affirm a glaring diversity of Muslim views on issues related to Islam and national identity. The survey explored several select dimensions of this subject; its focus of inquiry, however, was on two questions. (1) What was/were the object/s of each respondent's personal loyalty and national identity? (2) What did he/she desire to be the basis of Pakistani nationhood?[3] A study and analysis of the answers to these and other questions pointed to the presence of three types of "nationalists": the "Islamic nationalists," the "secular nationalists," and those who occupied a middle ground between these two whose position, for lack of a better term, could be called "Islamic-cum-patriotic."[4] The following describes some characteristic views associated with these three main types of "nationalists," distinguishes the subtypes among them, and notes their numerical distributions among traditional *ulamā* and the modern professionals. (For numerical distribution of the three main types, see Table 2.1.)

The "Islamic nationalist" solely or predominantly identifies with his Islamic faith and desires to see it as the only real collective bond among his Muslim countrymen. He rejects all other bases of nationhood as unworthy or threatening to his Muslim identity.

A fundamental assumption of the "Islamic nationalist" is that the factors that constitute the so-called natural communities have little significance for human beings, who are rational. Race, color, language, and birthplace are accidents of life. The only real basis of nationhood ought to be weltanschauung. The following passage illustrates such thinking:

TABLE 2.1
TYPE OF "NATIONAL" IDENTITY UPHELD BY
THE *ULAMĀ* AND THE PROFESSIONALS

| Social Category | *Type of Professed National Identity* | | | |
	Islamic	*Islamic-cum-* Patriotic	Secular	Row Total
Ulamā	24	1	0	25
	96.0%	4.0%	0.0	17.7%
Professionals	47	28	41	116
	40.5%	24.1%	35.3%	82.3%
Column Total	71	29	41	141
	50.4%	20.6%	29.1%	100.0%

For separate distributions of the professionals in East and West Pakistan, see Table 2.4.
Missing observations: 22.

My nationhood does not consist in the color of my skin or the texture of my hair or the language in which my mother spoke to me words of love when I was a little child. My nation is derived from my way of looking at the universe and awareness of my place in it. . . . I am deeply grateful that I was made aware of it by the first man of my nation — Muhammad, son of Abdullah, who was born in Arabia.[5]

To many Islamic nationalists it was not a matter of choice for the Pakistanis whether to build their nationhood on the foundation of Islam or on a common and truly secular cultural heritage: the latter, in their view, simply did not exist. Shariful Mujahid, a professor of journalism and director of the Quid-i-Azam Academy, wrote:

Our past is potently influenced by Islam. Our cultural heritage is Islamic; our social and moral code is no other. Our memories are all, again, Islamic: they revolve around either the triumphs or humiliation of Islam and its arms in the subcontinent. We rejoice at the victories won by M'ahmud Ghaznavi, Shihabuddin Ghori and Ahmad Shah Abdali; we mourn the annexation of the Punjab by the Sikhs, the defeat of Tipu Sultan and the humiliation of Sirajuddawla. We exult over the pride in the sacrifices that we made for the cause of freedom and of

Pakistan. On the other hand, we mourn the hundreds of thousands of Muslims butchered in cold blood by the enemies of Pakistan. Which means, our past is so far largely, if not wholly, Islamic. . . . Islam alone is the primary and most pronounced factor in making us into a nation: it is the basic sentiment in drawing and linking us.[6]

Even in the postdivided Pakistan, the Islamic nationalists continue to reject the cultural heritage of pre-Islamic Mohenjodaro and Gandhara civilizations, which flourished in the regions that now constitute Pakistan, as alien to Pakistanis:

Historically, we had no connection with those cultures. They left not even the faintest traces which could be found in our current national cultural heritage. . . . Those cultures had perished much before the arrival of Islam. . . . Indeed, the only culture which we have inherited is the one which was brought to Pakistan first by Muslim Arab conquerors and then by Muslim Afghans, Turks, and Iranis, and to this day that cultural heritage has the full imprint of Islam upon it.[7]

Islamic nationalists also continue to be critical and apprehensive of territorial and ethnic nationalisms. The following passage by Dr. Yousuf Abbas Hashimi, who frequently participated in television and radio discussions on Islamic matters, represents their concern:

When Western conception of selfish and narrow nationalism splits asunder Muslim social, political and economic morality, one can well imagine the further plight of the *millet,* divided by tribal, racial, parochial and territorial loyalties.[8]

One can survive plague and nuclear destruction but racial and parochial hatred must lead a community to total extinction and annihilation. . . . I dare say, that if we do not identify ourselves with the supreme and the noblest ideal, the *tawhīd,* conditions are bound to get worse and we shall, may Allah forbid, lose our honor and existence.[9]

Most of the "Islamic nationalists" regard the period of *khilāfa rāshida* (rule of the "rightly guided" caliphs who succeeded the Prophet Muhammad in leadership of the Muslim community in the seventh century A.D.) to be the golden age of their national history from which they seek inspiration and guidance. Almost all of the *ulamā* and a large majority of other "Islamic nationalists" of our sample considered it to be such. The few "Islamic nationalists" (ca. 13 percent) from the middle-class professionals who did not regard the period of *khilāfa rāshida* to be the golden age of their nation's history were in most cases Shī'ī Muslims, whose religious doctrine includes rejection of the first three caliphs as illegitimate.

Ninety-five percent of the "Islamic nationalists" of our sample claimed that the term *umma* indicated not simply a brotherhood of faith but also a community of ideals, requiring common political effort. About half of the "Islamic nationalists" (47 percent) would like the formation of some kind of Muslim commonwealth consisting of all Muslim countries of the world, while about 42 percent of them would like greater cooperation among the Muslim countries than that which exists today. Yet both of these groups held the formation of one great, unitary state of all the Muslims of the world to be either undesirable or an unachievable ideal under contemporary conditions. Only about 7 percent of the "Islamic nationalists" (the majority being from the *ulamā*, of whom they constituted about 17 percent) would still like to work for the formation of the greater Muslim state. But at the same time, just a few (5 percent) among the "Islamic nationalists" (all from the middle-class professionals) desired absolutely no Muslim political unity of any kind.

At the opposite pole from the "Islamic nationalists" were the "secular nationalists." They either rejected Islam totally or, in most cases, saw it strictly as a matter of personal, not national, identity. Beyond this, however, the "secular nationalists" were divided among themselves on various issues. The survey indicated at least four subtypes among them. (For numerical distribution of the various subtypes, see Table 2.2.) Two of their subtypes rejected all kinds of nationalism, for they declared their loyalties either to their economic class or to humanity at large and claimed to identify themselves mainly with one or the other of them.

The third subtype regarded secular culture and language of their own region to be the basis of their nationality. The respondents who thus boldly declared their secular, provincial identity in predivided Pakistan were a small minority (16 percent). However, it may be noted that even in 1969, before the division of Pakistan, their frequency in what is now Bangladesh was ten times higher than in the former West Pakistan. This group has been designated as "regional secularists" in Table 2.2.

The fourth subtype—"Pak-secularists"—regarded either the political

TABLE 2.2
SUBTYPE OF "NATIONAL" IDENTITY UPHELD BY THE *ULAMĀ* AND THE MIDDLE-CLASS PROFESSIONALS

Social Category and Region	Type of Professed National Identity							Row Total
	Islamic-cum-Patriotic			Secular				
	Islamic	Pak-Islamic	Regional Islamic	Economic Class	Humanist	Regional Secular	Pak-Secular	
Ulamā, East and West Pakistan	24	0	1	0	0	0	0	25
	96.0%	0.0	4.0%	0.0	0.0	0.0	0.0	17.7%
Professionals, West Pakistan	39	10	6	4	3	1	3	66
	59.1%	15.2%	9.1%	6.1%	4.5%	1.5%	4.5%	46.8%
Professionals, East Pakistan	8	6	6	6	2	8	14	50
	16.0%	12.0%	12.0%	12.0%	4.0%	16.0%	28.0%	35.5%
Column Total	71	16	13	10	5	9	17	141
	50.4%	11.3%	9.2%	7.1%	3.5%	6.4%	12.1%	100.0%

Missing observations: 22.

union that Pakistan was or the land of which it consisted as the foundation of their national identity. Again, though in minority in both the former "wings" of Pakistan, the occurrence of this subtype was six times greater in the former East Pakistan than in West Pakistan. Several "Pak-secularists" felt that though Pakistan did not yet have a national secular culture, such a culture would evolve in due course.

A large majority of secular nationalists held that "no period of our history can be regarded as golden, we must look forward rather than backward." Given their theoretical position, this is of course understandable. What is surprising is that almost half of those who belonged to "Pak-secularists," rather than "regional secularists," still held that *khilāfa rāshida* was the golden age of their past national history and a source of inspiration to them. If this did not reflect the extent of the confusion of some "secular nationalists," it must have indicated their helplessness due to the absence of those factors that are usually considered the bases of secular nationalism. Undivided Pakistan consisted of two, if not five or more, great ethnic groups. It had neither a wholly contiguous territory nor a substantially common secular culture, and it had experienced relatively short periods of history under common government. Only religion was common, but the secular nationalists necessarily rejected religion as a national bond. Yet so close is the association of early Islamic history with Islamic faith and so strong the legend of the just and righteous rule of the *rashīd* caliphs for the average believing Muslim that even a secularist Muslim cannot help identifying with it, even at the cost of inconsistency.

Most secular nationalists (ca. 71 percent) claimed that the *umma* was only a community of faith and simply a brotherhood of the Muslims of the world: it implied no political union. They desired no special relation with other countries merely because such countries happened to be Muslim and would reprove the "Islamic nationalists" for the latter's aspiration to world Muslim unity. As one secular nationalist puts it: "Idealism and cheap fraternalism have no place in international politics, and when we talk of a Muslim commonwealth based upon religion we neglect the past history of Islam and failure of previous attempts. Only a prophet would be able to organize the people under one banner and a prophet is never to come." [10]

Occupying the middle ground between the "Islamic nationalists" and the "secular nationalists" were those who saw no disparity between Islam and nationalism. Allama Alauddin Siddiqui, who was chairman of the Islamic

Ideology Council for several years during the government of General Ayub Khan, represented the feelings of many such "Islamists-cum-patriots" in Pakistan when he said:

> There is a strong misunderstanding that Islam, being an international and universal system of collective and co-operative living, is against nationalism. . . . No doubt the philosophy of life preached by Islam is universal, but Islam is not unmindful of the importance of a home for a family and a country for a nation. Usually we prefer going to the extreme in the consideration of the question of nationalism and universalism, or realism and ideals. To the protagonists of the idea of Pakistan, a homeland was the concrete demand, and universal peace and justice was the ideal for the propagation and preparation of which geographical entity was essential. The two considerations do not clash with each other as is sometimes feared. It is rather a very fortunate aspect of our national struggle that it is not without an "ideal" or "ideology." [11]

The "Islamists-cum-patriots" of our survey either identified with both Islam and secular objects, conceding to them their own specific places in national identity and integration, or they saw no difference between the two identities, holding them to be two aspects of the same national reality. The former approach (identifying with both Islam and a distinctive national culture) in its simplest form is represented by statements like the following:

> Our nationhood and our very existence as a political personality are entirely dependent upon Islam. "If we let go the ideology of Islam," says Dr. I. H. Qureshi, "we cannot hold together as a nation by any other means. . . . If the Arabs, the Turks, the Iranians, God forbid, give up Islam, the Arabs yet remain Arabs, the Turks remain Turks, the Iranians remain Iranians, but what do we remain if we give up Islam?" Islam no doubt is the unifying force in Pakistan but, in addition to this, our socio-cultural reactions and responses, our rituals and ceremonies, our family life, our respect for elders, our aversions to the tyranny of race, color and caste, our sense of tolerance, our pride in our past, our aspirations and hopes for the future, give us a distinctive stamp which is peculiarly our own. . . . All the above-mentioned characteristics and attributes are not found anywhere outside Pakistan in

any society, Muslim or non-Muslim. It is a combination of all these different facets of our life which is our identity and which we cherish and wish to preserve and pass on to our posterity.[12]

Some of the theoretical conceptualizations that illustrate the second approach—that Islamic faith and fatherland represent, in one way or another, two aspects of the same national reality or pursue the same national goals—are discussed below, in the next section of this chapter.

Among those who occupied the "Islamic-cum-secular" position, two subtypes were noted: one, the "Pak-Islamist," who identified with Islam along with the land or the political union of Pakistan; and the other, the "regional Islamist," who identified with Islam along with the culture or the land of his own region within the union. About 56 percent of both the regional Islamists and the "Pak-Islamists" held the period of the *rāshida* caliphate to be the golden era of their national history, while about 40 percent declared that none of the past national history could be regarded as golden.

The majority of "Pak-Islamists" in West Pakistan (60 percent) desired world Muslim cooperation or formulation of a Muslim commonwealth, while the two-thirds majority of "Pak-Islamists" in what is now Bangladesh wanted no special relations with other Muslim countries merely because they happened to be Muslim. Also, almost all "regional Islamists" in West Pakistan as well as the former East Pakistan desired no special relations with other Muslim countries.

SUPRANATIONAL ISLAMIC IDENTITY AMONG THE *Ulamā*

Table 2.1 presents numerical distribution of the three types of "nationalists" among the *ulamā* and the modern professionals. Two major points are indicated by the table. First, all but one of the *ulamā* held supranational Islamic identity; the *ulamā* of the former West Pakistan and what is now Bangladesh held similar views of their national identity (and therefore their numbers have been combined in the table). Second, among the modern professionals all three types were found—secular nationalists and Islamic nationalists, as well as the Islamists-cum-patriots.

How can one explain these differences? To begin with, what can explain the supranational Islamic identity of the *ulamā* and their remarkable consensus? What would explain the fact that all of them held the period of

khilāfa rāshida to be the golden age of their history and that all desired political unity of the Muslim World, though they differed somewhat on the
question of the extent of such unity?

To explore the association of the professed beliefs of respondents with
their social background, the author collected a wide variety of data about
their age, income, type and extent of education, medium of instruction, language of habitual reading, type of family, relation to and interest in kinship
group (*birādarī*), and province of residence. In most of these personal
characteristics—age, income, type of family, relation to and interest in kinship group, mother tongue, and region of residence—the *ulamā* differed
considerably among themselves. None of these characteristics were, therefore, found associated with the common views of the *ulamā*. A social property of the *ulamā* that—along with their occupation of traditional religious
instruction or mosque *imamate* (i.e., leading the congregational prayers)—
they shared completely was their traditional religious education. To this
alone, therefore, would one attribute the consensus of the *ulamā* in uphold-
ing Islamic national identity. However, inasmuch as the traditional Islamic
education is what sets the *ulamā* apart from the modern educated professionals, statistical or cross-tabular correlation of it with their Islamic identity amounts only to revealing the obvious. One would, therefore, want to
go a step further to explore how traditional Islamic education brings forth
the *ulamā*'s traditional Islamic identity and their remarkable consensus.

The typical *ālim* (singular of the term *ulamā*) is generally trained in traditional Islamic sciences at a *madrasa* or *dar al-ulum* (religious school or
seminary). All of the *ulamā* of our sample were trained at such seminaries.
These traditional religious schools differ greatly from one another in quality of instruction, degree of organization, and number of students. However, the curriculum at all the traditional schools in West Pakistan and
contemporary Bangladesh was, and continues to be, about the same. It includes studies of *hadīth*, *tafsīr* (interpretation of the Qur'ān), *fiqh* (traditional Islamic jurisprudence), and training in Arabic grammar and language. The texts are predominantly either of medieval origin or in the
medieval tradition. Instruction takes almost no notice of modern developments in natural and social sciences or of Western humanities. After the
completion of their studies, the bulk of the *ulamā* confine their reading to
traditional Islamic literature, which elucidates and reinforces the Qur'ānic

teaching that a Muslim's real identity is his faith and that differences in race and color are merely for social recognition.

The belief that the age of the first four caliphs was characterized by piety and justice in the highest degree became well accepted by the Sunnī Muslims in early Islamic times, and the period came to be called *khilāfa rāshida* (rightly guided caliphate). The belief in the excellence of this early period of the Islamic state was reinforced by what became the standard Islamic interpretation of history. According to that interpretation, the Prophet Muhammad's apostolic mission is seen as the climax of the march of history, after which came the anticlimax. Those who lived with and witnessed the Prophet Muhammad (i.e., his companions, or *sahāba*) are seen as the best of humanity and their times the best of times; those who saw the companions (i.e., the *tabi'ūn*) and the time in which they lived are regarded as the second best, after which, according to a *hadīth,* darkness was to engulf mankind.[13] This belief in the progressively deteriorating condition of humanity was reinforced by social instability and a profusion of sectarian violence in early Islamic history, but once it found a place in the religious— particularly *hadīth*—literature it acquired permanence. The more peaceful and happier times that followed the first two turbulent centuries of the Islamic era dimmed the darkness theme, but the idea that the *sahāba*'s was the best of times survived.

The influence of such developments aside, the historical fact is that justice, piety, and simplicity—to traditional Muslims the main qualities of an ideal Muslim ruler—were possessed by the first four caliphs (r. A.D. 632– 661) to a far greater degree than by most other Muslim rulers after them. Indeed, after the first four caliphs government became a possession of the families that often fell short of these qualities. It is but natural, therefore, that the pious Muslims would look back to those days with longing and with a great sense of respect. In the early Islamic history such respect was accorded only to the caliphate of the first two caliphs, Abu Bakr and Umar; later, in the typical conciliatory spirit of Sunnī Islam, the next two— Uthman and Ali—were also included on this list in deference to the Shī'ī sentiment for Ali and pro-Uthman sentiment of the Umayyads. Thus a mixture of fact, desire for sectarian reconciliation, and such contributory intellectual motifs as the Muslim view of history created and have sustained the belief that the period of the first four caliphs constituted the golden age of the Muslim past, and this belief has been perpetuated by Islamic literature, particularly by *hadīth*. Anyone who defines her or his national identity as "Islamic" naturally comes to regard that period as the best of her nation's past, which she considers to be the best period in Muslim history. All those who are educated in the traditional Islamic humanities are naturally most conscious of this equation.

Traditional Islamic literature also reflects the ideal of the political unity of the Muslim community. As has been noted by many writers on Islamic political theory, this ideal, as an ideal, persisted in Islamic history despite the actual political disintegration of the community. At the same time, however, for all practical purposes the reality of multiple sultanates came to be recognized after the fall of the Abbasid caliphate (A.D. 1258), if not earlier. Henceforth, and actually even before the fall of the Abbasid caliphate, the main concern of the *ulamā* came to be that the Islamic law (*sharī ʿa*) be enforced in the country and that the ruler be of the Islamic faith, so he may be relied upon to defend the Muslims against any non-Muslim aggression. Actual political unity of all Muslim lands continued to be only an ideal, but so long as the defense of the Muslim lands could be maintained by individual Muslim princes, the *ulamā* were reconciled to the multiplicity of Muslim states in medieval Islam.

Today's Muslim states are similar to those of the past in that these, too, are actually ruled by separate independent governments. But between the two there is one important difference. In medieval times, though Muslim states were many, citizenship for the Muslims residing in different states was one. A Muslim, unlike a non-Muslim, needed no visa (*amān*) to visit or reside in another Muslim country. He or she enjoyed the same legal status as native-born Muslims and a more privileged one than that of native-born non-Muslims. He could be given jobs that were theoretically denied even to the native-born non-Muslims. But in the modern nation-states, the Muslims of different countries are faced, except where regional arrangements have been concluded, with the usual limitations of foreigners, which severely restrict their physical mobility and socioeconomic activities. Even the performance of such a religious duty as *hajj* often requires a passport and a visa and, in some countries, the special permission of one's own government, which may further restrict the number of pilgrims in an effort to save foreign exchange.[14]

From today's perspective, therefore, even the reality of medieval political organization has become an ideal, albeit a less demanding ideal than that of creating a single Muslim state. Seen from this angle, the differences among the *ulamā* concerning the extent of Muslim world unity still reveal their significant agreement on the undesirability of such matters as the current mutual alienation of Muslims, restrictions on the number of pilgrims the Muslim nation-states allow each year, and the lack of concerted defense against the non-Muslim enemies, whether real or imaginary. All the *ulamā* of the survey sample, irrespective of the extent of Muslim world unity they desired, cited one or several of these reasons for their positions, though many of them also saw one political community of all Muslims as a necessary corollary of oneness of their faith. In this sense they all reflected the traditional ideal.

"NATIONALIST" ORIENTATIONS AMONG THE MIDDLE-CLASS PROFESSIONALS

If the traditional Islamic education of the *ulamā* perpetuates their supranational Islamic identification, what causes the new middle-class professionals to embrace their Islamic or secular national identity? Are there any variables significantly associated with the identities of these professionals? The survey found that age, occupation, and gender had no relation with either the secular or the Islamic identity professed by the middle-class professionals. Given the limited variation of monthly income of the professionals of the survey sample, economic status, too, made little difference. City of residence within the former West Pakistan (Lahore or Karachi) was also found to be of little consequence.

As could be expected, a lack of faith in Islam as a religion was found associated with a secular conception of collective identity, but the reverse association was much weaker: whereas most (84 percent) of the nonbelieving Muslims professed one of the four subtypes of secular "nationalism," only a small minority of all the "secular nationalists" were actually nonbelievers. (Only about 10 percent of *all* the professionals professed nonbelief in Islam as a personal faith.)

The frequency of the Islamic nationalists was found to be 28 percent higher among those professionals who migrated from India than among the native-born respondents (59 percent vs. 31 percent) and 19 percent higher than the overall frequency of the Islamic nationalists within the total sample of professionals (59 percent vs. 40 percent). Controlling the province of

TABLE 2.3
TYPE OF PREDOMINANT EDUCATION BY TYPE OF PROFESSED
"NATIONAL" IDENTITY AMONG *ULAMĀ* AND PROFESSIONALS

| Type of Predominant Education | Type of Professed National Identity | | | Row Total |
	Islamic	Islamic-cum-Patriotic	Secular	
Traditional	20 95.2% 28.2	1 4.8% 3.4%	0 0.0 0.0	21 14.0%
Equally Traditional and Modern	6 66.5% 8.5%	0 0.0 0.0	3 33.3% 7.3%	9 6.4%
Modern	45 40.5% 63.4%	28 25.2% 96.6%	38 34.2% 92.6%	111 78.7%
Column Total	71 50.4%	29 20.6%	41 29.1%	141 100.0%

Missing observations: 22.

residence did not much alter these relative differences. This is, of course, understandable. Almost all the migrants came to Pakistan around the time of the partition of the Indian subcontinent in 1947. Some of them left the places of their birth under pressure of communal riots and thus were painfully reminded of their Muslim identity even if they had not been conscious of it before. Theoretically, those who suffered because of communal frenzy could either turn against religious communalism itself or identify even more closely than before with their religious community. However, the fact that the incidence of the Islamic nationalists is indeed somewhat greater among the migrants indicates that the climate of thought prevalent at that time made most of them embrace their Islamic national identity rather than reject it. Other migrants who, without any pressure whatsoever, left their homes to reach Pakistan are likely to have already believed in their Islamic national identity.

Table 2.3 cross-tabulates the respondents by the types of their predominant education and professed national identity. It will be noticed that whereas almost all of those who received high, predominantly traditional Islamic education (i.e., the *ulamā*) hold supranational Islamic identity, only 59 percent of those who received modern education professed wholly or partly secular identity (34 percent totally secular and 25 percent "Islamic-cum-patriotic").

Obviously, traditional education is most likely to lead to a supranational Islamic national identification, but modern education in an Islamic or partly Islamic cultural milieu is not equally likely to lead to secular identification. Under the cultural circumstances that prevailed in Pakistan in 1969, modern education was found associated definitively with the lack of consensus on the nature of Pakistan's national identity. Its association with totally secular identification was weak, particularly if the two former provinces of Pakistan are treated as a whole.

DIFFERING ORIENTATIONS IN THE TWO FORMER "WINGS" OF PAKISTAN

Treating East Pakistan and West Pakistan separately, it was noted that a majority (60 percent) of the modern educated professionals of the survey's sample in what is now Bangladesh indeed professed secular "national identity." However, in West Pakistan an equal majority (60 percent) of the modern educated professionals professed Islamic, not secular, identity (see Table 2.4).

Despite the weak association between modern education and secular identity in West Pakistan, the influence of modern education on national self-identification is still significant since there were some "secular nationalists" among the modernly educated but none among the traditionally educated. Furthermore, if the numbers of those who upheld a partly secular identity are added with those who professed a wholly secular identity, they add up to about 40 percent in West Pakistan as against only 9 percent among the traditionally educated there. Other things being equal, the thrust of modern education would, of course, be toward secular identity. Supporting a union based on faith, "Islamic nationalism" implies a division of citizens into Muslim and non-Muslim, full and partial, or "natural" and contractual members of the state. Conversely, the ethos of modern Western social sciences and humanities—despite considerable racism in

TABLE 2.4
TYPE OF "NATIONAL" IDENTITY UPHELD BY THE MODERN
EDUCATED PROFESSIONALS IN THE TWO FORMER
"WINGS" OF PAKISTAN

Category of Respondent	*Type of Professed National Identity*			
	Islamic	*Islamic-cum Patriotic*	*Secular*	*Row Total*
Professionals, East Pakistan	8 16.0%	12 24.0%	30 60.0%	50 43.1%
Professionals, West Pakistan	39 59.1%	16 24.2%	11 16.7%	66 56.9%
Column Total	47 40.5%	28 24.1%	41 35.4%	116 100.0%

Missing observations: 18.

Western societies—is largely egalitarian, their orientation mainly secular. Both tend to lead toward a secular definition of citizenship and, therefore, of nationhood.

Other things, however, are not equal. Past history as well as present political, social, and general conditions may thwart, alter, weaken, enhance, hasten, delay, or otherwise modify the impact of modern Western education. It is in the light of these factors, therefore, that one might search for an explanation of the sharp contrast between the self-definitions of the modern educated middle-class professionals in West Pakistan and what is now Bangladesh. The contrast, noted above in Table 2.4, is evidenced, on the one hand, by a greater incidence of those in the former East Pakistan who described their nationality in terms of their country or ethnic group, not in terms of their Islamic faith (ca. 60 percent vs. 16 percent), and, on the other hand, by a greater incidence of those in West Pakistan who rested the foundation of their nationhood on their Islamic faith, not on ethnic group or territory (ca. 16 percent vs. 59 percent).

Though the secular national identity of some professionals, as already noted above, was associated in West Pakistan as well as in East Pakistan with lack of religious faith, the absence or presence of faith in itself can explain neither the higher frequency of the "secular nationalists" in East Pakistan than in West Pakistan nor the lower incidence of the "Islamic nationalists" among the professionals in East Pakistan than among similar professionals in West Pakistan. These differences and their relative proportion, indeed, remained significantly unaltered when the test variable on religious belief/unbelief was controlled. The immediate reason, therefore, has to be that most Bengali Muslims conceive of the social functions of religion differently from West Pakistanis. There are several reasons for this.

Historically, Islam was introduced in Bengal by the Sufis at a time when the power of the Muslim military was not securely established over the entire region. The character of Bengali Islam therefore reflected both the pliancy of the Sufi and his latitudinarian attitude toward Islam's social and political institutions. The culture of the traditional Muslim elite, that is, the *ulamā*, the generals (*umarā*), and the secretaries (*kuttāb*), was less infused among the general Muslim population, and, therefore, the ideological hold of the traditional Islamic culture over the minds of Muslim Bengalis was tenuous. In this sense, the position of the traditional Muslim elite in Bengal was weak, as was also the legalistic Islam. Furthermore, Bengal is geographically remote from the Middle East, which in the past was the locus of central, legalistic Islam, and frequently supplied scholars, administrators, and soldiers to such outlying areas of the Muslim world as India in the east and the Balkans in the west. In times of disintegration of Muslim India, Bengal was cut off from the source of human carriers of traditional Islamic outlook that would have reinforced the central, legalistic Islam.

The reverse is the story of West Pakistan. Historically, a greater part of this region was conquered by the Muslims first; the religion spread later. The *ālim* and the *qhazi* commander together established the social institutions of the Islamic *sharī'a*. Although here, too, the Sufis subsequently played an important role in spreading Islamic religion, the converts they won for Islam soon internalized the kind of Islam that they saw around them—one characterized by a relatively strict regard for the letter of the law and for the political supremacy of Islam. The development of a militant sense of Muslim paranationalism in the area was encouraged and perpetuated as the area became recruiting grounds for a line of Muslim military commanders who, either from their bases in Afghanistan and Turkestan or from the imperial capital at Lahore, Delhi, or Agra, invaded various regions of the Indian subcontinent that were predominantly populated by the

Hindus. Geographic contiguity with Afghanistan and Iran made possible a continuous flow of Muslim professional soldiers and civil servants as well as merchants and the *ulamā* who perpetually reinforced the central, legalistic Islam, which was already stronger in West Pakistan and in the urban areas of Delhi and Uttar Pradesh than in Bengal. Thus both the legalistic Islam and the traditional Islamic elite were strong in these regions.

With the coming of the British rule, the traditional Muslim elite was weakened everywhere in India, but in varying degrees. In Bengal it disintegrated not only earlier but also to a greater extent than in what came to be West Pakistan. Bengal was the first major province the British East India Company began to rule in the eighteenth century. Since the British East India Company took over the government from the Muslims, whom the British in the first part of the nineteenth century still considered a political threat, the company and the British civil servants followed a policy of active discouragement of the Muslims.

Again, the story of West Pakistan is different. Much of it was subjugated by the British in the nineteenth century at a time when the policy of active discouragement of the Muslims was about to be given up after the Indian War of Independence in 1857. Because British interest in the region was predominantly military, the British Indian government strove for significantly fewer cultural and intellectual changes in that area than in Bengal. In particular, the princely states were left alone after the 1857 war. Of the major Muslim princely states, several were located in West Pakistan, none in Bengal. Survival of the traditional elite meant survival of the traditional outlook, which, among other things, resisted ideological secularism. In Bengal, conversely, ideological secularism had a better chance of being accepted because of the weakened tradition.

In the survival of the traditional outlook in West Pakistan but in its further weakening in Bengal, language played a critical role. Persian and, to a lesser extent, Arabic were the literary and religious languages of premodern Muslim India. English became the language of administration in India in the nineteenth century. The places of Arabic and Persian as religious and literary languages came to be filled by local Indian languages, which until then had been either provincial dialects or mainly confined to light poetic, rather than serious scholarly, use. Among the several languages that came to prominence were Urdu and Bengali. The literature written in these two languages differed as much in thought-content as in linguistic characteristics.

Under the circumstances that prevailed in Bengal in the late eighteenth and early nineteenth centuries and under which the traditional Muslim elite disintegrated, the new literary medium, Bengali, became mainly a medium of Hindu, not Muslim, renaissance. This is evident from Bengali books written in the nineteenth and twentieth centuries as well as from Bengali journals. The contribution of the Bengali Muslims to Bengali literature is assessed to be as little as 5 percent. Thus the educated Bengali Muslims were unable to read and understand Persian, and their own language, which they read and understood, carried Hindu or secularist sentiment. The language that to some extent became the medium of the renaissance of Muslim Bengal was English, as is clear from the writings of two early modernist Muslims, Khuda Bakhsh and Sayyid Ameer Ali (1848–1928). To read English, though, required English education, and English education tended to inculcate liberal, secularist ideas. It is not surprising, therefore, that both these Bengali Muslim reformers upheld a secular, liberal interpretation of Islam.

Urdu, the new medium of serious intellectual dialogue and scholarly essay, was, from the beginning, mainly a medium of Muslim culture. It had been used for some time for poetical expression by the Muslims of northern and central India. As Arabic and Persian receded into obsolescence from the nineteenth century on, Urdu took their place in both religious and nonreligious literature. The close association of Urdu with Muslim culture is clear from both the content and authors of Urdu books from the nineteenth century to the present.[15] While it is true that the Aligarh school, with its liberal and secularist orientation, contributed one major stream of the new Urdu literature, it was only one such stream. The majority of Urdu writings reflect traditional Islamic values. So powerful was the traditional Islamic sentiment of the readers of Urdu literature that liberal essays in the Urdu language succumbed under its pressure. This is indicated by the decreasing number of liberal Islamic writings from their peak around the turn of the twentieth century to the 1930s. In the 1930s the "progressive literature" (*taraqqī pasand adab*) emerged to become a prominent movement within the modern Urdu literature; the secular liberal or secular socialist ideas in Urdu literature never reached the same level or acquired the same influence as in Bengali literature. Urdu continues to be a major vehicle of revivalist and traditional Islamic thought.

Urdu is closely related to Punjabi; according to many Pakistani historians of the language, it originally developed from Punjabi.[16] With the pass-

TABLE 2.5
LENGTH OF INSTRUCTION IN ENGLISH BY PROFESSED NATIONAL IDENTITY

| | Type of Professed Identity | | |
English-Medium Score	Traditional, Supranational Islamic	Nontraditional, Wholly or Partly Secular	Row Total
(A) West Pakistani Professionals English at Two or All Three Levels	8 47.0% 33.0%	9 53.0% 25.0%	17 28.3%
English at One Level Only	16 37.2% 67.0%	27 62.8% 75.0%	43 71.7%
Column Total	24 40.0%	36 60.0%	60 100.0%
(B) East Pakistani Professionals English at Two or All Three Levels	0 0.0 0.0	8 100.0% 20.5%	8 16.7%
English at One Level Only	9 22.5% 100.0%	31 77.5% 79.5%	40 83.3%
Column Total	9 18.75%	39 81.25%	48 100.0%

ing of traditional education in Persian and Arabic, Urdu became the literary language of the Punjab and, to lesser extent, of the Northwest Frontier Province. But Urdu is only distantly related to Bengali. It is not surprising, therefore, that though the British established a school at Fort Williams at Calcutta for the training of English civil servants in Urdu, the knowledge of Urdu among the educated classes in Bengal decreased with time, while in the Punjab it increased. This is again indicated by the publication of a growing number of Urdu books and journals in Lahore and their decreasing number in Calcutta throughout the present century.

The use of Urdu in place of Persian or Arabic in Delhi and Uttar Pradesh and in the region that became West Pakistan encouraged the continuation of traditional and revivalist Islam. In Bengal the recession of Persian and the emergence of Bengali greatly weakened the traditional Islamic outlook, an outlook that, for the historical reasons discussed above, was never as strong as in West Pakistan. Thus, both Bengali literature and the English education in Bengal supported a nonreligious orientation toward political institutions and statecraft.

This background explanation demonstrates that the kind of Islam that came to prevail in what is now Bangladesh was secularist—religion being understood as mainly a matter of personal experience and piety—while that which persists in West Pakistan is relatively nonsecular, that is, a religion that requires not only personal but also social and political demands. Yet this statement does not demonstrate why the majority of educated Bengali Muslims prefer a secular national identity. Indeed, they preferred a Muslim national identity about half a century ago, as shown by their support of the Muslim League and its two-nation theory before the partition of the subcontinent. However, the modern educated Bengalis discovered after the creation of Pakistan that to many modern educated West Pakistanis, particularly from Punjab and Karachi, an acknowledgment of Muslim identity implied a commitment to Islamic *sharī'a*. The Bengalis also discovered that the West Pakistani politicians, being aware of the strong Islamic sensitivities of West Pakistani masses, were all too ready to commit themselves to an Islamic state in order to bolster their own weak political support there. Furthermore, when the Bengali grievances grew over what the Bengali Muslims regarded as inequities and injustices, they perceived West Pakistani politicians as offering them not justice and redress of their grievances but lectures on Islamic solidarity. The Bengalis, therefore, believed that Islam was being used by the insecure and unfair governments in predivided Pakistan to deceive the people of both the former East Pakistan and West Pakistan. For example, in 1961 an East Pakistani intellectual, Dr. Syed Sajjad Hussain, lamented that "some people think that constantly reiterated emphasis on Islam might well serve as a substitute for practical measures on the material level in the interest of national integrity. . . . Many of us have exploited religious idealism in order to mask our inefficiency, misdeeds and our lack of faith in a national purpose." [17]

Thus, the young, new political leadership and the educated classes that emerged in East Pakistan in the 1950s and 1960s came to distrust all talk of

Islam—not only as a guide to political action but also as a basis of national identity. Doubtless, the inclination of the Bengali Muslims toward a secular interpretation of Islam made it easier, under such circumstances, to opt for a secular national identity.

After the separation of Bangladesh from Pakistan in 1971, one major grudge against West Pakistani "exploitation under the cover of Islamic solidarity" was removed, and soon Bangladesh began to perceive an over-bearing attitude from India. As a consequence, Bangladesh has developed increasingly friendly relations with Pakistan and has actively cultivated close relations with other Muslim countries as well. Islam is now conceded a greater share in the definition of its national self than it was allowed im-mediately following the separation. However, despite a relatively enhanced Islamic national awareness, Islam does not—and most likely will not—play as significant a role in political ideological matters in Bangladesh as in post-divided Pakistan, due in part to the historical and cultural reasons dis-cussed above.[18]

THE ISLAMIC-CUM-PATRIOTIC ORIENTATION

Table 2.4 demonstrates that, unlike the distribution of the Islamic na-tionalists and secular nationalists, which indicated widely different patterns in their proportional strengths in West Pakistan and East Pakistan, the frequency of the "Islamists-cum-patriots" was about the same (24 percent) in the two former provinces of Pakistan. Upon cross-tabulation of the "Islamic-cum-patriotic" attitude with the personal background and social properties of those who held it, it was noted that in both regions they were generally better off economically than the other two types of "nationalists." In Bangladesh, the "Islamic-cum-patriotic" attitude was found associated with migration from Indian Bengal. Perhaps the latter association is more significant than that of income. In both associations, however, the number of cases was too small to allow a generalization.

Perhaps an analysis of the thinking of the "Islamists-cum-patriots" would be more fruitful than a discussion of their quantitative distribution, since, of the three types of "nationalists," it is they who most feel the simul-taneous attraction of both Islam and nationalism. Faced with the problem of reconciling the rival claims of the two, they are seeking a new approach to collective identification.

Reconciliation involves several emotional and practical conflicts for anyone who experiences the two claims. Is one a Muslim first, or first a citizen of his country? What is the prime object of his devotion and sacrifice? Would not, for example, fighting and giving one's life for the honor or glory of one's linguistic or ethnic group amount to reverting to the days of *jāhiliyya* (i.e., "ignorance," or pre-Islamic tribal values)? Would not this be following the example of Abu Jahl (leader of the anti-Islamic forces against the Prophet Muhammad in the seventh century A.D.)? No doubt it was his consciousness of these conflicts that made Muhammad Iqbal, the eminent poet-philosopher (d. 1938), declare: "In tāza khudāōn men barā sab se watan hay; / Jo payrahan is kā hay voh madhhab kā kafan hay." Translated rather literally, the couplet means "Fatherland is the greatest of the new deities, whose garment is made of the shroud of religion."

The second aspect of the conflict between Islam and nationalism pertains to the relationship between Muslim and non-Muslim citizens of a country, as well as the relationship between the Muslims within and the Muslims outside the country. From a strictly traditional Islamic point of view, all Muslims, irrespective of their country and ethnic or linguistic attachment, are equal to one another and are like brothers. The non-Muslims are considered outside the Muslim community, even though they may live in the same country or belong to the same linguistic group as the Muslims. A well-accepted *hadīth* (saying of the Prophet Muhammad), "Al-kufr milla wāhida," has been traditionally understood to mean that all nonbelievers constitute but one community (i.e., basically different and separate from the Muslim community). In other words, there is a conflict between the universalism of Islam and the parochialism of nationalism in their attitudes toward the community of faith. But looking from the other side of the same phenomenon, it is a conflict between the liberalism of territorial nationalism and the sectionalism of Islam in their attitudes toward geographical or ethnic communities. For the great bulk of the Muslims of the Indian subcontinent who, before 1947, supported the creation of Pakistan, the demand for Pakistan resulted from their awareness of the differences between the two types of communities—based on faith and country—and from their preference of the former over the latter. Thus, Urdu-speaking Hindus from Delhi or Uttar Pradesh were taken by the Urdu-speaking Muslims of the same areas as being outside their community, but Pushtu- or Baluchi-speaking Muslims, from far-off provinces, are their compatriots.

The third aspect of the conflict between Islamic and national identities is related to delimiting state boundaries and defining foreign policy goals. If the only politically significant bond is Islam, why should not there be only one great Islamic state instead of several Muslim nation-states? If Islam is the true religion of God for the salvation of all Muslims, not to say of all humanity, then why should a Muslim state seek to pursue what are commonly regarded as national interests? Every one of these problems has been felt by the Muslims of the world with varying degrees of vagueness and intensity ever since modern nationalism began to attract them around the turn of the century.

That the Pakistanis have been faced with the problem of resolving these conflicts is reflected in their efforts to convince themselves and their fellow Muslims that there exists no problem of inconsistency between Islam and patriotism. Dr. Mahmud Husain (d. 1975), a former education minister and vice chancellor of Karachi University, obviously having in mind the Iqbal couplet quoted above, said in a seminar gathered in Dacca, East Pakistan, in 1961 to discuss problems related to national integrity: "To argue that religion has lost its place in the heart of man because the false gods have come to occupy it, is in a sense to misunderstand the nature of religion as well as that of nationalism." [19] That Dr. Husain felt the need to stress that Islam and nationalism were compatible only indicates the uncertainty of his audience. Further evidence for the pressure of such uncertainty and of awareness of the conflict between the two loyalties comes from numerous essays written by Pakistani Muslims to prove the consistency or inconsistency of Islam and nationalism.

How, then, have the Pakistani Muslims sought to reconcile Islam with nationalism? One finds several theories and patterns of arguments that they have developed to achieve a reconciliation of Islam and nationalism. Some of the theories can be traced back to the beginnings of the modern history of Muslims of the Indo-Pak subcontinent.

Apart from secularism, which reconciles Islamic and national loyalties by relegating Islamic identity to merely a personal level and which, therefore, repudiates the political significance of Islam altogether, one of the first Muslim attempts toward reconciling the two identities was made through what is commonly known as communalism. British rule, together with the gradual introduction of representative institutions in the subcontinent, presented the Muslims with an unfamiliar situation. Having lost their hegemony over India, they could no longer identify with the state, and being outnumbered by the Hindus in many areas, they had little chance for proportionate representation through general elections. The solution of this problem was found in separate electorates for the Hindus and the Muslims and in reserved quotas of community in the representative bodies of British India. The two communities thus assumed a political character. As the common subjugation to British rule along with similar Western education brought awareness of a common Indian nationality to some Hindus and Muslims, defining the respective places of the two loyalties, Indian and Islamic, became necessary. It was then, particularly during the years of World War I and immediately following it, when the Hindu-Muslim cooperation was strongest, that the difficult question was raised whether one was first a Muslim or an Indian.

Continuation of British rule in India solved this problem of categorically assigning priority to one or the other. The political activities and policies that were to become a bone of contention between Hindus and Muslims were temporarily hidden from view because of their preoccupation with securing from the British home rule for India and concern for the fate of the Ottoman caliph as the head of Islam. Upon being asked whether he was first a Muslim or an Indian, Muhammad Ali Jawhar (d. 1931), leader of the *khilāfat* movement of 1919–1924, replied that he was an Indian first, second, and third and at the same time a Muslim first, second, and third. So far as the question of political independence of India was concerned, he was an Indian first and last; but where the political rights of his own community within and without India were involved, he was a Muslim first and last. Such assigning of spheres of identities and zones of loyalties through the mechanism of communalism was thus one of the earliest methods of avoiding the conflict of national and Islamic loyalties.

In a sense, modern communalism resembled strikingly the traditional *millet* system (from *milla*, Arabic for religious community) with which the Muslims had long been familiar and which partly accounts for their quick and widespread acceptance of modern communalism. However, there was an important difference between the new communalism and the old *millet* system. Ironically, the Muslim *milla* was the least self-governing of all the *milla*s in the traditional Muslim state. While the past Muslim ruler allowed non-Muslim *milla*s certain rights in civic and fiscal matters and left the internal government of those *milla*s largely in their own hands, he mostly withheld such allowances from the Muslims. Under the autocratic rule of the sultans, this meant that the political participation by common Muslims in the affairs of their own community would be minimal. But by the rules of modern communalism, the method of representation approved by the British government was elective. The participation of the members of each community was progressively increased in British India as voting qualifications were liberalized. Paradoxically, therefore, the loss of imperial Muslim power and the introduction of representative institutions in British India made the Muslim community a more self-governing and politically participating nationality than it had been in most of its historic past.

The second major mode of reconciliation of Islamic and national loyalties that was also developed during the *khilāfat* years and later maintained by Jamiyyat al-Ulama-i-Hind and by those religiously oriented Muslims who stayed with the Indian National Congress even after the breakdown of the *khilāfat* movement was to show that nationalism was supported by the teachings of Islam itself. The argument followed two approaches. In its simplest version, it was no more than quoting the *hadīth:* "Love of the homeland is a part of one's faith" [hubb al-watan min al-īmān]. The *hadīth* is old, but a new meaning came to be assigned to the phrase "love of homeland." In the first place, the medieval Muslim understood *watan* to be the town or district where he was born and usually lived and not the entire country of his birthplace. In the second place, the two propositions of the nationalist—one, stating his identity, and the other, stating his demand for political independence and securing the boundaries of his nation-state—have no logical link with each other. The second proposition does not necessarily follow from the first. Obviously, the medieval Muslim did not primarily identify with his country, but even if he did, he was still one step removed from modern nationalism.

Despite the nonpolitical intent of the *hadīth,* however, it has been used in earnest to justify the political demands for self-rule and for the formation of a nation-state. And Indo-Pakistani Muslims were not the only ones who found political guidance in it. Turks and Egyptians much before them had used it either to sustain the existing integrity of the state or to achieve freedom from Western political intervention.

However, the Muslim nationalists in British India who opposed the joint Hindu-Muslim Indian nationalism and demanded an independent Pakistan rejected the political interpretation of this *hadīth.* Iqbal himself reiterated the traditional, nonpolitical meaning in repudiation of joint Indian nationalism.[20] It is ironic that after the creation of Pakistan, the same *hadīth* is occasionally suggested as an Islamic justification of Pakistani patriotism.

The second theory to support the argument that nationalism follows from the teachings of Islam itself was, like the first, developed during the eventful years of the *khilāfat* movement and reflects the unusual circumstances of Hindu-Muslim cooperation for ostensibly an Islamic cause of maintaining the integrity of the Ottoman caliphate. In what is commonly known as the Constitution of Madina, the Prophet Muhammad, sometime after his arrival at Madina in A.D. 622, laid down the terms of an agreement among the migrant Muslims, Arab tribes of Madina, and some Jewish tribes of Madina's surroundings, the three being allies of one another. The allies supported the common objective of peacefully resolving internal conflicts and of defending Madina against attacks by enemy tribes from outside Madina, particularly from the Quraish of Mecca. The Muslims and all the allied tribes at Madina are said in the constitution to constitute one *umma* (community). Mawlana Abul Kalam Azad (d. 1958), the late minister of education and the leading Muslim in the Indian National Congress, saw in this act of the Prophet an Islamic confirmation of joint Hindu-Muslim nationalism on the basis of their occupying common Indian territory and having a common political interest in freedom from the British yoke.

Mawlana Azad himself and particularly Shaikh al-Hind Mawlana Mahmud al-Hasan (d. 1920), the president of the first major professional association of the *ulamā* in British India, Jamiyyat al-Ulama-i-Hind, saw during the *khilāfat* years only a contractual basis of Hindu-Muslim cooperation in political matters and not a natural basis for the formation of nations. In other words, initially Hindu-Muslim cooperation was desired for strategic reasons, not because of any assumed national identity of the two communities. But, after the death of Mahmud al-Hasan in 1920 and subsequent breakdown of the *khilāfat* movement, Azad, and to some extent the new president of the Jamiyyat, Mawlana Husain Ahmad Madani (d. 1957), gradually drifted toward a position where the distinction between strategic consideration to achieve common interests and essential national unity, because of sharing common territory, melted away. Mawlana Husain Ahmad Madani made a distinction between *milla* and *qawm*, taking the former to be a religious community and the latter a territorial or ethnic community. He expressed the view that circumstances in the modern world required the formation of nations on the basis of common territory.

Mawlana Abul Kalam Azad applauded the Syrians who, he said, despite their differences of faith, had followed the principle that "religion is for God, but the *watan* [homeland] is for everyone" and who were united to win their national liberation. He deplored the fact that Hindus and Muslims of India were still holding communal prejudices and were thus blocking national progress.[21]

Thus, Abul Kalam and a few leaders of Jamiyyat al-Ulama-i-Hind slowly drifted toward a position where, for all practical purposes, "homeland" was conceded the first place in national identification. It must be said, however, that the majority of the Deobandi *ulamā,* who supported the Indian National Congress against the Muslim League and its demand for Pakistan, supported the congress not out of any natural sentiment for an "Indian nation" but for overwhelmingly strategic considerations. This is borne out by a discussion between some leading *ulamā* who supported the Indian National Congress and Mawlana Shabbir Ahmad Uthmani (d. 1949), who supported the Muslim League and the demand for Pakistan. In that discussion (held at Deoband in 1945), all the arguments given by the anti-Pakistan *ulamā* were in the nature of strategic considerations. Among these arguments, the necessity of joint Hindu-Muslim action against such a formidable enemy as British imperialism was emphasized, along with an objection to the impious character of most Muslim League leaders.[22] The third major consideration of those *ulamā* who were against the Pakistan scheme was for the anticipated helplessness of those Muslims who would be left in a divided India.

The basic assumption in all these discussions for the bulk of the *ulamā* remained that Muslims were a distinct community within India having their own collective social, cultural, and political interests. Only their political interests for the time being coincided with those of the Hindus and thus justified a concerted action with them against the British. The sentiment of the majority of so-called nationalist *ulamā,* therefore, was not nationalistic but communalistic. They justified not nationalism in itself but the use of the drive and strength of the nationalistic movement for the interests of the Muslims. Mainly in this sense did they conclude that nationalism is Islamically justified.

The means-and-ends relationship was also the justification of those who opposed joint Indian nationalism and championed the cause of an independent Muslim state in the subcontinent. However, there was a difference between conceptions of the two groups. Most of the Deobandi *ulamā* (i.e., the *ulamā* associated with the famous Islamic seminary at Deoband, India) and the nationalist Muslims regarded independence from British rule as the most urgent goal and held participation in the Indian nationalist movement to be its best means. But Muslim nationalists went one step further: they would have freedom not only from the rule of the British but also from the possible dominance of the Hindus. The more religiously oriented Muslims even entertained the hope of realizing the Islamic ideal of justice and of implementing the *sharīʿa* in its entirety. As a means to this end, they desired a territorial state consisting of a Muslim majority. Again and again this theme occurs in the history of the Pakistan independence movement and then in the history of independent Pakistan as an effort to reconcile the ideological and spiritual basis of Muslim nationhood with the demand for a territorial state.

Allama Iqbal, who first proposed in 1930 the idea of an autonomous Muslim state in the subcontinent, claimed that an autonomous Muslim state was needed for the opportunity it would provide for Islam "to rid itself of the stamp that Arabian imperialism was forced to give it, to mobilize its laws, its education, its culture and to bring them into close contact with its own original spirit and with the spirit of modern times." Fifteen years later, in 1945, a conference of the newly formed Jamiyyat Ulama-i-Islam, reportedly attended by five hundred *ulamā* and Sufi *mashayikh,* passed a resolution that regarded the creation of Pakistan as the only means to save the Muslims and the Islamic *sharīʿa* from the domination of non-Muslims and unbelievers.[23]

However, after the creation of Pakistan in 1947 the expectations for an Islamic utopia were mostly frustrated. The struggles that ensued between the so-called traditionalist and modernist Muslims were partly the result of past concessions made by the Muslim League high command for propaganda reasons and partly due to the differences in the conceptions of what constituted true Islam. The question of Pakistan's Islamic identity in an ideological sense was far from settled. The name "Islamic Republic" was dropped in 1958 from the state's nomenclature. It was not included in the

second constitution of Pakistan in 1962 either but a year later was reinstated, after considerable public debate. For those who took part in the
debate, the question was not simply that of nomenclature but of an Islamic
commitment or lack of it.[24] The question for them was one of identity:
whether Pakistan was an Islamic (or ideological) state or a nation-state. If
the interests of an Islamic state and a nation-state were to be equated, if
patriotism and Islamic brotherhood were to be reconciled, one needed a
theory. The same means-and-ends theory, therefore, was restated in the
second major phase (1958–1971) of Pakistan's political history. Professor
Taj Muhammad Khayal, for example, spoke for many "Islamists-cum-
patriots" when he said:

> Islam is a universal socioeconomic and socio-political system which
> lays down certain basic principles by following which man can reach
> the highest possible perfection. Islam is a religion for all people, for all
> times and for all climes. It cannot be identified with any particular ter-
> ritory. Yet we say that there can be a nation created on the basis of these
> principles; it is so because these principles cannot exist in a vacuum.
> Some people must imbibe them and put them into practice. . . . Islam
> needs individuals who in turn need a home where they can practice its
> high ideals and from where it could spread to other parts. In case of our
> people, I feel that Islam and nationalism are inseparable.[25]

Recognizing the importance of Islamic sentiment in Pakistan's national
identity, Dr. Mahmud Hussain laid emphasis, once again, on the necessity of a nation-state and nationalism to carry out the demands of Islamic
ideology:

> No doubt it was Islam which gave birth to Pakistan and Islam is likely
> to remain the most potent force in keeping it intact but however com-
> prehensive the claims of Islam on the believer may be, it is, in the twen-
> tieth century, generally conceded, that the claims can be made more
> real and they can be more expeditiously realized if they are stated in
> National terms.[26]

"Patriotism," he confirmed, "is an act of falling in love with one's country, its institutions and its practices, its people and their scheme of values —
a scheme of values, the purpose of which is to make accessible a fuller and
richer life to an ever increasing number of people."[27] His counsel to his

countrymen, like the counsel of many other "Islamists-cum-patriots," was "Let us then cultivate patriotism. Let us all be for Pakistan, and let Pakistan be for Islam."[28]

Immediately after the secession of Bangladesh from Pakistan in 1971, most Pakistanis, especially the Islamic nationalists, experienced a sense of great loss and betrayal. The "Islamic nationalists" still regret it greatly. However, the geographical contiguity and linguistic affinity of the remaining provinces of the new Pakistan offered greater potential for theoretical reconciliation of Islam and patriotism than in the past. Before the secession of Bangladesh, it was generally a secular or regional nationalist who pointed to the cultural differences between West Pakistan and East Pakistan, considering the two to be mainly incompatible. However, after the secession, some supporters of "Islamic-cum-patriotic" identity came to reconcile with the secession, which, they maintained, resulted in the emergence of Pakistan's real national identity. In 1973, at a conference on "The Quest for Identity," one participant speaker noted:

> The long and uneasy cooperation between East and West Pakistan had created a sense of unity, and the economy of both the wings was interdependent. The unexpected separation of East Pakistan by force from the rest of Pakistan has shocked every Pakistani. The sentiments have their value and should not be lightly cast off, nor can they be nonchalantly brushed aside. But hard realities and facts cannot be challenged and must be acknowledged. I believe that . . . the Pakistani nation . . . has eventually found its real identity that was chalked out for her by Chaudhry Rahmat Ali, Allama Iqbal and the Lahore Resolution of the Muslim League.[29]

Another participant, Professor Qudratullah Fatimi, reiterated that Pakistani nationalism ought to be based on religious as well as territorial consciousness.

Fatimi's definition of Pakistani nationalism represents the fourth type of theoretical formulation that seeks a reconciliation of the Islamic and the territorial bases of nationhood. The attempt consists essentially in finding a community of values between Islamic religion and the "national character," or a community of social goals between those inspired by religion and those pursued historically by a people inhabiting a given territory.

Accepting a basic distinction made by the ancient Hindu scripture

Dharma Shastra between the *madhya-desha* (middle land) and the *melec-cha-desha* (land of the impure) but reversing the normative characterization of the latter, Fatimi says that the Indo-Pakistan subcontinent is divided both geographically and culturally between a heartland (i.e., contemporary India), which has been historically the impregnable citadel of caste Hinduism (*varna dharma*), and the "rimland" (consisting of the former East Pakistan and West Pakistan), which has been historically the abode of Islam and, before that, of Buddhism. Whereas the heartland is associated with untouchability, inequality, and conservatism of caste Hinduism, the rimland has been associated with egalitarianism, a sense of moral justice, and an openness to healthy cultural influences.[30]

Speaking of the people of West Pakistan, Fatimi claims:

> Thus, all of us shared together the six-thousand-year-long historical experience in a very well-defined geographical environment. This produced a unity of character of our people, *viz:* "Their great love of equality and social justice, which made them withstand—to a very great extent—the onslaughts of the Brahmin caste system and its cruel code of untouchability. (It was this ideal of equality and social justice which also made them accept the noble and humane message of the Buddha, and when Buddhism lost some of its pristine egalitarianism they embraced the brotherhood of Islam); their resilience which made it possible for them to live through invasions and recurrent political upheavals; their great adaptability by which they assimilated different and divergent cultures and faiths; their ruggedness which was the outcome of their continuous touch with the simplicity of the primitive societies of invading hordes and their unmistakable characteristics of a 'Frontiersman,' which is the inevitable result of the geographical location of the whole country, not only the highlands of the Pathans, who are, of course, frontiersmen par excellence."[31]

Fatimi concludes that the above characteristics of Pakistanis "can lay the foundations for the cultural and ideological harmony of modern Pakistan— the cultural symphony and not the self-righteous, boorish monotony. We can meet the challenge of regional prejudices by rediscovering this common character and by conscious and concerted effort to develop it."[32] It is obvious that Fatimi views Islam mainly as a set of moral values, chief among which are equality, fraternity, and social justice.

Identification with the ancient, pre-Islamic cultural traditions of West Pakistan, even when these traditions are interpreted as having a community of ideals with Islam or as having contributed to an Islamically worthy "national character," continues to be a rare attitude in postdivided Pakistan. Most "Islamists-cum-patriots" continue to view the relationship between Islam and country as that of the end and its means, or they accept the nation-state simply as a practical concession to the political norms of the twentieth century.

MODERNIZATION AND ISLAMIC NATIONALISM

Inquiries about the impact of modernization on religiously based traditional communal identity have often relied on the secularization theory. In brief, the theory maintains that traditional societies—characterized by agrarian economies and religious worldviews—succumb under the mighty impact of industrialization and modern sciences, giving way to the emergence of modern societies, which are characterized by rationalism and secularism. As a consequence, secular nationalism displaces the eroded religious communities and discredited religious worldviews.[33] Ernest Gellner took a similar position in his work *Nations and Nationalism.*[34] He regarded the secularization theory to be as much applicable to Islam as to other major religious and cultural traditions of the world. In his recent study, *Postmodernism, Reason and Religion,* Gellner continues in general to support the secularization theory.[35] At the same time, however, he takes the view that Islam is an exception to the rule, since it is the only tradition that has been resistant to secularization. "At the end of the Middle Ages," Gellner writes, "the Old World contained four major civilizations. Of these, three are now, in one measure or another, secularized. . . . But in one of the four civilizations, the Islamic, the situation is altogether different."[36] Arguing further, Gellner says, "We see a pre-industrial faith, a founded, doctrinal, world religion in the proper sense, which, at any rate for the time being, totally and effectively defies the secularization thesis. So far, there is no indication that it will succumb to secularization in the future either, though of course it is always dangerous to indulge in prophecy."[37]

The position that I have taken here supports neither the universality of the secularization process, as claimed by the orthodox secularization theory, nor the exclusion of the Islamic tradition from all secular consequences of modernization.

There can be no denying the obvious truth that major economic, social, and intellectual changes in a society lead to other sociocultural changes in that society. Nor can the fact be disregarded that the consequences of a major sociocultural development in one society are likely to be, in identical conditions, analogous to those in another, similar society. The difficulty with the orthodox secularization theory, as many critics have pointed out, is that it supports, in effect, a universal and unilinear correlation of economic modernization with secularization.[38] Development of secular nationalism is understood to be a necessary consequence of modernization in a given society. Although the proponents of the theory explicitly recognize the distinct social, economic, political, as well as intellectual aspects of modernization, the modernization process and its consequences nonetheless continue to be treated as a single integrated syndrome. Empirical research presented here suggests that various social, political, and intellectual processes that are subsumed under modernization can individually lead to different, at times even conflicting, sociocultural consequences within a society. Some of these processes promote secular nationalism; others, under certain conditions, hinder it.

In order to evaluate both the extent and the nature of influence of major historical developments and social processes on matters of collective identity, one must recognize a basic distinction. Collective identification consists of two, analytically separable aspects: the first is the feeling or sentiment for a group that is seen as the "nation," and the second is a view that defines the boundaries of that group. The nature of the former is essentially affective; that of the latter, primarily intellectual. These two aspects of collective identification are not necessarily affected in a similar way by a major social process or historical development. A major historical development may lead to an increase or decrease in the intensity of the sentiment without substantially altering the cognitive view of the nationalist. Witness, for example, the decrease in intensity of the national sentiment in peacetime and its increase in wartime, without a substantial change in the basic definition of the nation. Alternatively, a historical development may warrant a change in the cognitive view of the community without altering the intensity of the sentiment for collective identity. The sentiment of belonging to a community is partly a response to the human need for security. It has been argued that this need is likely to be felt to a greater extent by societies at a time when they undergo relatively rapid social change, since social change brings uncertainties about the future as well as considerable social or physical dis-location. Breakdown of traditional social structure, which once provided a sense of security and protection, could accentuate the need for cohesion.[39] To the extent that the introduction of modern technology, transportation, and social structure may encourage, promote, or force the breakdown of traditional groups or alienate individuals from their group in one or several ways, industrialization can be seen as indirectly productive of an increased need for collective identification.

However, the new group that may become a major object of the individ-ual's collective identity may be religious or secular, political or nonpolitical. Which large group will indeed become the major focus of identification for the bulk of a society may only partly be suggested or determined by indus-trialization and modern technological and economic developments. The rest would depend on many other variables. First among these variables is the intellectual climate of the time, in the formation of which technology and industrialization are only indirectly related: the spirit of inquiry and the worldview implicit in modern sciences are likely to undermine religious faith and thus reduce the likelihood of its continuing to be the basis of "nationhood." The second variable is the availability of the groups that could be the potential foci of national identity. In this, again, industrializa-tion may play only a partial role and mostly a negative one. The groups that totally disintegrate under its pressure would, of course, stand no chance of becoming the objects of "national" identification. The third variable is the degree of importance that the bulk of the population of a society attaches to a given group. The extent of the importance of such a group is itself likely to correspond to the extent of a shared culture and the range of social com-munication among members of that society.

These factors can lead in different directions. For example, a Bengali Muslim may have greater community of culture with the Muslims of the Middle East but greater social communication with his Hindu neighbors. Which factor actually proves to be decisive depends on the combined influences of other factors.

The decision whether the "nation" is defined in religious or in secular terms, or a combination of both, is likely to be further influenced by (a) the value and the role that a religious tradition assigns to political organization as well as the actual role of the state as manager of social services and orga-nizer of resources: the greater the role a religion assigns to such political organization, the greater the chances would be for religious nationalism; *(b)* the presence or absence of the peoples of different faiths in a society, along with the degree of importance of these faiths in the eyes of their followers; and *(c)* the extent to which one faith may recognize or reject the truth or validity of another, and the extent to which it may allow or restrict social relations with the followers of other faiths: the greater the exclusive character of a religion, the greater the obstacles would be for secular nationalism.

Searching for these factors in Islamic civilization and the Muslim societies in the traditional past, one notices that in comparison with the governments of contemporary modern states, the traditional Muslim government did very little for the bulk of its subjects, including its Muslim subjects. The services actually provided by historic Muslim governments — distinguished from what the Islamic political ideal demanded — often did not go beyond providing law and order, establishing some trusts (*awqāf*) for religious, educational, or charitable purposes, and patronizing the literati and the artists. Beyond the defense of the Muslim community against the attacks by non-Muslim states, protection from lawlessness and anarchy caused by criminals or political adventurers, dispensation of penal justice and enforcement of Islamic civil laws, the state had little use for its average members. Despite the reality of the actual role of the government and realistic expectations from it, the ideal role of government continued to be upheld as that of an instrument of social justice and moral reform. This idealist strand persisted in Muslim consciousness and was revitalized occasionally by some Islamic movements in the premodern period.

As for the claim to truth, Islam's is total. Of all the non-Muslims only the "people of the book" are recognized as believing in partially correct religion. In the context of India, the Hindu, of course, unlike the Jew and the Christian, was considered a total infidel, although legally he was, like the Jew and the Christian, allowed the status of a *dhimmī* (member of a protected community) in premodern times.

In social relations, Islam supports considerably egalitarian norms, but even Islam forbids marriage with pagans. Apart from the weight of the Muslim tradition, which tended to sway Muslims toward an Islamic identification, the added factor of the presence of a Hindu majority in the Indian subcontinent and the caste-related social norms of the Hindus further strengthened them in their Muslim identity.

Which new changes and societal processes in contemporary Pakistan and Bangladesh—or their predecessor in British India—have influenced those aspects of the Islamic tradition described above as relevant to conceptions of "national" identity? Of the potentially several, the following may be noted here.

A process that was operative until recently in the modern Muslim history was the secularization of the law. With the coming of British rule in the Indo-Pakistan subcontinent, the provisions of the *sharīʿa* were progressively replaced by the secular law of British origin. The sphere of the *sharīʿa* eventually came to be confined to personal and family law. This had two social effects. First, some specifically Muslim social and public institutions (e.g., the court of the *qāḍī*, or Islamic judge) passed away, and to that extent one social-structural dimension of the *umma* was demolished. Second, the portion of the *sharīʿa* law that became nonoperational fell from the active memory of the Muslims. And to the extent it was forgotten, one cultural dimension of the *umma* was damaged. For a long time after the creation of Pakistan in 1947, its government talked much of reviving and reformulating the Islamic law, but it did little beyond paying lip service. Under the rule of General Zia-ul-Haq (r. 1977–1988), however, the process of "Islamization" began to take specific and concrete shape in Pakistan. By a series of ordinances, the government reintroduced with minor changes some laws of the traditional *sharʿī* in the country. The reintroduction of the Islamic *sharīʿa* in Pakistan has been piecemeal and so far partial. It is, of course, too early for these laws to become a part of the living culture and thus to fully influence the national consciousness. In time, however, if the process of "Islamization" continues and such *sharʿī* laws are earnestly implemented, the *sharīʿa* could potentially resume the place it once had in the "national" consciousness.

The partition of the Indian subcontinent in 1947 and the widespread communal violence that accompanied it all but eliminated Hindu and Sikh populations in West Pakistan as these people fled to India. The almost exclusively Muslim character of West Pakistan that resulted from this flight has made it easier for the Pakistanis to equate the interests of the Muslim community with the interests of the state. The same fact of flight of the Hindu community to India, along with the flight of a part of the Muslim community from India to Pakistan, emphasized the equation of the rival community (Hindu) with the rival state (India) in the minds of the Pakistani

Muslims. In both cases, therefore, religious sentiment seems to support an aspect of territorial nationalism, or at least the secular part of the "Islamic-cum-patriotic" orientation.

The obvious political reality of the time is that the boundaries of most states in the world are drawn not along confines of religious faith but along the lines of territorial or ethnic communities. Thanks to modern transportation and communication, an increasing number of people are becoming aware for the first time of what lies beyond their village, district, or town and eventually their country. This new awareness is conducive to accepting the given boundaries of the country as the boundaries of the nation and, thus, conducive to accepting a definition of the nation that is not purely religious.

Never in the past, except in the arid river valleys where irrigation was essential for the very survival of the population or in the territorially small city-states of classical antiquity, did the government play so large a role as it assumed in the twentieth century, whether in the democratic West or in what was, until recently, the communist East. In the countries of the Third World, too, the functions of the state are larger than what they were in premodern times. In the Indo-Pakistan subcontinent, since the beginning of the British rule, the government has had an increasing role in providing or regulating many services in the society. Not only are new means of communication and transportation, such as telegraph, telephone, radio, television, and railways, managed by government, but old services such as irrigation, education, and finance have come under increasing control of the state both in Pakistan and Bangladesh. As the services provided by the state as well as the number of those who use public services grow, so will grow the people's realization of the importance of the state and, with it, the national identity associated with that state.

These societal processes should work for a greater acceptance of secular or partly secular national identity in Pakistan and Bangladesh. However, due to the several historical and cultural factors discussed above, future prospects are uncertain. Secular nationalism is not intrinsic to these societies, as it has been to the societies of Europe and America in recent times. Initially a result of partial acculturation of modern Western ideas, nationalism continues to be a borrowed element only uncomfortably and incompletely adopted by a section of the society in Pakistan as well as Bangladesh.

Indeed, despite the large role of nationalism in the independence movements in the twentieth-century Muslim World, it constituted neither as thorough a commitment nor as comprehensive a movement as in the modern European experience. Thoroughgoing nationalism requires an unchallenged supremacy of the nation over religion as well as over all large social groups. In Europe it came naturally: as the old large groups disintegrated, the nation assumed importance; as religion fell from the heart, nationalism moved in. (Cases of conflicting religious-ethnic nationalism as Catholic-Irish nationalism in Ulster would, of course, constitute exceptions.) But in such Islamic lands as Pakistan neither have the traditional large groups so disintegrated as to make their members helplessly seek an alternate identity, nor has the secularly oriented Western rationalism been accepted to a degree that would seriously undermine religious faith and, therefore, religious consciousness.

Finally, the modern educated class, which is the main bearer of nationalism (to the extent it does bear it), is still not only small in relation to the whole society, but also far from stable.

3 ❋ *The Islamic State*

About a quarter of all the independent countries in the world today contain Muslim majorities. The political systems of these countries represent a wide spectrum, ranging from conservative monarchies to radical republics, from self-proclaimed "Islamic states" to fully secular and quasi-secular states.

In many of these countries, the issues of secularization and Islamization are far from settled. After World War One, the Turkish government zealously followed the path of secularization. Under the secular nationalist leadership of Kemal Ataturk (r. 1923–1938), Turkey developed a constitution as well as basic governmental and legal institutions that completely removed religion from the public sphere. After Ataturk, several Muslim leaders, in Iran, in the Arab world, and elsewhere, pursued secularization, although none as aggressively or as successfully as Ataturk. Secularization continued to be a part of the reformist programs sought by nationalist governments in many Muslim countries through the 1960s. Since then, however, secular nationalist goals and programs have been increasingly challenged by Islamist activists and intellectuals. In several Muslim countries, the notion of a "people's republic" is countered by the notion of an "Islamic republic" or "Islamic state."

In Pakistan the controversy between the Islamists and the secularists over both the character and the desirability of the "Islamic state" ensued much earlier than the sixties. Indeed, the concept of the Islamic state has dominated religio-political thinking in Pakistan ever since the creation of that country in 1947. It was the first major ideological issue that engaged the attention of a great many Pakistanis. From 1949, when the first Indo-Pakistan war over Kashmir ended, to March 1956, when the first constitution of Pakistan was passed by its National Assembly, the issue was debated in newspaper columns and magazine articles as well as in the National Assembly and became a central theme of numerous political speeches in public rallies as well as countless Friday sermons in mosques in Pakistan.

After the military coup d'état of 1958, General Ayub Khan's government imposed martial law in the country, abrogated the constitution, and initially dropped the term "Islamic Republic" from the formal nomenclature of Pakistan, thus signaling a rejection of its Islamic commitment. However, as soon as the restraints of martial law were eased in the early sixties, the debate about the secular or Islamic nature of the state of Pakistan reemerged in earnest. In the seventies the popular discourse favored the use of such terms as *nizām-i-Islam* (Islamic system) and *nizām-i-Mustafā* (the Prophet's system), both, however, closely linked with the concept of an Islamic state.

Debates and discussions in Pakistan on the desirability and nature of the Islamic state have covered several political topics, four of which have engaged most attention: (1) the functions of the state, (2) democratic values, (3) the character and form of government, (4) the law and legislation. Islamic political attitudes in Pakistan and Bangladesh have been formed around these four topics.

This chapter examines the various individual political attitudes on the above four subjects, notes their quantitative distributions among the different strata of the survey sample, compares the observed attitudes with some traditional Islamic views on the same issues, and searches for identifiable patterns or typologies among the observed attitudes.

MAJOR ISLAMIC POLITICAL ORIENTATIONS

Some familiar typologies that are commonly employed to characterize political orientations in general include progressive and reactionary, liberal and totalitarian, liberal and conservative. The problem with many such terms is that they are context-specific, closely associated with the ideas and institutions that are part of the Western political experience. Unavoidably, they bring to mind characteristics that would be fully true mainly of the Western political systems.

Another typology, suggested recently by Gabriel Almond, Emmanuel Sivan, and Scott Appleby, characterizes the politically active religious movements around the globe essentially as "fundamentalist" and "fundamentalistlike."[1] Each of these two kinds of movement is said to relate to the "world" outside itself as "world conqueror," "world transformer," "world creator," and/or "world renouncer."[2] This new scheme, which reduces diverse religious approaches to a forced dichotomy, can lead to some obvious inaccuracies and indistinctions. When the conceptual criteria suggested by this scheme are applied rigorously, the two very different religious movements in Pakistan, the politically active Jamaat-i-Islami and the politically aloof Tablighi Jamaat, despite their contrasting visions and approaches, are to be theoretically grouped together with "fundamentalist" movements. One could be a little more discerning by employing the concepts that the modern Western scholarship of Islam has already developed.

Western analysts of Islam have often used the terms traditionalist, fundamentalist, and modernist to distinguish various religio-political orientations among contemporary Muslims. The criteria employed to characterize these types are varied, sometimes including cultural and theological as well as political elements.

For purposes of this discussion, it appears best that the distinguishing criteria be reduced to exclusively political attitudes, and to as few characteristics as possible. Keeping this in mind, one may start by distinguishing two major types of contemporary Muslims: the "political secularists" and the "political Islamists." Their respective positions, which are identified by the survey findings as well as by much of the Muslim writings on religio-political matters, may be defined and characterized as follows.

The "political secularists" exclude Islam as irrelevant to, or undesirable in, statecraft. A political secularist, however, need not necessarily be a "secular nationalist"—as defined in the previous chapter—because the two are concerned with different questions, the former relating to the conduct of the state, the latter relating to the identity of the political community.

The "political Islamists" may be defined as those who believe that Islam makes some political demands on them and who, therefore, would like to pursue what they consider Islam's political teaching in matters of statecraft. As with the two types of secularists, an "Islamic nationalist"[3] may not *necessarily* be a "political Islamist" as well, or vice versa, since, once again, the two deal with different subjects. The "political Islamists" may be further classified into the three familiar types according to their orientations: traditionalists, modernists, and revivalists, a term that is used in this work in preference to the term "fundamentalists." The connotations of these categories in the context of this chapter are, however, narrower than what is generally assumed.

The "modernists" may be defined as those who would like to reinterpret Islamic tenets, particularly its legal rules. The "revivalists" want mostly to revive rather than to reinterpret Islam. Theoretically, both the modernists and the revivalists grant the validity of *ijtihād* (reasoning to determine specific Islamic rules), but while the modernists would like to apply it freely, the revivalists want to keep its field severely limited and its application strictly regimented (see the section on law and legislation below for elaboration). Consequently, despite their claim to go back to the Qur'ān and the Prophet for guidance, Islamic revivalists seek, in effect, to revive the bulk of the medieval Islamic law, a large part of which was developed by the Muslim jurists more than a century after the death of the Prophet. The traditionalist position resembles that of the revivalists so far as the attitude toward the substance of the law goes; but it differs from the revivalist stand in conceding the theoretical validity of *taqlīd* (mandatory acceptance of legal formulations of Islamic law found in medieval schools of juristic thought). The traditionalists permit *ijtihād,* at the most only in matters that are related entirely to new developments in Muslim society. (This subject will be fully treated below in the section on law and legislation.)

The three "Islamist" positions are roughly associated with three groups. Traditionalism in Pakistan continues, as in many other Muslim countries, to be most espoused by the *ulamā;* the revivalist stand in Pakistan has been articulately and enthusiastically supported by the religio-political party Jamaat-i-Islami, and particularly by its founder, Sayyid Abul Ala Mawdudi (1903–1979). Modernism is associated with the writings of Dr. Fazlur Rahman (1919–1988), Ghulam Ahmad Parwez, Khalifa Abdul Hakim (d. 1958), and others. The following discussion of individual attitudes toward different political issues includes summaries of the answers received from respondents during the survey and from the published statements of individuals generally identifiable with the three positions among the "political Islamists," as well as from some appropriate collective statements.

THE NEED FOR AN ISLAMIC STATE

Proposing in 1930 the idea of creating a Muslim state in the northwest of the Indian subcontinent, Dr. Muhammad Iqbal (d. 1938) stated two major goals of his proposal: one, to solve the communal problem in India by achieving internal balance and giving the northwestern Muslims of India a sense of responsibility; and two, to provide the Muslims "an opportunity to rid Islam of the stamp that Arabian imperialism was forced to give it, to mobilize its law, its education, its culture, and to bring them into closer contact with Islam's original spirit and the spirit of modern times."[4]

Ten years later, in 1940, when the Muslim League passed the Pakistan Resolution for the creation of "autonomous and sovereign states" for the Muslims in India in the region where they constituted majorities, no mention was made of Islam, either as a final objective whose interests a Muslim state could serve or as a source of religious compulsion that could demand the creation of an independent state. However, in the same Muslim League session, the president of the league, Quaid-i-Azam Muhammad Ali Jinnah (d. 1949), argued that Muslim autonomy in the subcontinent alone would avoid rivalry between the Hindu and the Muslim communities in India and prevent domination of the Hindu majority over the Muslim minority, thus making democracy workable in India; it would lead to mutual goodwill and harmony among the Muslims and the Hindu communities in India. Apart from these considerations of expedience, however, Jinnah also said in justification of the creation of Pakistan: "We wish our people to develop to the fullest our spiritual, economic, social, and political life in a way that we think best and in consonance with our ideals and according to the genius of our people."[5]

Though Jinnah did not specifically mention Islam, the context of this statement made it clear that the "ideals and genius of the people" of which he spoke had much to do with Islam. Certainly, the efforts of the Muslim League to win the Muslim masses to the demand for Pakistan after 1940 included the argument that the purpose of the new state would be to provide the Muslims an opportunity to put Islam's cherished ideals and political principles into practice.[6]

In view of this historical background of the Pakistan national movement, the author sought to assess how the Pakistanis generally conceived the purpose of their state. The following question was employed as part of the survey questionnaire to explore this subject:

With which of the following propositions do you agree?

a. Political organization (i.e., the state) should be based on expedience and should aim at utilitarian ends.

b. Political organization is required by Islam and should further the cause of Islam.

If you agree with neither or take exception to such a dichotomy, what is your own view on this subject?

As in the case of the question of "national" identifications, the attitudes of West Pakistani professionals differed greatly from those of the professionals in the former East Pakistan. Only 8 percent of the Bengali professionals held that a polity ought to seek the ends of Islam, while 50 percent of the West Pakistani professionals thought so; the bulk of the Bengali professionals (ca. 72 percent) considered either general utility, the interest of the working classes, or social justice to be the desirable aim of the state (see Table 3.1). As against this, only about 38 percent of the West Pakistani professionals considered one or more of these secular objectives that they held to be the desirable goals and bases of the polity. About 20 percent of the professionals in the former East Pakistan considered the interests of Islam along with the interests of the working class, or social justice, or general social utility to be the desirable goals of the state, but only about 8 percent of the professionals thought so in West Pakistan. All the *ulamā* in both of the former two "wings" of Pakistan said, of course, that the state should seek to serve Islamic ends.

When the respondents were asked further if they would like Pakistan to be an Islamic state, the majority of professionals in West Pakistan included in the survey conducted for this study in 1969 gave an affirmative answer, the majority in what is now Bangladesh, a negative one; all of the *ulamā*, of course, said "yes" (see Table 3.2).

In Pakistan the revivalist party Jamaat-i-Islami has been most committed to the idea that Islam needs a state. Since the creation of Pakistan in 1947, no group has so persistently tried to Islamize politics as the celebrated Jamaat. But the traditionalists and Islamic modernists also generally regard the state to be a necessity for Islam.

For an elaboration and illustration of the political attitudes noted above, one may turn now to the longer answers of the respondents as well as to the published statements made by Pakistani Muslims on related matters. The reasons given by the Muslims in Pakistan for the necessity of an Islamic state are several and are not exclusively attributable to any single school of thought. One can, however, distinguish three main lines of argument, which are summarized below.

One of these arguments justifies strictly the need for good government,

TABLE 3.1
PURPOSE OF THE STATE AS DESCRIBED BY *ULAMĀ* AND THE PROFESSIONALS

Social Category		Purpose of the State								Row Total
	Utility	Islam	Social Justice, Interest of Working Class	Utility, Islam, and Interest of Working Class	Islam and Social Justice	Islam and Utility	Social Justice and Human Brotherhood	"I Don't Know," Etc.		
Ulamā	0	19	0	0	0	10	0	0		29
	0.0	65.5%	0.0	0.0	0.0	34.5%	0.0	0.0		19.4%
Professionals, West Pakistan	11	36	15	1	1	4	1	2		71
	15.5%	50.7%	21.2%	1.4%	1.4%	5.6%	1.4%	2.8%		47.3%
Professionals, East Pakistan	18	4	18	2	4	4	0	0		50
	36.0	8.0%	36.0%	4.0%	8.0%	8.0%	0.0	0.0		33.3%
Column Total	29	59	33	3	5	18	1	2		150
	19.3%	39.3%	22.0%	2.0%	3.3%	12.0%	0.7%	1.3%		100.0%

TABLE 3.2
DESIRABILITY OF AN ISLAMIC STATE

Social Category	Desirability of an Islamic State			Row Total
	Not Desirable	Muslim State Is Desirable	Islamic State Is Desirable	
Ulamā	0	0	29	29
	0.0	0.0	100.0%	22.8%
Professionals, West Pakistan	14	2	34	50
	28.0%	4.0%	68.0%	39.4%
Professionals, East Pakistan	40	0	8	48
	83.3%	0.0	16.7%	37.8%
Column Total	54	2	71	127
	42.5%	1.6%	55.9%	100.0%

Missing observations: 36.

but inasmuch as goodness in the minds of many Muslims is closely associated with Islam, it has been seen as justifying the need for an Islamic government. The argument is based on the image of government as a potent and effective agency that unavoidably influences social life—for good or ill—according to its own character. In a passage discussing the moral effects of a government's rule, Mawlana Mawdudi revealed his thinking about the extent of the importance of government:

> If we take a penetrating look at all those evils comprehended by *fitna* (oppression) and *fasād* (injustice), it will be seen that every one of them is the creation of a truthless, non-God-fearing, wrong principled system of government. Even if in the case of some particular evil such government is not responsible for its coming into being, its persistence and imperviousness to reform most certainly are owing to the wickedness of that government. . . . Through its agency wrongdoers and tyrants will find power to carry out their evil deeds. Laws that corrupt morals and ravage social justice will be enacted by it.[7]

But, on the other hand,

> if leadership and power of command are vested in God-fearing and
> righteous people, then it is inevitable that the entire system of life
> should proceed in terms of goodness, righteousness, and fear of God.
> Even evil people will be obliged to remain upon good paths. Virtue will
> increase and flourish, and evils, if they are not altogether obliterated,
> at least will not multiply.[8]

Such a conception of the moral role and power of government moves the
revivalist Muslims to underscore the necessity of controlling the government in the interests of Islamic causes.

The *ulamā* generally see the Islamic need for government, and therefore
for the state, in the argument that only by establishing conditions of peace,
security, and justice is it possible for the Muslims to live Islamic lives.[9]

The second major statement to justify the thesis that Islam needs a state
is the argument that some goals of Islam cannot be realized except in an organized society. This attitude is shared by the modernists as well as the traditionalists and the revivalists. To the *ulamā*, as for the rest of the Muslims,
the Islamic *sharīʿa* not only teaches the believer the rules of pious conduct
before his Lord, but it also seeks to regulate his behavior toward his fellow
men. Except for some sectarian *khawārij* who believed that both personal
and social teachings of the Islamic *sharīʿa* can be fully observed without the
benefit of a government, the Muslims in general and the *ulamā* in particular have held throughout Islamic history that the full implementation of the
sharīʿa requires a government that may enforce its dictates. This justification of the state is still upheld by the *ulamā*.[10]

Similar reasoning, though less committed to traditional *fiqh*, comes from
the modernist quarters. Khalifa Abdul Hakim wrote, for example: "Islamic
spirituality has a twofold aspect: toward God it leads man to personal relation; but toward humanity it signifies social rights and responsibilities."[11]
For him, too, "the question how religion should inspire, inform, and discipline life naturally gets related to the question as to how it should be related
to the highest organization of the society called the state."[12]

The third argument, which resembles the second but is actually distinct
from it, is that Islam makes certain social demands not only upon the
Muslims individually that they should conduct themselves in a certain way
but also upon the Muslim community collectively that it seek certain social
goals.

One of the modernist statements of this approach comes from Dr. Fazlur Rahman, the former director of the Islamic Research Institute, Pakistan. Rahman argues that though Islam recognizes individual responsibility as well as the basic and ultimate worth of the individual, it also holds the society as a whole responsible for the creation of an Islamic social order.[13] The creation of such "Islamic social order," says he, "cannot be achieved immediately without there being a directed society,"[14] a term he prefers in this context over the usual "state." It appears, however, that according to Rahman, while the creation of an Islamic order is an Islamic responsibility, the creation of a state to fulfill that responsibility is not essentially Islamic but only a pragmatic consideration. The traditionalist version of this argument makes establishment of a government, and hence normally of a state, a *fard kifāya* (a duty that is deemed fulfilled if some members of the community perform it, but, if left unattended, all members may be held responsible) and, thus, it makes establishment of the state a social responsibility of the *umma*.[15]

FUNCTIONS OF THE ISLAMIC STATE

If Islam demands the creation of a state, what functions does it expect the state to carry out? Mawlana Mufti Muhammad Shafi, one of the most respected *ulamā* in Pakistan until his death in 1977, reflected widely held attitudes among the traditionalists and the revivalists in Pakistan when he described the following functions of the state in his *Basic Principles of the Qur'ānic Constitution:*

   a. To establish justice and equity for all the citizens of the state;

   b. To ward off internal disorder and external aggression;

   c. To organize for the Muslims the institution of prayer and the collection and distribution of *zakāt;*

   d. To endeavor actively for the establishment of *al-maʿrūf* (i.e., that which is morally right) and the effacement of *al-munkar* (i.e., that which is wrong).[16]

This list at once brings to mind the duties of the Muslim ruler as described by the medieval Muslim political theorists and in particular the theories of government associated with Islamic jurisprudence. The celebrated Abul Hasan al-Mawardi (d. 1058), whose classic treatise, *Ahkām al-Sultāniyya* (The ordinances of government), seems to have influenced both the *ulamā* and the Jamaat-i-Islami in Pakistan, states ten duties of the ruler. A comparison of Mufti Shafi's description with al-Mawardi's list shows, however, that their differences are as significant as their similarities.[17]

The first duty of the ruler described by al-Mawardi reads as:

> He must maintain the religion according to the principles established and agreed upon by the earliest Muslims (*salaf al-umma*), and if an innovator appears, or someone with dubious opinions who deviates from those principles, then he must clarify matters by logical proofs, and show him the correct way, and finally apply the rules and punishment to which he is bound, that religion may be preserved from disorder and the community from stumbling.[18]

Other jurists of the *imamate* (Islamic rule) describe the same duty of the ruler as "to guard religion in its principles and beliefs, to put down innovation and heretics, and encourage the religious science and study of the law."[19] These two methods of preserving Islamic religion, positively through education and negatively through "putting down innovations and heretics," theoretically may be, and in the past actually were, included under the general function of the state "to order what is right and forbid what is wrong" [amr bi'l-ma'rūf wa nahī 'an al-munkar]. However, a reading of Mufti Shafi's *Basic Principles of the Qur'ānic Constitution* shows that the sole method he describes to safeguard the faith is the positive one: education. Article 11 of his *Qur'ānic Constitution* reads: "It shall be the duty of the Islamic state to organize and enforce a system of universal and compulsory education wherein every Muslim citizen shall obtain requisite knowledge of the Islamic principles and practices."[20]

The absence of a provision to protect the Islamic faith through "putting down innovations and heretics" does not indicate that such a function of the state is no longer considered as part of the ideal desired by the *ulamā*. Indeed, the civic disturbances of 1953 and 1974 were partly the result of a set of demands made by a coalition of political and religious groups. One of these demands was that the government declare the Ahmadis to be a non-Muslim minority, although this new sect considered itself Muslim.[21] Several *ulamā* not only supported this demand but were also among the leaders of the popular movement that was launched to achieve the demands. The declared objective of the *ulamā* was to preserve the purity of Islamic faith by indicating that the Ahmadi belief against the finality of Muhammad's prophethood was an innovation and not a part of the true Islam. Another demand was to deprive the Ahmadis of the full rights of full Muslim citizenship, and particularly of their high governmental positions. The expectation, therefore, that the government authoritatively declare (upon the recommendation of the *ulamā*) what ought to be considered beyond the pale of Islam and thus protect Islam's purity is by no means absent among the traditionalist *ulamā,* and many of them found themselves supporting "direct action," that is, violent protest against the government, to exact such a declaration from it. Public protest in 1974 was far less violent than in 1953. So pressing were the anti-Ahmadi demands, though, particularly in the Punjab province, that the National Assembly of Pakistan meeting in September 1974 declared—without specifically mentioning the Ahmadis— that those who rejected the Islamic doctrine of the finality of Muhammad's prophethood were to be considered non-Muslims.

The ambivalence of the *ulamā* in matters of sectarian tolerance has historical roots. In Islamic history there have been theoretical bases both for toleration and forceful rejection of differing religious opinions. Any religion that claims exclusive truth and sees the state as its agent, as does Islam, is likely to have a theoretical bias for using state power in the interests of religious purity. Indeed, some differing sects in Islam's early history sought to "put down heresy" forcefully, as the question "who is a true Muslim?" became one of their prime concerns. However, after witnessing the fratricidal consequences of several civil wars fought over a hundred years, due in part to the disagreement upon who could be regarded a true Muslim, the Sunnī majority came to rally around those who counseled for leaving the matter of a Muslim's purity of faith to God Himself. The theoretical basis for this tolerant attitude was found in the dictum "He who says: 'There is only one God' will enter paradise" [man qāla lā ilāha illā Allah, dakhala al-jannah]. Thus, the bias toward "putting down heretics" was balanced and soon outweighed by this attitude of tolerance.

The practical implication of the early Muslim historical experience and the resulting Islamic doctrinal approach has been twofold.

On the one hand, the dominant Sunnī interpretation of Islamic religious doctrine was not generally imposed forcefully over other Islamic sectarian interpretations. Indeed, throughout most of the subsequent Islamic history, intersectarian tolerance continued to be a persistent policy of the Sunnī leadership.[22] By and large, only those religious movements that combined a political threat with a religious one (e.g., the movement of the Assassins in the eleventh to the thirteenth centuries A.D.) were repressed or challenged by the state. Other purely religious dissidents were designated by a Muslim state as non-Muslim subjects generally when they viewed themselves as outside the Muslim community. A few radical *ulamā* here or a zealous revivalist movement there in the Muslim world often did entertain the thought, but the bulk of the *ulamā* did not actually seek to uproot all religious differences through the physical sanction of the state.

On the other hand, there have been occasions when some *ulamā,* as well as a section of the public, did actively seek to use state sanction to preserve "the purity of the faith," especially against groups that they perceived actively proselytizing and seeking political influence for their sect. The *ulamā*'s, as well as popular, support of the anti-Ahmadi demands and agitation in Pakistan points to the limits and the weaknesses of religious toleration of popular Islam. The historical and cultural reasons for this limitation include the fact that the *ulamā*'s policy of toleration did not so much result from their recognition of the validity of diverse approaches to the truth—for that characterized the thinking of the Sufis rather than of the traditional *ulamā*—as from their fear of the conflict and bloodshed to which religious intolerance within Islam could lead. Due to that mostly utilitarian basis of doctrinal tolerance, it is easy for some *ulamā*—especially for those who have little knowledge of Islam's historical experience—to yield to the temptation of using state sanction to guard the purity of the faith.

Jihād AS NATIONAL DEFENSE

The second major function of an Islamic state as described by Mufti Shafi is maintenance of law and order and defense of the state's territories.[23] Muslims of other orientations—the revivalists as well as the modernists—also assign prime importance to defense. "Above all," wrote Rahman, "it is the duty of the State to effectively guard the frontiers of the country and guarantee the integrity of the territories of the Muslim State. In fact, this is the first charge laid upon a Muslim State."[24] Given the authenticity of the Islamic state and the honesty of its commitment, all efforts of the government as well as the citizens to enhance defense preparedness have an Islamic merit; they are a form of *ibāda,* that is, service to God:

> An effective Armed Force, equipped with the most modern and powerful weapons, has always to be kept as a stand-by. It should be borne

in mind that, according to Islam, devoted public service is a genuine form of *ibāda*. . . . But to serve the nation in guarding its integrity, i.e., to work selflessly in the Armed Services of the State, is a paramount form of *ibāda*. Whereas the Qur'ān speaks of fasting only in one passage, almost one-third of the entire Qur'ān is devoted to the building of an effective power-machine to safeguard the Muslim interests and territories, and the Qur'ān insistently says that God is theirs who are prepared to lay down their lives for the sake of the defense of the Muslim territories.[25]

Traditionally, the defense of an Islamic state has been seen by the Muslims as *jihād* (generally translated as "holy war," literally, "virtuous struggle"). As is clear from the above quotation, defense of an Islamic state is considered nothing less by contemporary Muslim "Islamists." Although the concept *jihād*, as popularly understood in the Western world, is associated with fanatic militancy, unprovoked aggressiveness, and anti-Western obsession, the actual attitudes of contemporary Muslims toward *jihād* fall into various categories.

Apart from the continued acceptance of the Sufi concept of "the greater *jihād*" as an individual's moral struggle against his own baser self and moral vices, there are diverse Muslim interpretations of *jihād* even in the sense of military campaigns. Of course, all Muslims of nonsecular orientations consider Muslim self-defense against non-Muslim aggression a virtuous struggle, that is, not just a practical necessity but a religious obligation as well. Beyond this, however, the opinions are divided. The modernists generally reject the permissibility of offensive—as against defensive—war even when it is waged ostensibly in the interests of Islam. "The Muslims are forbidden from transgressing others" is seen by the modernist Muslims as an essential Qur'ānic teaching that rejects the acceptability of offensive war.[26] According to their understanding, the many battles that the Prophet Muhammad fought during his lifetime were all defensive in nature.

Muslim revivalists and traditionalists, however, reject this interpretation of Islamic history; some see in it evidence of the apologetic servitude of Muslim modernists who seek to justify Islam according to the "fake liberalism of the West." For example, quoting Shah Waliallah's (d. 1762) opinion on the question of *jihād* as one of the duties of the state, Mawlana Muhammad Idris Kandhalwi, the late professor of *hadīth* and Qur'ānic exegesis at Jamia Ashrafiyya, Lahore, wrote: "More of those wars which the Prophet fought were initiated by him, than the ones whose purpose was merely self defense. . . . Persons who claim Islam allows only defensive war reject the Qur'ān and *sunna* and conceal the facts of history. They manifest servility of mind, and their statements are unreliable." [27]

The traditional historical theory supports, of course, both types of *jihād:* war in self-defense, as well as war for extension of the Islamic rule. Some medieval Muslim theorists even prescribed the minimum frequency of military activity that a Muslim ruler must undertake. Ibn Jamaa (d. 1333) wrote, for example, "The fifth [duty of the Muslim ruler] is to wage *jihād* himself and with his armies at least once a year, if the Muslims have strength enough, and oftener than that if necessity demands it." [28] Other theorists merely describe the obligation for *jihād* without specifying the frequency of the obligation. Al-Mawardi (d. 1058), for instance, said in his *Ordinances of Government:* "He [the ruler] must struggle with holy war against those who have been invited to join Islam and rejected it, until they either convert or enter into the status of tribute-paying non-Muslim subjects, to make victorious the truth of God over every [other] religion." [29]

While the contemporary Muslims of the revivalist and the traditionalist orientations in Pakistan continue to support this historical interpretation of *jihād* in theory, few of them, if any, actually recommend it as a Muslim pursuit today. Even the term *jihād* was conspicuous by its absence in the resolution on the basic principles of the Islamic state passed by a convention of major *ulamā* of Pakistan in 1951—a resolution that has been reaffirmed repeatedly by the major *ulamā*-supported political parties since then. Most recommendations for military preparedness in the manifestos of the religiously oriented political parties are intended to enhance the capability for self-defense of the country, none to impose Muslim rule over non-Muslims.

The contemporary Muslim attitude in Pakistan toward the non-Muslim world favors a policy of coexistence, subject only to intervention in the affairs of the Muslim countries by non-Muslim powers. Not only the modernists but also a number of the revivalists and the traditionalists have made declarations that they would support efforts for the maintenance of world peace. The election manifesto of a major *ulamā*-dominated political party, which is at the same time also a professional association of the *ulamā*, Jamiyyat Ulama-i-Islam, stated, for example, that the foreign policy of Pakistan "will support [the efforts] to promote the general welfare of the entire humanity and to maintain world peace." [30] At the same time, the manifesto also promised support for liberation efforts of all countries from the imperialist yoke, especially for independence movements in the Muslim majority regions that continue to be under non-Muslim rule.[31]

Indeed, almost all *jihād* campaigns in the twentieth century in the Islamic world, as in the nineteenth century, have been for the liberation of the Muslim countries that were subjected to non-Muslim domination. In the context of the Indo-Pakistan subcontinent, the religiously oriented Muslims have generally considered Pakistan's war against India as *jihād* both on grounds of Muslim self-defense, and—in the case of the first two wars—as the rightful efforts to liberate the Muslims of the disputed Kashmir. Mawlana Mawdudi, leader of the revivalist Jamaat-i-Islami, refused to declare Pakistan's initial military involvement in the first Indo-Pakistan war of 1948–1949 as *jihād,* partly because the proper procedures—such as making a formal declaration of war before initiating the hostilities—were not observed by the Pakistani government and partly because the government of Pakistan had not, until that time, committed itself to the principles of the Islamic polity. In the absence of such commitment, according to Mawlana Mawdudi, the war amounted to a secular, nationalistic war, conducted by a secularist government. Yet the Mawlana fully shared the view of other nonsecularist Muslims, that all wars for Muslim liberation—if supported by an Islamic commitment—were truly a form of *jihād.* In keeping with this view, the Jamaat and its revivalist following considered Pakistan's second war with India—which began as an effort to help the liberation of the Muslim Kashmir from Indian rule—as a *jihād,* and recently it strongly supported the Afghan resistance movement against Soviet occupation as *jihād* as well.

To the revivalist, the term *jihād* has an additional connotation. It is the effort to Islamize the political institutions and the law within the Muslim countries by all necessary, including political, and—in the last resort—forceful, revolutionary means. Such efforts are linked to the concept of *tajdīd* (renewal) and the movements that appeared repeatedly in Islamic history seeking restoration of what these movements considered pure Islam. Under the twentieth-century circumstances of the postcolonial legacy of secular Western values and institutions in the Muslim countries, the Muslim revivalists consider the reintroduction of Islamic laws and institutions most urgent. Most revivalists in Pakistan have decided to complete this transition from secular to Islamic institutions peacefully, unless the secularist forces themselves initiate violence against them. Still, the spirit of devotion and the willingness even to give one's life in the struggle to re-Islamize the institutions are ideally to be as great as in *jihād* for the defense of the Muslim territory. The main objective of both kinds of *jihād*— whether in defense of the Muslim territory or for restitution of the Islamic institutions — is the same, namely, securing conditions in which God's will can be fully implemented.

ISLAMIC EDUCATION

Defense and administration of justice, indeed, are the two major functions of the state over which there exists a consensus among the traditionalists, revivalists, and modernists alike. Two other functions over which agreement in principle exists are social welfare and education. Views of the *ulamā* and of the modern educated professionals on the question of social welfare will be discussed below in the chapter on economic orientations. As for education, the statement of Mawlana Mufti Shafi, which represents the view of most *ulamā* as well as of the revivalists, has already been noted above. But the modernists, too, generally agree upon the importance of public education, though they have their own different notions of what exactly constitutes Islamic education. The "Directive Principles of State Policy," a part of three successive constitutions of Pakistan, speaks of making the teaching of the Qur'ān compulsory for the Muslims and of "providing facilities whereby they may be enabled to understand the meaning of the Qur'ān and the *sunna*."[32] These and some other "Islamic provisions" of the three successive constitutions of Pakistan may be taken to represent the points of compromise between the traditionalists and the modernists. But modernist support of the state's direction of Islamic education is confirmed by several other modernist statements as well. The Commission on National Education, representing Islamic modernist sentiment, recommended in its report:

> Our educational system must play a fundamental part in the preservation of ideals which led to the creation of Pakistan, and strengthen the concept of it as a unified nation. . . . The moral and spiritual values combined with the freedom, integrity, and strength of Pakistan should be the ideology which inspires our educational system.[33]

Another function of the state on which the three types of "Islamists" in Pakistan — the traditionalists, the revivalists and the modernists — generally agree is what the three constitutions of Pakistan have described under the "Directive Principles of State Policy" as "endeavoring to preserve and strengthen fraternal relations among the Muslim countries based on Islamic unity."[34] The attitudes toward, and the desired extent of, world Muslim unity have been reported at some length above in the context of the discussion on Islam and nationalism (see Chapter 2).

Some *ulamā* have included guaranteeing the basic civic rights of all citizens as one of the functions of the state; this subject is discussed in the next section on the attitudes toward democratic values and the latter's place in an Islamic state.

ISLAM AND DEMOCRACY

The belief that Islam is democratic seems to be widely upheld by those who desire an Islamic polity. In response to the survey question "With which political systems among democracy, dictatorship, fascism, etc., is Islam closer in spirit?" a majority of those who said that political organization was required by Islam, or that it should serve the cause of Islam, considered Islam closest to democracy, or close to both democracy and socialism (see Table 3.3; for distribution of responses to this question by social categories, see Table C.11 in Appendix C).

However, the majority of those who saw a close kinship between Islam and democracy said the two differed as well as resembled each other (see Table C.12 in Appendix C).

The interviews and literature on the subject at once suggest that those who regard Islam as democratic perceive democracy in two different ways: as a set of values and as a system of government. The middle-class professionals, as well as the *ulamā*, regard elected government, egalitarianism, civic liberties, and socioeconomic justice as features of Islam in common with democracy (see Table 3.4).

There is considerable agreement between the traditionalists, the revivalists, and the modernists concerning these ideals, but not on all of their implications. The most conspicuous sources demonstrating this agreement are the relevant portions of the three successive constitutions of Pakistan. In declaring that "the principles of democracy, freedom, equality, tolerance, and social justice as enunciated by Islam should be fully observed" in Pakistan,[35] the preambles of the constitutions at once state the feelings both of the traditionalists and the modernists, the former insisting on an Islamic interpretation of democracy, the latter on a democratic interpretation of

TABLE 3-3
SIMILARITY OF ISLAM TO OTHER POLITICAL SYSTEMS AS SEEN BY THE *ULAMĀ* AND THE PROFESSIONALS*

| | The Political System That Resembles Islam | | | | | | | | |
Social Category	Democracy	Socialism	Democracy and Socialism	Dictatorship and/or Fascism	"True Islam Is Democratic; Actual Islam Is Dictatorship"	Islam Is Similar to None	Islam Is Not a Political System	Refused to Answer	Row Total
Ulamā	24	0	0	0	0	4	0	0	28
	85.7%	0.0	0.0	0.0	0.0	14.3%	0.0	0.0	18.4%
Professionals, West Pakistan	43	9	8	5	0	3	0	2	70
	61.4%	12.9%	11.4%	7.1%	0.0	4.3%	0.0	2.9%	46.1%
Professionals, East Pakistan	12	4	24	4	4	0	4	2	54
	22.2%	7.4%	44.4%	7.4%	7.4%	0.0	7.4%	3.7%	33.5%
Column Total	79	13	32	9	4	7	4	4	152
	52.0%	18.6%	21.1%	5.9%	2.6%	4.6%	2.6%	2.6%	100.0%

*Responses to the question: To which of the following in your opinion is Islam closer in spirit?
a. Democracy; b. Socialism; c. Dictatorship; d. Fascism; e. Any other.

TABLE 3.4
COMMON FEATURES OF ISLAM AND DEMOCRACY, AS DESCRIBED
BY THOSE WHO DESIRE AN ISLAMIC STATE*

Social Categories	Common Features of Islam and Democracy					Maxi- mum Number
	Egalitarianism	Economic Justice	Civic Liberties	Constitutional Govt., etc.ᵃ	Considering People's Interest	
Ulamā	7	5	9	13	6	25
	28.0%	20.0%	36.0%	52.0%	24.0%	
Professionals,	22	8	12	17	2	32
West Pakistan	6.8%	25.0%	38.7%	53.1%	6.3%	
Professionals,	2	0	2	6	2	8
East Pakistan	25.0%	0.0	25.0%	75.0%	25.0%	
	31	13	23	36	10	65
Total	47.7%	20.0%	35.9%	55.4%	15.4%	

*Responses to the question: What features does Islam have in common with democracy? Each column records the number and percentage only of those who described that particular item as common between Islam and democracy. The number and percentage of those who did not mention that item are not shown in the table but may be figured from the percentage of those who did.

ᵃConstitutional government, elected government, democratic government, people's supremacy.

Islam. The qualifying phrase "as enunciated by Islam" should not, in the opinion of this writer, be taken as merely a device of the secularists to camouflage secular democracy plain and simple. While the intentions of some of those who formulated the constitution of Pakistan may indeed have been to disguise their secular notions, the findings of the survey confirmed that associating democratic values—even though superficially—with the teaching of Islam represents a widely diffused belief common to educated Pakistanis, including the traditionalist and the revivalist Muslims.

Even the *ulamā* seem to have accepted, in principle, the modernist formulation of democratic values about the fundamental rights of the citizens. The 1951 convention of the *ulamā* unanimously passed a resolution that contained their concept of the basic principles of an Islamic state. The resolution recommended certain statements that the *ulamā* considered fundamentally important and that they sought to include in the national consti-

tution that Pakistan's Constituent Assembly was formulating at that time.
One of the recommended articles of the constitution reads:

> The citizens shall be entitled to all the rights conferred upon them by
> the Islamic law, i.e., they shall be assured, within the limits of the law,
> of full security of life, property, and honor, freedom of religion and be-
> lief, freedom of worship, freedom of person, freedom of expression . . .
> benefit from public services.[36]

Another recommended article states: "No citizen shall, at any time, be deprived of these rights, except under the law, and none shall be awarded any
punishment or any charge without being given full opportunity of defense
and without the decision of a court of law."[37]

EQUALITY AND THE RULE OF LAW

Respect for law and the due process of law have, indeed, long been hall-
marks of traditional Islam's political ideal, excepting, of course, those sectarian interpretations of Islam that theoretically set the ruler above the law.
It is, therefore, not surprising that this Islamic ideal receives, in a world
climate of democratic ethos, fresh affirmation not only from the modernized Muslims but also from the traditional *ulamā*.[38] Traditional Islamic
attitudes toward equality and freedom, however, have been uneven. While
equality of all Muslims in the eyes of God is generally conceded, and the
Qur'ānic criterion of piety is recognized as the only standard of man's
worth,[39] both the traditional Islamic law and social sentiment have long
accommodated social, and in some cases also legal, inequality.

Though the legal status of women in medieval traditional Islam was
superior to their status in many of its contemporary civilizations, the traditional Islamic law—most provisions of which concerning the status of
women are fully accepted by contemporary *ulamā*—conceded inequality
of women in several legal matters. For example, a woman's witness in a
court of law, according to traditional Islamic law, carries only half as much
weight as that of a man's. Unlike the total commitment to the rule-of-the-
law ideal, therefore, acceptance of the legal equality of women by Islamic
revivalists and traditionalists is limited and subject to qualifications.[40]
According to Mawlana Kandhalwi, women should not even be allowed to
vote in elections of the national parliament.[41] The modernist sentiment,
however, generally recognizes the equal legal status of women for civic and
political rights.

Another aspect of the traditional political theory of Islam that puts further limits on the principles of equality concerns the status of non-Muslims. Generally, in most societies and on most matters, the law is more liberal than the practice; however, the practice of the Muslim state in the medieval past was far more liberal than the traditional Islamic law. Although the traditional Islamic law allowed considerable civic and religious autonomy to non-Muslim communities (*millets*), it still subjected non-Muslim citizens of a Muslim state to considerable theoretical restrictions.

According to the traditional medieval legal theory, the non-Muslim citizens (*dhimmīs*) of an Islamic state were required to pay a special poll tax (*jizya*) for their protection by the Muslim government. The legal theory also required that the non-Muslims not be allowed to build their houses higher than those of the Muslims or to wear saddles on their horses, and that they give way to a Muslim on public streets. These and other provisions of the law concerning disabilities of the non-Muslims were often disregarded by the Muslim rulers. The traditional medieval legal theory dictated further that the non-Muslims not be appointed to high executive positions in the government. This provision of the legal theory, too, was ignored by many caliphs and sultans in premodern times who appointed some non-Muslims to high executive posts. Unlike the disregard of the social disabilities of the *dhimmī*, which was taken lightly by the *ulamā*, the disregard of his civic disability was occasionally protested by them. The religious restrictions on the *dhimmīs* included the provisions that they not build new churches or temples without the permission of the Muslim government nor propagate their religion to convert others to their faith. Of all the legal disabilities, the last—proselytization to non-Islamic religion—was consistently enforced by most Muslim rulers in the premodern period and was most strongly demanded by the *ulamā*.

The extent of actual discrimination in premodern Muslim states did not generally reach the level of intolerance. Furthermore, the same legal theory that justified discrimination insisted on granting some basic rights and privileges to the non-Muslim communities. As Bernard Lewis notes:

> The level of willingness to tolerate and live peaceably with those who believe otherwise was, at most times and in most places, high enough for tolerable coexistence to be possible, and the Muslim did not therefore feel the imperative need felt by the Christian to seek an escape from the horrors of state-sponsored and state-enforced doctrine. . . .

By a sad paradox, the adoption in the nineteenth and twentieth centuries of democratic constitutions, guaranteeing equal rights for all citizens, in the Ottoman Empire, in Iran, Egypt, and elsewhere, on the whole weakened rather than strengthened the position of minorities.[42]

Contemporary attitudes toward the rights of non-Muslim citizens in Pakistan differ according to religious orientations. But even the most traditionalist of the *ulamā* do not approve of all the disabilities of the non-Muslims that the traditional Islamic law contains. The modernist sentiment clearly concedes the religious freedom of the non-Muslims, including their right to religious propagation, and recognizes no social or civil disabilities of the non-Muslims in Pakistan. The successive constitutions of Pakistan reflect the contemporary liberal Islamic sentiment in this respect, as they recognize complete religious freedom of all citizens: "Subject to law, public order and morality: *(a)* every citizen has the right to profess, practice and propagate any religion; and *(b)* every religious denomination and every sect thereof has the right to establish, maintain, and manage its religious institutions."[43]

None of the successive constitutions of Pakistan recognizes any special tax to be collected from the non-Muslims. Some Pakistanis, however, did entertain the idea of collection of *jizya,* even though they would otherwise allow full legal equality of non-Muslim citizens with Muslim citizens. Khalifa Abdul Hakim wrote, for example:

> The non-Muslims, if they become peaceful and loyal subjects of the state, are to be granted complete liberty of religious belief and practice. In lieu of a small and reasonable tax for protection, which they shall pay to the state, their equality before the law is to be guaranteed. A non-Muslim can sue even the president of the republic in the court, as it actually happened during the reign of the early khalifas. The life, honor and property of the non-Muslim subjects of an Islamic state shall receive full protection and no Muslim will be allowed to plead a privilege against them.[44]

Some of the Muslims who still favor the payment of *jizya* by the non-Muslim citizens of an Islamic state appear to have been caught between the demands of traditional *fiqh*—whose theoretically overriding authority they acknowledge—and the modern democratic values to which they are at-

tracted. Trying to satisfy both, they have sought to reconcile the two demands. Some say that the Muslims in an Islamic state have to pay the *zakāt*
tax, which obviously could not be collected from non-Muslims; collection
of *jizya* from them, therefore, would amount to no discrimination against
non-Muslims.[45] Others indicate that *jizya* is a monetary consideration in
lieu of the military service of the country's defense, from which the non-
Muslims are exempt, in view of the ideological nature of the Islamic state,
while a Muslim is subject to conscription.[46]

Many Pakistani Muslims desirous of an Islamic state character talked of
jizya in terms that seemed to lack the kind of conviction and commitment
that characterized their discussion of most other Islamic matters. Others,
including most of those who supported the idea of an Islamic state, did
not even mention it, either considering it—as do some modernists—too
far-fetched an idea to be valid in the twentieth century or finding it—as do
some *ulamā*—so offensive to the taste of the modernist Muslims as to dam-
age whatever chances there could be for compromise between the *ulamā*
and the modernists on other, more important aspects of the Islamic state.
Undoubtedly, it is due to this last consideration that one finds no mention
of *jizya* in the constitutional recommendations of the 1951 convention of the
ulamā.[47] Yet for those among the *ulamā* and the revivalists who distinguish
between the Muslims and non-Muslim citizens of the state, the distinction
is a necessary part of the Islamic character of the state. It would be unreal-
istic and unreasonable, they say, to expect the non-Muslim to serve Islamic
goals. For this reason, and following the traditional Islamic legal concepts,
the *ulamā* and the revivalists insist that key positions in the government of
a Muslim state should not be assigned to non-Muslims.[48] For them, this,
too, is a necessary corollary of the Islamic character of the state:

> The Islamic state means a state which is run on the exalted and excel-
> lent principles of Islam. . . . It can only be run by those who believe in
> those principles. People who do not subscribe to those ideas may have
> a place in the administrative machinery of the state but they cannot be
> entrusted with the responsibility of framing the general policy of the
> state or dealing with matters vital to its safety and integrity.[49]

As against this, the modernists, by and large, would concede no such exclusion of the non-Muslims from any administrative positions. The three
constitutions of Pakistan representing, again, in this respect, the liberal

modernist sentiment, declare: "No citizen otherwise qualified for appointment in the service of Pakistan shall be discriminated against in respect of
any such appointment on grounds only of race, religion, caste, sex, residence or place of birth."[50] The only exception that the consecutive constitutions of Pakistan make—an exception upon which the *ulamā* and the revivalists insisted and that the modernists willingly accepted—is that the
president of Pakistan and since 1973 its prime minister must be Muslims.[51]

In most other matters, the traditionalists and the revivalists have sought
to emphatically recognize the rights of non-Muslims with regard to religious worship and cultural autonomy. The 1951 convention of the *ulamā*
declared:

> The non-Muslim citizens of the state shall have, within the limits of the
> law, complete freedom of religion and worship, mode of life, culture
> and religious education. They shall be entitled to have all their matters
> concerning Personal Law administered in accordance with their own
> religious code, usages and customs.[52]

Similar statements are found in other traditionalist and revivalist writings.[53]
One may conclude by saying, therefore, that though the extent of equality
that the traditionalists in Pakistan would concede according to their understanding of Islam is still partial and limited, it is less limited than what
the tradition itself allowed. Certainly, the contemporary ethos of equality
has affected not only the modernist Muslims but, to some extent, also the
most traditionalist of them. One reason for this greater allowance, at least
in the sphere of religious rights of the non-Muslim minority, may be the recent historical experience of the Muslim community of the Indo-Pakistan
subcontinent.

More than a hundred years of British rule over India, which recognized
full religious rights of all communities in the subcontinent not just in practice but by law as well, must have familiarized the *ulamā* with a wider range
of religious rights than Islam's own *millet* system granted earlier. The realization of the value of full legal equality in matters related to religious freedom, which benefited the Muslims despite their subject status, could not
entirely escape the *ulamā*.

Besides outside Western influence on the contemporary Muslim understanding of the ideal of equality, internal factors were also influential. The
Islamic tradition offered, with the exceptions discussed above, an egalitar-

ian ideal of considerable range. In the medieval age, its sensitivity to human equality far exceeded that of Islam's contemporary civilizations. As an ideal, it recognized no class privileges and no caste or race differences. Social prejudice in Muslim societies, therefore, was, and in some important matters still is, less significant than in some other contemporary societies. And there existed even in medieval Islam some basic motifs that to some Muslim Sufis were suggestive of a wider egalitarianism than traditional Islam actually conceded. Doctrinal acceptance of the contemporary concept of equality, therefore, has been relatively easy for those modernists who sought its accommodation or—from the liberal Islamic point of view—its restoration in Islam. Ghulam Ahmad Parwez, for example, quoting the Qur'ānic verse "Verily we have honored every human being" (17:70), stated: "As human beings, all men are equal; every one possesses that precious jewel, the human self." [54]

FREEDOM AS A DEMOCRATIC VALUE

The third democratic value, freedom—in the modern sense of civil liberties of thought and expression—was rather unfamiliar in medieval Islam. Bernard Lewis notes that "freedom" (Arabic: *hurriyya*) in classical Islamic literature is used in a legal and social and, exceptionally, in a philosophic sense. In the legal sense, it connoted the status of a free man as against that of a slave, and in the philosophic, the freedom of the will. However, Franz Rosenthal concludes in his study, *The Muslim Concept of Freedom,* that "freedom as an ideal was not unknown [in medieval Islam]; yet, as a political force it lacked the support which only a central position within the political organism and system of thought could give it." [55]

The considerably accommodating spirit of traditional Sunnī Islam, which tolerated a great variety of religious and legal opinions among the Muslims, has been noted above. However, several points must be noted in this respect. First, whereas past doctrinal departures from the norm eventually came to be accepted by the majority Sunnī Muslim community as alternate understandings of Islam, the same Muslim communities often resisted new theological assertions that originated in their own times. Second, such disagreement as was accepted right away was usually confined to legal questions of minor importance. Third, whenever new dissent on questions of basic, doctrinal importance was tolerated, it was tolerated mainly to avoid conflict and not in recognition of any fundamental rights of man.

It is therefore not surprising that even though the *ulamā* would allow the non-Muslims in an Islamic state complete freedom in doctrinal matters, they would wish to severely restrict freedom of thought and expression for the Muslims themselves. The recommendations of the 1951 convention of the *ulamā* asserted: "The propagation and publicity of such views and ideologies as are calculated to undermine the basic principles and ideals on which the Islamic state rests, shall be prohibited."[56]

Some *ulamā,* particularly those of West Pakistan, consider freedom of expression a common characteristic of Islam and democracy (see Table 3.4 above). However, it became clear from their full responses, during the interviews conducted for the survey, that by freedom of expression they actually mean freedom to criticize the Muslim government, not the Islamic ideology. The majority of those among the non-*ulamā* who support the idea of an Islamic state also subject freedom of thought and expression to the restraints of what they consider the Islamic ideology.[57] Table C.32 (in Appendix C) presents the responses of *ulamā* and professionals to the following question, which sought to assess their attitude on this matter:

To which of the following propositions do you subscribe?
a. The Muslims in Pakistan must share the fundamentals of our Islamic Ideology. The non-Muslims must respect them.
b. The citizens of our country, both Muslims and non-Muslims, should be allowed every right to oppose and object, in good conscience, even to what could be regarded by others as the fundamentals of Islamic Ideology.

Table 3.5 presents the same responses of those among the *ulamā* and professionals who want the state to serve secular or Islamic interests. As noted in Table 3.5, a vast majority (ca. 80 percent) of those who desired an Islamic state demanded that Pakistani citizens recognize and respect the fundamentals of Islamic ideology. In place of the ideal of freedom of the individual (whether of thought, expression, or association), traditional Islam emphasized the values of consensus and solidarity of the Muslim community. In modern times, due to the colonial experience of many Muslim lands and under the influence of national liberation movements, the awareness of the need, as well as the value, of solidarity and unity was likely increased. It is perhaps for this reason that, after a brief period of popularity of liberal democratic values among the modern educated Muslim intelligentsia in the

TABLE 3.5

CONSENSUS ON ISLAMIC IDEOLOGY DEMANDED BY THE SUPPORTERS
OF ISLAMIC AND SECULAR STATES

The Type of State Desired	Consensus on Islamic Ideology			Row Total
	Not Demanded "B"	Demanded "A"	Qualified "A" and "B"	
Muslim, Islamic	11 15.9% 19.6%	55 79.7% 93.2%	3 4.3% 60.0%	69 57.5%
Secular	45 88.2% 80.4%	4 7.8% 6.8%	2 3.9% 40.0%	51 42.5%
Column Total	56 46.7%	59 49.2%	5 4.3%	120 100.0%

late nineteenth and early twentieth centuries, liberalism began to wane everywhere in the Muslim world as the focus shifted from the freedom of the individual to the freedom of the community, the achievement of which required solidarity. This trend has continued after the achievement of national liberation. Dr. Fazlur Rahman neatly and concisely presents the democratic values of Islam: equality, in itself a fundamental value, and freedom, more of a means to other social goals, namely, cooperation, brotherhood, and self-sacrifice. Here is a liberalism based on Islamic sources:

> The Qur'ān . . . enunciates certain fundamental principles of social organization. These principles are those of social justice, cooperation, brotherhood and self-sacrifice for the sake of the common good. Human equality belongs to the very essence of this teaching and, in effect, the entire Islamic movement and the teachings of the Qur'ān can be seen as directed towards the creation of a meaningful and positive equality among human beings. As such the Islamic purpose cannot be realized until genuine freedom to human beings is restored and freedom from all forms of exploitation — social, spiritual, political and economic — assured. It is only then that real cooperation, brotherhood and self-sacrifice can become realities.[58]

ISLAMIC GOVERNMENT

In response to the question, "What are the minimum requirements of an Islamic state?" the *ulamā* and the middle-class professionals gave diverse answers (see Table 3.6). Among those who desired an Islamic state the four most frequent responses of the *ulamā*, in descending order, were: enforcement of the *sharī'a*, rule of just and righteous government, Islamic faith of the ruler, and meeting the dictates of economic justice. The most frequent responses of West Pakistani professionals, in their order of priority, were economic justice, *sharī'a*, righteous government, and democracy; of the former East Pakistani professionals, *sharī'a*, democracy, righteous government, and economic justice. Obviously there is agreement on some ideals among those who desire an Islamic state. However, the extent of agreement on these ideals as well as their exact conception and formulation varies from one social category to the other.

Thus, some of the responses describing the nature of an Islamic state are related to democratic values (such as equality), some to the character of government, and still others to conceptions of the law and legislation. Of these, democratic values have already been discussed in the preceding section, and attitudes related to the law and legislation will be discussed in the next section. This section examines three major questions related to the institution of government: its legitimacy, formation, and form.

The issue of governmental legitimacy loomed large in political thought and controversy in medieval Islam. The prevalent medieval Sunnī legal theory preferred "election" of the ruler to the dynastic principle of inheritance. Some Muslim legal theorists in medieval times stated the qualifications of those who may be chosen to govern the Muslim state. These qualifications of the ruler are sometimes reinstated by contemporary *ulamā* in Pakistan.[59] The qualifications may be categorized in three classes: (1) minimum qualifications that are explicitly or implicitly required by the law in most societies whether Muslim or non-Muslim, for all candidates, such as soundness of the senses and the adult age; (2) those that the citizen populations of most societies usually value in or expect from the head of their government: wisdom, understanding, a brave and just disposition; and (3) those that have a peculiar reference to Islam: the Islamic faith and knowledge of Islamic sciences.[60]

The distinction between what can stand a legal test (e.g., soundness or

TABLE 3.6
MINIMUM REQUIREMENTS OF THE ISLAMIC STATE AS DESCRIBED BY THOSE WHO DESIRE IT

<table>
<tr><td rowspan="2"></td><td colspan="9">Requirements of an Islamic State[a]</td></tr>
<tr></tr>
<tr>
<td>Social Category of Respondent</td>
<td>Implementation of the Shari'a</td>
<td>Just and Righteous Ruler</td>
<td>Democracy, Equality</td>
<td>Muslim Head of State</td>
<td>Economic Justice, etc.</td>
<td>General Honesty and Fairness among Officers and/or Citizens</td>
<td>Muslim Majority</td>
<td>Ulamā's Role in Interpreting Islamic Law</td>
<td>Maximum Number</td>
</tr>
<tr>
<td>Ulamā</td>
<td>20
71.4%</td>
<td>19
69.9%</td>
<td>6
21.4%</td>
<td>17
60.7%</td>
<td>10
35.7%</td>
<td>1
3.6%</td>
<td>3
10.7%</td>
<td>6
21.4%</td>
<td>28</td>
</tr>
<tr>
<td>Professionals, West Pakistan</td>
<td>6
50.0%</td>
<td>8
25.0%</td>
<td>13
14.6%</td>
<td>6
18.8%</td>
<td>19
59.4%</td>
<td>13
40.6%</td>
<td>12
37.5%</td>
<td>1
3.1%</td>
<td>32</td>
</tr>
<tr>
<td>Professionals, East Pakistan</td>
<td>4
50.0%</td>
<td>2
25.0%</td>
<td>4
50.0%</td>
<td>0
0.0</td>
<td>2
25.0%</td>
<td>1
12.5%</td>
<td>0
0.0</td>
<td>0
0.0</td>
<td>8</td>
</tr>
<tr>
<td>Column Total</td>
<td>40
58.8%</td>
<td>29
42.6%</td>
<td>23
33.8%</td>
<td>23
33.8%</td>
<td>31
45.6%</td>
<td>15
22.1%</td>
<td>15
22.1%</td>
<td>7
10.3%</td>
<td>68</td>
</tr>
</table>

[a] Each column records the number and percentages only of those who described that particular item as a minimum requirement. The number and percentage of those who did not mention that item are not shown in the table but may be figured from the percentage of those who did.

impairment of the senses) and what can only be a matter of subjective judgment (wisdom) is often not made in classical Islamic literature on this subject, nor always by the contemporary *ulamā* of Pakistan. This is, of course, partly a reflection of the general character of Islamic law, in which religio-moral values imposed by one's Islamic conscience and rules of law enforceable by an Islamic state were in some cases discussed together within the same chapters of legal treatises. Such treatment of the law is in itself a reflection of the fact that the real validity of Islamic law—as of laws in several other religious traditions—is seen by the believer as resting on God's commands, irrespective of whether a state enforces it or not, and even whether it is enforceable by a state or not. In this sense all religious norms are, from the standpoint of the faithful, essentially the same, whether they are observed by conscience alone or enforced by the state as well.

This is, of course, not to suggest that the traditional Islamic law made no distinction at all in any respect between the commands enforceable by the state and those observable by the personal conscience. It did so distinguish in several cases where practical necessity demanded it, but the practical necessity of distinguishing the two spheres in respect to the choice of the ruler shrank and became almost nonexistent because of the reality of medieval Muslim politics, which willy-nilly sustained dynastic rule or de facto power. The judicial system that developed in medieval Islamic history could not, therefore, realistically apply the Islamic legal provisions concerning a ruler's legitimacy against a king under whose very protection it existed, even though the king was, from the viewpoint of the ideal theory, obviously less than a fully legitimate ruler. The legal theory, thus freed from realistic expectations, dispensed altogether with the need to distinguish legal requirements from the socially desirable characteristics of a legitimate ruler.

Even the "Views" of the Board of Talimat-i-Islamiyya, Pakistan, whose active membership consisted of three *ulamā* and two modern educated (but traditionally inclined) Muslims, failed to categorically distinguish between qualifications that may be judicially enforceable and those that may only be left to the subjective, personal judgment of the voter.[61] The failure is particularly remarkable in view of the fact that the board stated these views as its recommendations for the first constitution of Pakistan to the Basic Principles subcommittee of the first National Assembly of Pakistan, a subcommittee that was assigned an important role in formulating the constitution and that created the board as a source of expert advice on Islamic constitutional matters. The board's recommendations consisted essentially of a rephrasing of traditional qualifications.[62]

The *ulamā* in Pakistan have been rather insistent on two qualifications of the ruler that medieval *ulamā* often, though not always, took for granted: the Islamic faith and male gender of the ruler. The reason that the traditionalists give for the necessity of Islamic faith of the ruler is the same one they give for the necessity of Islamic faith of those who may occupy high administrative offices generally, namely, only a Muslim can be expected to work for the glory and welfare of Islam, while a non-Muslim will tend to work for the promotion of his own faith, since it is a natural human tendency that one would promote the interest of one's own faith.[63] In the case of the chief executive, however, the necessity is seen to be even greater since he has the supreme responsibility of implementing the *sharīʿa*.[64]

The second condition, the male gender of the ruler, is said to be necessary because women, in the view of some traditionalists, are naturally "weak and fickle-minded"; because their natural monthly cycle, pregnancy, and delivery are likely to interrupt the business of the state; and above all, because ordinances of the *sharīʿa* forbid their going out of their homes.[65]

The contemporary traditionalist conception of the qualifications of the ruler significantly departs from al-Mawardi's description in one significant way. Al-Mawardi requires of the ruler such knowledge of Islam as may be needed for independent judgment (*ijtihād*). The *ulamā* of today would, in effect, reduce the extent of the required expert knowledge to such general understanding of Islam as is needed for him "to honor the ways of Islam, propagate the Islamic *sharīʿa*, and maintain Islamic sciences."[66] For most *ulamā* either the need of *ijtihād* simply does not exist or they consider a body of the *ulamā* alone to be fit for *ijtihād*.

The revivalist position on the qualifications of the ruler is mainly similar to that of the *ulamā*, though not necessarily to their reasoning.[67] It may be noted, however, that the revivalist Jamaat-i-Islami, despite its doctrinal position on the requirement of the male sex of the ruler, supported the candidacy of Miss Fatima Jinnah (sister of Quid-i-Azam Muhammad Ali Jinnah, the founder of Pakistan) for the Pakistani presidency in 1964. This was justified as a means of getting rid of a greater evil: the dictatorship/presidency of General Muhammad Ayub Khan. Even more remarkable is the fact that in both postdivided Pakistan and Bangladesh female prime ministers came to power through popular elections and have effectively ruled their countries for several years. Obviously, the caution against female leadership has limited popular appeal, and that caution is easily diluted by popular attachment to the surviving family of a favored, dead leader. Benazir Bhutto in postdivided Pakistan led the People's Party that her late father, Prime Minister Zulfiqar Ali Bhutto, founded. She became the prime minister of Pakistan in 1988, was removed from that office in 1990, but returned to power in 1993. Begum Khaleda Zia is the widow of the assassinated president of Bangladesh, General Ziaur Rahman. She became prime minister of her country in 1991.

The modernist Muslims in Pakistan do not pay so much attention to the question of qualifications of the ruler as do the traditionalists and the revivalists. They generally reject the necessity of such qualifications of the ruler as ritual piety and knowledge of traditional Islamic sciences that are emphasized by the traditionalists and the revivalists.[68] It would be correct to say that generally the modernist as well as the secularist notion of a good ruler bears more resemblance to an efficient prime minister or president in a Western country, but with a marked sense of decency and honesty, than to a caliph-sultan of the *ulamā*'s conception.

Apart from the occasional philosophical eclecticism of some individual modernists that suggests idealization of autocracy, there appeared to exist among the educated Muslims in predivided Pakistan considerable agreement on the ideal of elected government. Not only do the secularist and modernist Muslims uphold this ideal, but the revivalists do too. What is even more significant is that the *ulamā*, too, are moving in this direction. Mufti Shafi's *Qur'ānic Constitution* states that "the power to appoint and depose the head of the state shall vest in the people, who shall use it through their elected representatives."[69]

The Board of Talimat-i-Islamiyya, Pakistan, favored elected government, consisting of a popularly elected legislature and a president who is elected, in turn, by the legislature.[70] However, one notices some hesitation on the part of the *ulamā* to accept the full implications of the elective principle in the choice of government. Whereas they are willing to accept popular election as a valid and, under contemporary conditions, a desirable method, they do not consider it to be the only acceptable method. The 1951 convention of the *ulamā* used more general terms. "The head of the state shall always be," states the resolution of the convention, a person "in whose piety, learning and judgement the people or their elected representatives have full confidence."[71]

Confidence, indeed, is what the traditional Sunnī theory takes to be a criterion of legitimacy, not the specific method of expressing that confidence. Apart from the arrangement that the Islamic legal tradition worked out to knowingly—even though somewhat unwillingly—legitimize usurpation in order to avoid the danger of armed conflict and anarchy, the medieval theorists allowed three methods of succession to legitimate caliphate: acclamation, nomination of the next caliph by the previous caliph, and nomination by an electoral council that is appointed by the previous caliph. The three methods are taken to be valid on the grounds that selection of the first three *rashīd* (rightly guided) caliphs took place according to these three methods, respectively.[72] Whatever the method of the initial choice, it is, theoretically, to be followed by a demonstration of confidence of the people through the institution of *bay'a* (acclamation; shaking hands to indicate acceptance).

The contemporary understanding of the Muslims that Islam favors elective principle in the choice of government is mainly based on two points: one, the Qur'ān's characterization of the Muslims as those "who conduct their affairs with mutual consultation";[73] and two, the precedent established by the Madinese Muslims as they acclaimed Abu Bakr to be the caliph after the death of the Prophet (A.D. 632), which was followed by a public *bay'a*. However, according to the prevalent, that is, Sunnī, medieval interpretation, the acclamation (or election) was to be accomplished by *ahl al-hall wa'l-'aqd* (the people of loosening and binding) alone. In medieval traditional literature, the *ahl al-hall wa'l-'aqd* are generally described as "amirs and *ulamā* and chiefs and leaders of people."[74] Ibn Jamaa (d. 1333) further limits their number by adding one qualification: ability to attend the acclamation ceremony in the city of the caliph's residence.[75] No limit to the number of such people is specified, and the likelihood of disagreement among them is usually ignored by medieval writers. The acclamation was to take the form of *bay'ah* representing a contract (*ahd*) between the acclaimed caliph and the *ahl al-hall wa'l-'aqd* concerning their mutual obligations in accordance with Islam.

Obviously the modern electoral process is several steps removed from this medieval Muslim understanding of "election" of the head of the state. Not just the traditional Islamic practice but even the traditional Islamic ideal amounted to a process that was essentially acclamation by a small group of influential people, not election by the entire citizenry. Many medieval jurists speak of a second, public *bay'a* or acclamation, but this acclamation is to be for confirmation, with no choice of alternate candidate. Other jurists simply dispense with the need of the public acclamation and suggest that even those important people in the provinces whose presence is not practical at the capital are legally bound to agree with the choice, if the chosen ruler is worthy of the office.[76] Seen in this background, the acceptance of the elective principle, even though with some hesitance, by contemporary *ulamā* in Pakistan represents a significant departure from medieval interpretation of Islam's political teachings. However, for the modernists (and in this case even for the revivalists, who are less committed to the medieval interpretation of Islam than the *ulamā*), acceptance of the elective principle constitutes not a departure from but a return to what the Islamic ideal has always sought.

Finally, it should be noted that, for the *ulamā*, confidence of the people as a criterion of legitimacy of a government is secondary to the criterion of the Islamic quality of law that the government enforces. If the choice were between an honest king or a dictator who enforced the laws of the *sharī'a* and a government that was duly elected by the people but that cared little for what the traditional law required, then there would be no doubt that for the *ulamā* such a king or dictator would be preferable. The same would be the position of the revivalists. The kind of Islamic democracy supported by them is meaningful only after the fundamental principle of the supremacy of the *sharī'a* is granted. Indeed, apart from the inherent appeal of some democratic aspects of Islam for the traditionalists and the revivalists, one strategic reason for their support of the elective principle in government in Pakistan has been their realization that the popular sentiment of the people is pro-Islamic, and therefore an elected government is likely to be an asset in Islamization of law and the social order.

Making Islamic legitimacy of the government and Islamic quality of its rule the two main conditions, the non-secularly oriented Muslims in Pakistan, including the *ulamā*, hold that neither the presidential nor the parliamentary form of government (i.e., executive) is un-Islamic. Many *ulamā* do, however, consider the presidential cabinet to be nearer to the spirit and ideals of Islam since, in their view, a parliament could unnecessarily check and limit the powers of the head of the state.[77] Yet the *ulamā* insist on the principles of consultation in the discharge of administrative duties. "The function of the Head of the State," declared the 1951 convention of the *ulamā*, "shall not be autocratic but consultative."[78] And "the head of the state shall have no right . . . to run the administration in any other way but on consultative basis."[79] In the final analysis, however, the requirement for the head of the state to consult the council in executive matters is not, in the view of the *ulamā,* absolute, and once the counsel is given to him, he is free to accept or discard it.

The consultative council (*shūrā*) may take any shape, formal or informal. Some traditional *ulamā* would prefer to leave it to the head of the state to individually consult those whom he considers competent in the field of expertise in which the counsel is sought.[80] Others would insist on proper election of a formal parliament.

A principle in the organization of government that all Muslim "Islamists"—the traditionalists, the revivalists, and the modernists—seek to stress is independence of the judiciary.[81] They underscore the importance of two judicial principles: one, that the same laws be applied to all, including the head of the state, as well as other public officials; and two, that all officers of the state be tried in the same courts of law as the ordinary public. Discussion about these principles in contemporary Islamic literature is often subsumed under the subject of independence of the judiciary.[82]

ISLAMIC LAW AND LEGISLATION

The area in which the Muslims of various orientations differ most significantly is that of Islamic law and legislation. As has been noted above, the concept of an Islamic state in the traditional Muslim thinking is most closely associated with the implementation of the *sharīʿa* law.

The secularists are, of course, opposed to the very notion of Islamic law beyond matters of "personal status" (i.e., matters related to marriage, divorce, inheritance, and child adoption). A ranking civil servant of secularist persuasion in Pakistan, when asked whether he would like to see the law in Pakistan be Islamized, said: "The [Islamic] laws of inheritance are already enforced in Pakistan; the rest are tribal customs."[83] In contrast to the secularist disregard of the traditional Islamic law, the traditionalists and the revivalists hold Islamic laws to be either directly revealed by God or indirectly based on His revelation. The fact is that not only do the secularists and the Islamists hold radically opposed views, some of them also lack a full appreciation of each other's feelings, reasoning, and ethical orientations.

Apart from the law pertaining to family matters (marriage, divorce, adoption, inheritance), and the *awqāf,* the prevailing law in predivided

TABLE 3.7
ISLAMIC CHARACTER OF THE LAW IN PAKISTAN AS PERCEIVED BY THE *ULAMĀ* AND PROFESSIONALS

Social Category	Perceived Islamic Character							Row Total
	Mainly Islamic	Partly Islamic	"Not Repugnant to Islam"	"Islamic Character Is Uncertain"	Mainly Un-Islamic	Totally Un-Islamic	"I Don't Know" or Refused to Answer	
Ulamā	0 0.0	6 20.7%	0 0.0	0 0.0	18 62.1%	2 6.9%	3 10.3%	29 22.1%
Professionals, West Pakistan	20 29.0%	4 5.8%	1 1.4%	1 1.4%	27 39.1%	6 8.7%	10 14.5%	69 52.7%
Professionals, East Pakistan	0 0.0	7 21.2%	20 60.6%	0 0.0	4 12.15%	2 6.1%	0 0.0	33 25.2%
Column Total	20 15.3%	17 13.0%	21 16.0%	1 0.8%	49 37.4%	10 7.6%	13 9.9%	131 100.0%

Pakistan was, and in good part still is, of British origin. Most conscious of the un-Islamic origin of such laws have been the *ulamā* and the revivalists.[84] To the modernists, however, non-Islamic origin of the law does not by itself indicate its non-Islamic character; to some of them, any just law can be considered Islamic.[85] To assess the attitudes toward the prevailing law in predivided Pakistan in 1969, the following question was included in the survey questionnaire:

> How would you describe the present laws of Pakistan with reference to their Islamic character?
>
> *a.* Mainly un-Islamic.
> *b.* Mainly Islamic, for those laws that do not originate from the *sharī'a* are nevertheless based on the Islamic principles of justice and equity.
> *c.* Totally un-Islamic.

Table 3.7 presents the distribution of the three categories of respondents by their conceptions of the Islamic character of the law. Table 3.8 presents the responses to the next question, whether the respondent wanted to see the prevailing law in predivided Pakistan Islamized.

The survey data confirmed, once again, a greater propensity of the West Pakistani professionals toward a sociopolitical understanding of Islam than that of the Muslim Bengali professionals, a difference that was also indicated in respect to the "national" identity and the functions of the state. It should be noted, however, that even in the former East Pakistan the frequency of those who held all Islamic laws undesirable was less than the frequency of secular nationalists there (ca. 33 percent vs. 60 percent: compare Table C.13 given in Appendix C with Table 2.4 presented in Chapter 2). Almost half the East Pakistani professionals (47 percent), including some who otherwise appeared to be political secularists and secular nationalists, wanted to retain fully the Islamic law concerning family matters. Since these matters have long been considered a part of personal matters—as opposed to social, economic, or political matters—and were considered so even during the British rule in India, their regulation by religious laws is not seen as a compromise of their secularist position. The British policy to allow these matters to be governed by the religious law in their otherwise secular rule of the Indo-Pakistan subcontinent must have led to an even closer association of such laws with matters of personal faith

TABLE 3.8

DESIRABILITY OF ISLAMIC LAW BY PERCEIVED CHARACTER
OF LAW IN PAKISTAN

Desirability of Islamic Law	Perceived Character of the Law in Pakistan			Row Total
	Mainly Islamic	Partly Islamic	Un-Islamic	
	4	10	3	17
Undesirable	23.5%	58.8%	17.6%	15.0%
	21.1%	26.3%	5.4%	
	3	11	5	19
Partly Desirable	15.8%	57.9%	26.3%	16.8%
	15.8%	28.9%	8.9%	
	12	17	48	77
Desirable	15.6%	22.1%	62.3%	68.1%
	63.2%	44.7%	85.7%	
	19	38	56	113
Column Total	16.8%	33.6%	49.6%	100.0%

and, as such, to their relatively unchallenged accommodation within a secular legal framework. However, this leads to a situation—paradoxical by one standard—that in respect to the sanctity of the traditional Islamic law on matters of "personal status," some secularists support an essentially traditionalist stand.

Those among the sample of the survey in 1969 who desired to Islamize the law beyond matters of "personal status" identified four major spheres of the law that they would specially seek to Islamize (see Table 3.9).

Foremost among these is the sphere of social morality. Drinking, gambling, and prostitution were the social evils the eradication of which was most urgently sought through the implementation of Islamic law. The *ulamā* generally also included cinema, theater, coeducation, and nonobservance of the veil (*purdah*) among the practices they regarded as social evils. During the survey, a few of the *ulamā* further indicated that they would also like to see enforced by state law the obligation of five times daily prayers (*salāt*) and fasting (*siyām*) in the month of Ramadan.

The second major area in which Islamization of the law was sought

TABLE 3.9
"SPHERES" OF THE LAW WHICH THOSE WHO ARE DESIROUS OF ISLAMIC
LAW WOULD SPECIALLY SEEK TO ISLAMIZE[a]

Social Category	"Spheres" of the Law to Be Specially Islamized[b]				
	Social Morality, Piety	Economic Justice, etc.	Criminal Law, Administration of Justice	Honest and Fair Administration	Maximum Number
Ulamā	22	7	9	4	29
	75.9%	24.1%	31.0%	13.8%	
Professionals, West Pakistan	29	24	24	3	47
	61.7%	55.8%	54.5%	7.0%	
Professionals, East Pakistan	7	8	0	7	16
	43.8%	50.0%	0.0	43.8%	
Column Total	58	39	33	14	92
	63.0%	44.3%	37.1%	15.9%	

[a] Responses to the question: In what spheres would you particularly like to see the law Islamized?
[b] Each column records the number and percentage only of those who stated that particular "sphere" they seek to specially Islamize. The number and percentage of those who did not mention the item are not shown in the table but may be figured from the percentage of those who did.

covered matters relating to economic justice. Many professionals in the two former "wings" of Pakistan spoke generally of social or economic justice, which they sought through implementation of Islamic laws; some specifically named elimination of interest and collection and administration of zakāt by the state as the objectives that must be achieved in accordance with Islamic laws. Almost all of those ulamā who spoke of economic matters mentioned only usury and interest, elimination of which they sought through enforcing the Islamic law. (These subjects will be treated at some length in the chapter on economic orientations.)

Islamizing the country's criminal law and honest and free administration of justice constituted the third major area in which enforcement of Islamic law was urgently sought. Concern for the criminal law, of course, reflects the fact that punishments for some crimes are specified by the Qur'ān itself, which is considered to be the first and the most authoritative source of Islamic law. A greater compulsion is, therefore, felt for enforcing Islamic

laws to prevent crimes that are strongly condemned by the Qur'ān itself—
crimes such as theft and murder.

Honest and efficient administration of justice, too, has been a prime concern of the classical Islamic legal tradition. It was, indeed, one of the most
important criteria the Muslim public applied in judging the character of a
government. Traditional Muslim legends and literature are full of refer-
ences to judicial sagacity and honesty, as respected qualities of the *qāḍī*, as
well as to an unqualified commitment to justice as a prime quality of a good
sultan. The contemporary traditionalist and revivalist literature, too, em-
phasizes the Islamic importance of honest and efficient administration of
justice.[86]

Both the traditionalists and the revivalists are strongly critical of the
system of trial attorneyship and court fees. Considering them to be both un-
Islamic and unjust, they wish to abolish both systems.[87] The concern of the
ulamā for fair administration of justice reflects not only Islam's general
concern for honesty and justice but also the fact that *qudāt* (judges of the
Muslim courts) were, in the premodern period, mainly nominated from
amongst the ranks of the *ulamā*. The *ulamā* seek not only implementation
of Islamic laws but would also like to carry out the administration of such
laws, as they did in the past.[88] These factors aside, the administration of
justice in the lower courts of Pakistan has been so strained with obstruc-
tionism and bribery—which is generally sought and accepted by peons,
typists, and clerks of the court and sometimes even by the judges—as to
make justice not infrequently a mockery. The defects of the present judicial system have been evident to all, especially to those who wish to fully
Islamize the law.

Bribery, dishonesty, and general betrayal of public faith by civil officials
were also included among major administrative problems by those survey
respondents who wanted to reform government by Islamizing the administrative law. However, those who pointed to corruption as a reason for
Islamizing the law were half aware that what they actually disapproved of
was the un-Islamic behavior of public officials (betrayal of trust, etc.) rather
than a deficiency of the existing non-Islamic laws, which also declared such
behavior criminal. The feeling of some who sought to Islamize the law was
that those evils in government and administration would be more efficiently
controlled under Islamic laws because the people have far greater moral
commitment to the *sharīʿa* law than to the laws of British origin.[89]

Although the modernists, as well as the traditionalists and the revival-

THE ISLAMIC STATE • 93

ists, have desired to Islamize the law, their conceptions of the Islamic law differ substantially. For the traditionalists and the revivalists, the bulk of Islamic law already exists in the books of compiled *fatāwā* (juristic opinions) and learned commentaries on *fiqh*. The major need, according to them, is mainly organization and systemization of this material to achieve easy accessibility. For them, therefore, Islamization of the law means mainly full implementation of those laws in place of the British Indian laws in Pakistan.[90] For many modernists, a large portion of the law included in the *fiqh* books is obsolete. They argue that Islamic law ceased to grow long ago in medieval times, as *ijtihād* came to be thoroughly confined within the established legal schools of Muslim law.[91]

To a very limited extent, the traditionalists and the revivalists also concede the need of a new formulation of the Islamic law, but only in those matters that are not covered by traditional laws, such as those that resulted from entirely new historical developments.[92] Mufti Muhammad Shafi (d. 1977), for example, granted, at least in theory, that in a few cases implementation of some rules of the traditional *fiqh* might appear difficult; in such cases *ijtihād* might be exercised to meet the difficulty.[93] However, in interviews with the author the *ulamā* made no such exception. By and large, the traditionalist position remains that the provisions of those traditional laws upon which the learned and pious doctors of Islamic law agreed in the early centuries of Islamic history must be enforced unaltered. Additionally, the *ulamā* prefer, some even insist on, enforcing the provisions of their own legal persuasion or school of thought (*madhhab*) concerning those matters in which the interpretation of their school is different from that of another.

The position of the revivalists on matters of interschool differences is much more liberal, as they suggest a free, pick-and-choose method for compiling laws from compendia of the four legal Sunnī schools of traditional Islamic *fiqh*. They are guided, they say, mainly by the principle that whatever appears to be closer to the Qur'ān and the *sunna* is preferable, irrespective of its *madhhabī* origin.[94] They also advocate freely dropping, when and as contemporary needs demand, those laws from the traditional corpus of the law that are based on custom and expedience of the Muslim communities,[95] as distinguished from the laws that are believed to be based on the Qur'ān, *hadīth*, *ijmā* and *qiyās*. However, in view of the great number of the *hadīth* of a wide-ranging legal content, the traditional laws that cannot be potentially related to one or the other *hadīth* or previous *ijmā* would be relatively small.

The traditionalists do not simply limit formulation of the new Islamic laws mainly to matters relating to the few new developments. They differ radically from the modernists in their very conception of the means and method of formulating the Islamic law. While talking of Islamizing the law, both the traditionalists and the modernists use the same two terms derived from traditional Islamic jurisprudence, *ijtihād* and *ijmā,* but their conceptions of the terms are essentially different. In the first place, according to the traditionalists, both *ijtihād* and *ijmā* refer primarily to past decisions of the learned pious among the *umma.* To them, *ijmā* is mainly the consensus of the learned pious over the norms either that the *umma* has been practicing for ages or that exist in the traditionally accepted law books. The superior validity of one *ijmā* over another is established according to the temporal proximity to the Prophet. The *ijmā* of the companions (*sahāba*) of the Prophet, therefore, has preference over the *ijmā* of those who succeeded the companions (*tābiʿūn*); and the latters', over those who succeeded the successors (*tābiʿūn al-tabiʿīn*), and so on. *Ijmā* thus interpreted is mainly a method that validates the past; it authenticates the present only to the extent that the present conforms to the past agreement. According to the traditionalist understanding, therefore, it is, in effect, an essentially recessive concept. According to the modernists' understanding, however, *ijmā* is a progressive concept. To them, it mainly means contemporary consensus on the validity of an act or rule of law that is either presently practiced or is envisaged for future practice.

Ijtihād (literally, exertion) is an even more disputed concept, meaning different things to contemporary Muslims of different orientations. Its technical meaning in premodern books of Islamic jurisprudence is generally defined as "exhaustive endeavor in understanding the derivative principles of the *sharīʿa* by means of detailed argument."[96] The use of *ijtihād* that most of the *ulamā* would allow today is confined to what may be more appropriately called research: to uncover opinions and findings of the past doctors of Islamic law concerning those matters on which neither the Qurʾān nor *hadīth* contains specific and obvious legal guidance. *Ijtihād* for the contemporary *ulamā,* therefore, is mainly *ijtihād* of the great jurists of the past, and as such this, too, is, in effect, a recessive concept. In those few cases where opinions of the past jurists of the same legal school differ on minor details, the *ulamā* would allow limited freedom of choice. This restricted *ijtihād* (*ijtihād muqayyad*) has been identified by Shah Waliallah of Delhi (d. 1762) as *ijtihād al-futyā* (*ijtihād* in decisions) and *ijtihād fiʾl madhhab* (*ijtihād* within one's school of law, i.e., confined to the choice of one of the several differing opinions within that school).[97] Freedom beyond this the *ulamā* in Pakistan would generally not allow. Formulation of new laws through the use of *ijtihād* is limited, as noted above, exclusively to those matters on which traditional laws do not already exist in traditional Islamic literature.

This is also more or less the position of the revivalists. The main difference between them and the traditionalist *ulamā* is that, for the latter, following the *ijtihād* of the past doctors of law (*fuqahā salaf*) is almost a principle of faith; for the revivalists, it is rather a matter of wise policy. Several arguments are given for accepting the *ijtihād* of the past doctors of law. Past *ijtihād,* says Mawlana Zafar Ahmad Ansari, has been accepted by the Muslim *umma* for centuries, and therefore its continuing acceptance will help maintain a sense of historic continuity among the *umma;* it is, says Amin Ahsan Islahi, the safest way because the moral character and motivations of the early doctors of law were sound, something that may not be matched by the contemporary *mujtahid*s; it represents, says Mawlana Mawdudi (d. 1979), the efforts and understanding of the Muslims over centuries, and as such it is invaluable.[98] Both the *ulamā* and the revivalists insist on proper qualifications of the *mujtahid* (one that exercises *ijtihād*), who must have knowledge of Arabic, must be fully conversant in the Islamic sciences, and must be of proven piety and character.[99]

The modernists, and particularly the secularists, characterize such insistence as mullaism and theocracy, insinuating that the *ulamā* are concerned with their own power and interests.[100] To the modernists, *ijtihād* implies independent understanding and interpretation of the Qur'ān and the *sunna,* unfettered by the *ijtihād* and *ijmā* of the past Muslim jurists.[101] They are prepared to learn from the past doctors but surely do not feel bound to follow what they learn.[102]

Islamization of the law, whether free and unfettered, as the modernists would like, or severely restricted and strictly guided by the traditional *fiqhī* methods, as the revivalists and the traditionalists would like, requires the sanction of the state. Since most Muslims, including the *ulamā* in Pakistan, have come to generally accept the principle of elected legislature, the question arises: what is the position of an elected parliament in a process of Islamization of the law or in legislation generally?

For the traditionalists and the revivalists, "legislation in an Islamic state is a limited activity insofar as the function of an Islamic state, based as it is on the idea of sovereignty of Allah, is primarily to execute whatever has been ordained by Allah."[103] However, in an age when no clear consensus among the Muslims of various orientations exists on what exactly Islamic laws are, neither the phrase "sovereignty of Allah" nor the statement "to execute whatever has been ordained by Allah" dispenses with the need for legislation. Some competent authority must decide which rule the state will endorse.

In modern democratic states, the agency that declares that a rule be supported by the sanction of the state—thus making it a law properly so-called—also discusses and debates the variant proposals in an effort to reach consensus and refine the rule that is to be ultimately promulgated as the law. Many *ulamā* would like to divide these functions between two separate bodies: one, a popularly elected legislative assembly, and the other, a committee consisting, in effect, of major *ulamā,* preferably from all over the Muslim world, who would have the responsibility to discuss, develop, and organize the ordinances of Islam, which may then be enacted by a modern legislative agency or by the executive.[104] Or, alternatively, they suggested the formation of a committee or board of experts on Islamic *sharī'a* within, or attached to, a regular legislative assembly.[105] If differences over the Islamic character of a bill or act arose, the board's decision would prevail.[106] (See survey findings in Tables C.16, C.17, and C.18 in Appendix C.) Many *ulamā* suggested that the members of this body could be elected by the *ulamā* themselves or by the legislature; alternatively, the executive could nominate its members either from amongst the leading *ulamā* exclusively or from the *ulamā* plus modern educated Muslims.[107]

The *ulamā* of Pakistan worked for the establishment of such a body in the early years of Pakistan without fully realizing their objective. A committee of the first Constituent Assembly did create a Board of Talimat-i-Islamiyya in 1949, but the board's recommendations were confined to the topics on which the parent committee solicited the board's views, and they were to be purely advisory. The two recent constitutions of Pakistan (1962, 1973) provided for a Council of Islamic Ideology to advise the government on Islamic fitness of matters; but the majority of its members, nominated by the government, did not consist of graduates of *dār al-ulūm*s, as are the typical *ulamā.* The council, furthermore, tendered its opinion, and still does, only when asked by the government, and its opinions are binding neither on the legislative nor the executive.[108]

The modernist attitude in Pakistan has been in favor of entrusting the national assembly of the Islamic state with all the functions of legislation. The attitude rests on a reinterpretation of the classic Islamic concepts of *ijtihād, sharīʿa,* and *ijmā,* along with an acceptance of the modern forms of representative government. In the Indo-Pakistan subcontinent, Iqbal first supported this idea to achieve, in his own words, a forward thrust for Islam and to bring Islam closer to the democratic spirit. He declared:

> The growth of republican spirit and the gradual formation of legisla-
> tive assemblies in Muslim lands constitute a great step in advance. The
> transfer of the power of *ijtihād* from individual representatives of
> schools to a Muslim legislative assembly, which in view of the growth
> of opposing sects, is the only possible form *ijmā* can take in modern
> times, will secure contributions to legal discussion from laymen who
> happen to possess a keen insight into affairs. In this way alone we can
> stir into activity the dormant spirit of life in our legal system, and give
> it an evolutionary outlook.[109]

However, Iqbal suggested in the same lecture that "the *ulamā* should form a vital part of Muslim legislative assembly, helping and guiding free discussion on questions relating to law."[110] The contemporary modernist sentiment in this respect tends to favor the idea that some *ulamā* should, through the regular process of election, find their way into the legislature; but, by and large, it does not care to concede them a "vital part" of its membership, and it does not expect any guiding role from them.[111]

Though most modernists allow public debate as a matter of course, some modernists would reserve major discussion of sensitive issues concerning a reinterpretation of the *sharīʿa* for the national legislature:

> It is obvious that the only place where discussions can take place in
> connection with the reinterpretation and re-orientation of the *sharīʿa*
> is the legislature, because as the supreme representative of the people,
> the legislature alone can speak for them and accept on their behalf what
> seems rational and proper out of the mass of arguments and commen-
> tary putting forward different points of view.[112]

Despite the prominence of some politically active *ulamā,* the majority of the *ulamā* generally shy away from assuming the role of legislators themselves.[113] However, most of them do consider it their collective responsibility to advise the legislature on Islamic legal matters, as well as to pass the final judgment on Islamic acceptability of any bill that is to be enacted as an Islamic law.[114]

The *ulamā*'s insistence that the experts of the Qur'ān and the *sunna* must be allowed, in effect, the role of an umpire or guide in the process of Islamic legislation is based on their self-image as the guardians of Islamic *sharī'a* who have preserved the purity of Islamic orthodoxy through their age-old scholarly consensus.[115] As against this, the modernist argument has been that the entire *umma* is the guardian of itself in all of its affairs, including legislation. Dr. Fazlur Rahman, the former director of the Islamic Research Institute and a former member of the Advisory Council of Islamic Ideology, said:

> Legislation in Islam is the business of the community *as a whole*. It is, therefore, the function of the representatives of the people who sit in the legislative assembly to make the laws. The claim of many *ulamā* that Islamic legislation is a function properly belonging to the *ulamā* is not only patently wrong but is equally falsified by the formative phase of the development of Muslim law in history. . . . However, it is also to be admitted that expert advice will be needed on some technical aspects . . . for which adequate institutions are to be provided.[116]

Dr. Rahman's statement reflected his concern for a democratic interpretation of Islam, as well as the popular desire at once for Islam and democracy. This desire was shared by many Pakistanis some three decades ago. As we approach the beginning of a new millennium the concern and the desire are experienced by an increasing number of persons in Muslim countries. Reconciliation of Islam and democracy has indeed emerged as a central theme of practical politics in the Muslim world. As John Esposito and John Voll commented recently:

> The dual aspirations of Islamization and democratization set the framework for most of the critical issues in the contemporary Muslim world. When one looks at the issues of Islam and democracy, it becomes clear that the most important questions revolve around the compatibility of Islam and democracy and the role of the new-style movements in the political evolution of Muslim societies.[117]

4 ❋ *Islam and Economic Orientations*

A number of Muslim countries today have financial institutions that are experimenting with "Islamic banking." The underlying imperative of Islamic banking is substitution of interest by profit sharing.[1] In some of these countries, *zakāt* (religiously obligatory payment by Muslims for the welfare of the poor) is now collected in some situations by the government. These two recent developments, related to banking and distribution, reflect what many Muslims believe to be Islam's concern for social justice and its rejection of usury.

In a country like Saudi Arabia, there has been a historical continuity on the legal ban on usury, in conformity with the specific norms of the traditional Islamic *sharīʿa*. However, in most other countries where the noted measures concerning banking and distribution have been recently adopted, these economic measures have been associated with a revived awareness of Islam's social demands in general.

In Pakistan, the experiment with both "interest-free" banking and government-sponsored collection of *zakāt* began in 1979. The new laws regulating the two matters were preceded by a national debate more than a decade before the actual legislation. Indeed, the public discussion on economic issues that took place in the 1960s can be itself seen, for the purposes of this study, as one dimension of the continuing ideological debates involving the sociopolitical implications of religion that have characterized the short history of Pakistan ever since its creation in 1947. In the 1950s, as the new nation struggled to formulate a constitution to run its government and define its values, the question of what characterized an Islamic state became the focus of a lengthy ideological controversy. In the late 1960s, the focus shifted to Islam's economic teachings. The questions came to be, which economic system could best help achieve distributive justice and economic progress in Pakistan, and how did such a system stand in relation to the demands of Islam? Although as early as 1948 Mohammed Ali Jinnah and the prime minister, Liaqat Ali Khan, vaguely spoke of Islamic socialism, economics then was by no means an Islamic or ideological issue. But soon after June 1965, when a member of the National Assembly proposed nationalization of major industries in accordance with socialistic principles that he thought were consistent with Islam,[2] an unceasing discussion, often heated, and arguments, sometimes leading to violence, came to occupy newspaper columns, magazine pages, and public rallies.

This chapter describes some major positions taken in undivided Pakistan on these economic and Islamic issues. Specifically, it discusses two subjects: one, the relative popularity of different economic systems among the *ulamā* and the modern middle-class professionals in predivided Pakistan; and two, the basic concepts and major arguments offered in support of differing, at times conflicting, Muslim interpretations of Islam's economic teachings.

As in the case of the previous two chapters on "nationalism" and political attitudes, the information and analyses presented here are based partly on the findings of a survey that the author conducted between January and July 1969 in Karachi, Lahore, and Dacca and partly from ideological tracts and magazine articles written by Muslim supporters of different economic interpretations of Islam.

DIFFERING PREFERENCES FOR THE ECONOMIC ORDER

The respondents were asked to describe the main features of the economic system they believed to be most desirable for Pakistan. They were requested to state their position concerning three specific matters: one, the desirability of the institution of private property and the extent to which nationalization was advisable; two, the scope of public and private enterprise; and three, the society's collective responsibility for providing the basic needs of the poor.

By combining and collating the responses to the questions dealing with these issues, the author sorted the economic arrangements desired by respondents into three familiar categories, namely, free market economy, mixed economy, and socialist economy.[3] (The survey questions on economic issues—numbered 19 to 26—are included in Appendix A; responses to these specific questions are recorded in tabular form in Appendix C, Tables C.16 to C.28.)

Since popular conceptions of the three main types of economies differ considerably, classification of respondents, as supporters of one or another type of economy, is not based here on their self-proclamations; it is based exclusively on their positions on specific economic issues. The following criteria are employed here to distinguish the three main categories. (1) Designated as "in favor of a socialistic economy" are those respondents who declared themselves in favor of nationalization of the major, though not necessarily all, sources of production and who wanted distribution of wealth on the basis of need as well as merit. (2) Included among the supporters of a free market economy are those who held that the individual's right to all kinds of property was inviolable and who would allow no nationalization and no arrangement for social insurance, except private charity. (3) Counted as supporters of a mixed economy are all those who, despite their opposition to forceful or large-scale nationalization, would like the government to participate in some sectors of the national economy and who favored establishing a social security system to meet the needs of the poor.

Judged from these criteria, a large majority of the *ulamā* both in the former East Pakistan and the former West Pakistan (91 percent and 70 percent, respectively) opted for a free market economy, allowing only a minimal participation of the state in economic enterprise and conceding almost no governmental responsibility to provide for the basic necessities of its citizens, except whatever might be accomplished through the institutionalized charity of *zakāt* (see Table 4.1). However, about one third (29 percent) of the *ulamā* in the former West Pakistan would like to have a mixed economy with the state taking responsibility for some kind of social security scheme. None favored a socialistic economy.

Among the professionals, on the contrary, the survey found a large majority inclined toward either a socialistic or a mixed economy. Indeed, less than 7 percent of professionals in the former East Pakistan declared themselves in favor of a free market economy, while more than half (56 percent) desired a socialistic economy, and another 37 percent opted for a mixed economy. In the former West Pakistan socialism was less popular among these categories of professionals than in the former East Pakistan. There, only about one fifth (19 percent) wanted a socialistic system. However, when one includes with them another two fifths who desired a mixed economy, they add up to a significant majority that was against a free market

TABLE 4.1

ECONOMIC SYSTEMS DESIRED BY THE *ULAMĀ* AND THE
MIDDLE-CLASS PROFESSIONALS IN PAKISTAN

Category of Respondents	Desired Economic Order			Row Total
	Free	*Mixed*	*Socialist*	
Ulamā, East Pakistan	11	1	0	12
	91.7%	8.3%	0.0	7.9%
Ulamā, West Pakistan	12	5	0	17
	70.6%	29.4%	0.0	11.3%
Middle-Class Professionals, East Pakistan	4	22	33	59
	6.8%	37.3%	55.9%	39.1%
Middle-Class Professionals, West Pakistan	26	25	12	63
	41.3%	39.7%	10.0%	41.7%
Total Number	53	53	45	151
Percent	35.1%	35.1%	29.8%	100.0%

economy (see Table 4.1 above). The overwhelming majority of those who wanted a socialistic order described it in terms that fall short of a totally socialized economy. They desired nationalization of major industries and businesses but would leave small businesses and workshops free. Less than 10 percent of all socialists sought to completely abolish private enterprise, big and small, and thus make the state the sole employer.

DIFFERING CONCEPTIONS OF ISLAM'S ECONOMIC ORDER

The arguments and theoretical orientations of those who claim no Islamic sanction for their views on economics or who find Islam irrelevant to such matters were found to be roughly similar to those of the supporters of free, mixed, and socialistic economies in the Western world. These do not concern us here. Of primary interest to this study are the views and the interpretations of those Muslims who accept any given set of economic relations on Islamic grounds. The basic questions explored here therefore are:

TABLE 4.2
RESPONDENT'S OWN DESCRIPTION OF THE ISLAMIC CHARACTER OF THE
ECONOMIC ORDER HE/SHE DESIRED

Category of Respondents	Islamic	Implied by General Islamic Teachings	Not Against Islam	Islam Is Impractical	Against Islam	"I Don't Know"	Row Total
Ulamā, East Pakistan and West Pakistan	29 100.0%	0 0.0	0 0.0	0 0.0	0 0.0	0 0.0	29 19.2%
Middle-Class Professionals, East Pakistan	15 25.9%	12 20.7%	7 12.1%	2 3.4%	16 27.6%	3 10.3%	58 38.4%
Middle-Class Professionals, West Pakistan	46 71.9%	5 7.8%	6 9.4%	0 0.0	3 4.7%	4 6.3%	64 42.4%
Column Total Number Percent	90 59.6%	17 11.3%	13 8.6%	2 1.3%	19 12.6%	10 6.6%	151 100.0%

The Stated Islamic Character of the Desirable Economic Order

What economic arrangements do the contemporary Muslims conceive to be the defining features of Islam's economic order, particularly with reference to ownership, production and distribution of wealth? What Islamic concepts and arguments do those Muslims cite whose understanding of the Islamic order bears similarity to a free, socialistic, or mixed economy?

In order to determine how the respondents view the economic demands of Islam vis-à-vis the economic arrangements that they themselves hold desirable, the author asked them to outline Islam's economic system. As could be expected, 100 percent of the *ulamā* described Islam's economic system in terms that were identical with what they personally held desirable. Similarly, 80 percent of the professionals in West Pakistan and 47 percent in East Pakistan saw the economic order they preferred as either required by Islam or implied by its general moral teachings. The rest either rejected Islam's economic demands or recognized none—a position that may be conveniently described as secularist (see Table 4.2 for details).

TABLE 4.3
PROFESSED BELIEF IN "ISLAMIC SOCIALISM" AMONG SUPPORTERS
OF DIFFERENT ECONOMIC ORDERS

Response to the Question: "Do You Believe in Islamic Socialism?"	The Economic Order Actually Desired			
	Free	Mixed	Socialist	Row Total
"Yes"[a]	4 11.8% 7.5%	12 35.3% 23.3%	18 53.0% 41.8%	34 23.1%
"No"[b]	48 45.3% 90.5%	34 32.1% 66.7%	24 22.6% 55.8%	106 72.2%
Refused to Answer[c]	1 14.3% 1.9%	5 71.4% 9.8%	1 14.3% 2.3%	7 4.7%
Column Total	53 36.1%	51 34.7%	43 29.3%	147 100.0%

[a] Alternate response: "Complete Islam includes socialism."
[b] Alternate responses: "No, but in Islam's socialism"; "No, but in scientific socialism"; "No, but in democratic socialism."
[c] Alternate responses: "I do not know"; "The concept is ambiguous."

This obviously reveals a greater preoccupation of the West Pakistani middle-class professionals with the sociopolitical demands of Islam than that of their counterparts in East Pakistan, who, as a whole, reflected a rather secular orientation toward public issues.

Among the supporters of socialistic interpretations of Islam some identify their stand as "Islamic socialism." Others, though they hold similar views, would give it a different name, nizām-i-rubūbiyyat (divine or providential system) or musāwat-i-Muhammadī (Muhammadan equality). For the purposes of this discussion, however, such differences in nomenclature have been ignored here, due to the substantive similarity of their supporters' views. Conversely, counted here among the supporters of a free or mixed economy are all those who, despite claiming the title "Islamic socialism" for their stand, actually described it in terms that amounted only to a free or mixed economy. Indeed, only about half (53 percent) of those who gave a positive answer to the question "Do you believe in Islamic socialism?" actually described the economic system they desired in terms that amounted to socialism, while the description of 35 percent amounted to a mixed economy and of 12 percent to a free market economy (see Table 4.3 and Table C.25 in Appendix C).

ISLAM AND SOCIALISM

The proportion of those who described Islam's economy in socialistic terms was not large, only about 13 percent of our total sample of professionals in 1969. Even among the socialist professionals they formed a minority of about one third in each of the two former provinces of Pakistan. Thus, only one in every three real socialists claimed Islamic justification for his socialist views.

Yet the socialist understanding of Islam among the middle-class professionals merits attention for two reasons: one, the seriousness with which supporters and opponents of socialistic interpretation of Islam engaged each other in arguments, and two, the danger of political conflict and civil strife that the confrontation of the two positions posed in a Muslim country like Pakistan.

SOCIALISTIC INTERPRETATION OF ISLAM

Basic to the thinking of all those who favor a socialist interpretation of Islam is their nontraditional approach to religion. By and large they reject as deviation from the right Islamic principles that portion of the traditional Islamic law that recognizes the institution of private property and free enterprise. Real Islam, they claim, requires a socialistic order. In support of this claim they point to a number of Qur'ānic verses which they believe have a socialistic content. Here are a few major examples of their reasoning.

Some Islamic socialists quote the Qur'ānic verse "Man is entitled only to what is due to his effort" (53:39). This means, they claim, that like modern socialistic theories, Islam too holds labor to be the sole value in economic production and concedes to invested capital no share in profits.[4] All those laws and practices that allow any such share violate this principle and are therefore un-Islamic. For the same reason the system of private enterprise is also un-Islamic, as its very foundation is permissibility of the capitalist's share.[5] But socialism, through its denial of private property and private enterprise, helps enforce the above-mentioned Qur'ānic dictum. Thus, Islam demands a socialist economy.[6] Islamic socialists find further support for this view in Islam's disapproval of usury. The traditional *ulamā* themselves uphold such disapproval. But the Islamic socialist, picking up the thread where the *ulamā* leave it, argues that the very reason why Islam forbids interest is that interest is a concession to capital and not a reward for labor. The profit derived from a commercial or industrial enterprise, he adds, is also in reality a premium on the invested capital and is, therefore, in no way different from interest.[7] The implication of Islam's denial of interest is thus obvious to him: the institution of private entrepreneurship is as harmful and un-Islamic as is the practice of lending money for interest.

Another Qur'ānic verse that the Islamic socialists see as clearly pointing in the direction of a socialistic economy would translate as "land belongs to God" (7:128). They argue that if land belongs to God, no human can legally own it. At the same time the Qur'ān further tells us, they say, that God has created the earth for the livelihood of all humanity. Thus men, though they cannot own land and its resources, can still use it. But even this limited right is not a private right of an individual but the collective right of humanity at large, and it is subject to the condition of equal use and enjoyment by all humans. It follows that no individual or group may be allowed to monopolize the resources of the earth and thereby deny anyone his equal right to use them. Since capitalism inevitably results in such a denial, it may not be allowed. Only the government, acting as the representative of the entire society, can rightfully regulate the use of land for the benefit of all.[8]

Along with the above legalistic approach, some Islamic socialists emphasize the general moral concern of Islam. Some say, for example, that as a comprehensive religious and moral system, Islam sees its mission to eradicate all injustices and cruelties from society. Since the preservation of a system of private property and enterprise, they say, does indeed lead to social injustices that are morally intolerable to Islam, capitalism should not be allowed to govern social relations.[9] Some of those who take this approach see Islam basically as a socioeconomic movement. Among them is Muhammad Sarwar, who wrote frequently in the late 1960s on the subject of Islamic socialism. Finding support in the ideas of Shah Waliallah (d. 1762), he viewed the role of Prophet Muhammad essentially as that of a revolutionary leader. The Prophet's immediate mission, he said, was to put an end to the capitalist exploitation of the Quraishi merchants of Mecca, on the one hand, and to disestablish the corrupt royalty and bureaucracy of Byzantium and Persia, on the other. Muhammad and other prophets of God, he wrote, differed from the leaders of secular social revolutions in only one important respect: they made greater allowance for human nature, and hence the system they established survived longer than those established by the leaders of secular social revolutions. Nonetheless, the major goals and methods of both kinds of leaders are the same, namely, the establishment of socioeconomic justice and the declaration of war against the unrepentant oppressors and exploiters of the helpless and the poor.

A less popular and somewhat eccentric theory of Islamic socialism gives new meaning to Islamic eschatology. Traditionally, Muslim theologians have taken heaven and hell to be metaphysical abodes to which men are destined in the life after death. But Ghulam Ahmad Parwez and Faqir Muhammad Bugti, without totally rejecting those connotations, understand these terms to imply mainly two types of human societies in this life. According to the Qur'ān, they claim, hell (*jahannam*) is that society in which men, dominated by its evil socioeconomic system, struggle to accumulate wealth. Men in such a society thus become the victims of their own mutual competition and enmity whose fire eventually consumes them.[10] The extreme pain and anxiety associated with the traditional Islamic concept of hell are seen by Parwez and Bugti as the result of social conflict and class war in this type of society.[11] They define heaven as a society free from distinctions of social classes and characterized by justice, peace, and cooperation.[12]

Social conflict and class war are seen in their turn as the work of Satan — another term to which Parwez and Bugti give nontraditional meaning. They define Iblīs (i.e., Satan) as that human impulse that induces man to use his mental faculties in contravention of the divine laws.[13] This impulse pushes man to seek wealth and power, causing mutual conflict.[14] Both Parwez and Bugti find support for this view in the Qur'ānic (and biblical) story of the fall of man, which they interpret allegorically. They take the "forbidden tree" to be a symbol of wealth on the grounds that it was an object of utility. They further argue that the tree was "forbidden" because in its acquisition lay a potential source of conflict. For Parwez and Bugti, therefore, the fundamental social message of the Qur'ān is that ownership is the source of social conflict and hence ought to be avoided, or else life will be like hell.

Conversely, a heavenly society — one characterized by peace and com-

fort and by cooperation instead of social conflict — is established when a socialist economy is practiced, when the government, instead of individuals,
owns and manages the property. In such a heavenly society individuals
work and toil not for themselves but for the society, receiving only their assigned shares from the government.[15] In support of their suggestions for a
centralized socialistic economy, Parwez and Bugti quote another Qur'ānic
verse: "Allah has bought the lives and belongings of the Muslims in return
for paradise" (9:111). They claim that here Allah means the government;
and paradise, of course, is the ideal society where peace and justice reign.
They interpret this verse to be an exhortation to the believers to surrender
all of their possessions and commit their lives to the society at large for the
sake of peace and justice. The government of the state, in its capacity as
God, that is, representative of the society, must then collect the fruits of
everyone's labor in the central treasury and from it meet the needs of all, irrespective of their contributions.[16] Parwez and Bugti thus confirm the socialistic principle "From each according to his capacity and to each according to his needs"; in the process they almost deify the government.
Preference for a dominant dictatorial government is not, however, typical
of Islamic socialists. Indeed, the majority of those of our survey who believed in Islamic socialism indicated a desire for a democratic government.

The argument that socialism is needed for the solidarity of the nation —
a stand taken by some supporters of Arab socialism in the Middle East[17] —
has been rather uncommon among the Islamic socialists in Pakistan.
Though the two concerns — for social justice and national solidarity — are
by no means exclusive and may be experienced simultaneously by the same
individual, by and large it is the first concern (social justice) that moves
most Islamic socialists in Pakistan. Even Parwez and Bugti, who consider
unity and cooperation chief traits of a socialist society, did not see a socialist order as a means of buttressing Muslim national unity. Among those few
Islamic socialists who did is Muhammad Hanif Ramey, a former chief minister of the Punjab province. As editor of the weekly *Nusrat* and as a writer
of many tracts on Islamic socialism for the Pakistan People's Party, of whose
Basic Principles Committee he was once a member, Ramey helped considerably to popularize the notion of Islamic socialism in Pakistan in the late
1960s.

Ramey maintains that socialism is necessary to achieve national solidarity, that a Muslim nation divided between the oppressors and the oppressed,

the rich and the poor, cannot achieve solidarity.[18] Muslim nationalism, he says, needs socialism today because in the contemporary circumstances Islamic goals of a just social order and a united, egalitarian society can be achieved only through socialism.[19]

ISLAM VIS-À-VIS COMMUNISM

Most supporters of Islamic socialism hold it to be basically different from communism. Only one of the respondents in the survey (3 percent of those who profess it) took Islamic socialism to be similar to any non-Islamic socialism. Emphasizing the differences between Islamic socialism and communism, almost all of the rest claimed that Islamic socialism is theistic and/or that its concern for social justice originates from spiritual values rather than from the self-interest of the economically deprived class. Only one distinguished Islamic socialism from non-Islamic socialism on the basis that the former allowed greater freedom to private economic effort. Another distinguished it on the basis that it allowed greater civic liberties than communism.

In their writings, too, the Islamic socialists profess a clear distinction between Islam and communism. Here again, the difference they most emphasize is the religio-moral foundation of Islam. Not only do many of them reject dialectical materialism, they also hold, after the late philosopher-poet Sir Muhammad Iqbal (d. 1938), that "the highest socialist objectives can be realized only through Islam's spiritual and moral principles" and that the communist worldview is incapable of supporting the heavy burden of a socialist economy.[20] Some further claim that because of this lack of spiritual foundation, communist societies are not truly free from social stratification and racial prejudice and are still deficient in internationalism and humanism.[21]

None of the survey respondents indicated any difference between Islamic and non-Islamic socialism with regard to the strategy for achieving a socialist society. In their writings, however, some Islamic socialists do discuss this issue, taking significantly different stands. Many, perhaps a majority, take for granted a democratic, evolutionary approach as essential to the kind of socialism that Islam proposes.[22] Others would grant the use of violence against the capitalists to achieve a socialist society, but only after peaceful means had failed. Professor Ghulam Dastgir Rashid says, for example, that in hopeless circumstances the suffering poor of a society are entitled to exercise physical force to bring about a social revolution. How-ever, in his view, such circumstances would exist in a society only when two conditions obtain: when the basic needs of the poor—food, shelter, medi-cal care, and education—go unfulfilled, and when the rich do not volun-tarily meet their social obligations toward the suffering poor nor does the government employ the sanction of the state to force them to contribute their share (in the form of taxes, etc.) for the welfare of the poor.[23]

Such, in brief, was the thinking of those who professed an Islamic com-pulsion toward a socialistic order in the 1960s and the early seventies. Some of those who shared a more or less socialistic interpretation of Islam, yet re-jected the term "Islamic socialism," argued that a description of Islam's col-lective economy as "socialist" would subject it to non-Islamic impulses of a materialistic worldview.[24] Indeed, some opponents of Islamic socialism claimed the term was being shrewdly exploited by those who pay no more than lip service to Islam to sugarcoat a communist ideology. Whatever the truth in this allegation, it would be difficult to assess the number of such pseudo-Islamic socialists or the extent of their influence on those whose Is-lamic motivation was genuine.

REASONS FOR THE RELATIVE POPULARITY OF A SOCIALISTIC INTERPRETATION OF ISLAM IN THE 1960S

As noted at the beginning of this chapter, the attraction of the Indo-Pakistani Muslims to socialism is by no means new. Indeed, since the 1920s there have been those who saw Islam as genuinely socialistic and those who accepted the label socialist without accepting its content.[25] But, whereas before 1960 the former of these trends seems to have been limited to very small circles, in the sixties and the early seventies it came to attract a significant number of the members of the new middle class.

One probable reason for this attraction was the growing popularity of socialistic ideas in Western Europe, particularly in Britain, in the early six-ties, a popularity reflected in predivided Pakistan. It seems that popular Western ideas influence the thinking of the Western-educated Muslims in developing countries such as Pakistan in two ways. Those who are inclined toward a secularist interpretation of Islam readily accept the major so-ciopolitical ideas current in the Western countries, provided such ideas are claimed to have a universal validity and involve nothing that may be derogatory to the self-respect of either their Muslim or national identity. But even those Muslims who see Islam as a complete code of life are sometimes influenced by the ideological tides enough to look for, and find, a message in Islam reflecting contemporary ideological currents in the West.

This relatively easy adoption of popular Western ideas of the day has been made possible only by some internal developments in the structure of Islamic religious thought. The most important of such developments is that modernist Muslims early in the twentieth century freed themselves from the restraints of the traditional Islamic jurisprudence. At the core of the contemporary modernist thinking is the realization that Islamic religion (*dīn*) and Islamic law (*fiqh, sharī'a*) are two different things. *Dīn,* in such thinking, implies moral and spiritual values and is, therefore, of permanent validity. The *fiqh,* on the contrary, is considered merely a set of rules of social conduct that were developed mainly by the medieval Muslim jurists. The Muslim modernist thus concludes that the value of the *fiqh* is relative both to time and place, and that the new conditions in the contemporary world indeed demand its reformulation. Such reformulation, he believes, can be accomplished through a return to the essential teachings of the Qur'ān, and the use of personal judgment and enlightened reasoning (*ijtihād*).

Because of this theoretical formulation, with an emphasis on a return to the essential teachings of the Qur'ān and the need for *ijtihād,* Muslim modernists have acquired a capacity for accommodating within Islam virtually all ideational changes that they hold desirable. The Qur'ānic teachings themselves are general enough to allow a wide variety of interpretations. Parliamentary institutions, monogamy, and rejection of slavery were confirmed by Muslim modernists in the early decades of this century on the basis of general Qur'ānic teachings and *ijtihād,* despite the opposition or disapproval of the traditionalists at that time. In the sixties a socialistic economy was recommended on the same grounds. Hanif Muhammad Ramey, for example, who accepts the above-mentioned modernist stand, declares socialism to be a *sharī'a* that complements and best realizes the eternal values of Islamic religion (*dīn*) in the contemporary world.[26]

Also increasing Islam's capacity to adopt new ideas is another modernist view that a portion of the traditional *fiqh* not only fails to realize the Islamic goals today but has consistently frustrated them ever since the early history of Islam. In this connection, some modernist Muslims point to the institutions of autocracy and private ownership, which, they contend, were recognized by the traditional Islamic law in violation of the essential socioeconomic teachings of Islam. They therefore see the establishment of social democracy as no more than a correction of the medieval distortion of Islam.[27]

In their protest against the traditional handling of Islam's sociopolitical message, the modernists are not alone. Even in the medieval period voices were occasionally raised against the traditional understanding of Islam. The modernists, therefore, have found support for their beliefs within the Islamic tradition. The Islamic socialists in Pakistan are attracted to, and sometimes guided by, two famous Muslim theologians of the past: Ibn Hazm (d. 1064) and Shah Waliallah (d. 1762), both strongly sensitive to the sufferings of the poor and to Islam's mission to remove such suffering.

Unevenness of socioeconomic development affected the receptivity to socialist ideas. It appears from the available statistics that from 1955 to 1965 the number of college and university graduates in Pakistan increased five and six times, respectively.[28] With the expansion of education, a much larger number of people entered the job market, but the economy over the same period of time increased by comparatively meager proportions. Industrial production over the same ten years only doubled, as did trade and commerce.[29] Obviously, the numbers of new jobs these two major urban sectors of the economy could offer were proportionally limited. Government and defense-related jobs probably grew by even smaller proportions, once the large-scale recruitment of the first few years immediately following Pakistan's creation in 1947 was over. Under these conditions unemployment among those with higher education must have risen considerably. And though exact unemployment statistics for Pakistan are not available, the large number of applications that businessmen, industrialists, and government agencies are generally known to receive in response to a single advertised position indicates a huge surplus of unemployed or marginally employed college and high school graduates. In such circumstances, intense competition and economic insecurity are but natural and an attraction to an alternate economic system that promises social justice understandable.

However, the fact remains that despite the considerable appeal of a socialistic economy among the Muslims of predivided Pakistan, the belief that Islam does not seek a socialistic economy seemed in 1969 to be widely accepted in the former West Pakistan as well as the former East Pakistan. The survey indicated that almost 98 percent of the respondents who favored a free market economy described it as either required by Islam,

TABLE 4.4
PROFESSED ISLAMIC CHARACTER OF THE DESIRED
ECONOMIC ORDER

| Desired Economy | *The Islamic Character Claimed by Respondent for the Economic Order He Desired* | | | | | Row Total |
	Islamic	*"Not Against Islam"*	*"Islam Is Impractical"*	*Opposed to Islam*	*"I Don't Know"*	
Free	51	1	0	0	0	52
	98.1%	1.9%	0.0	0.0	0.0	35.6%
Mixed	38	6	0	2	7	53
	71.1%	11.3%	0.0	3.8%	13.2%	36.3%
Socialist	14	5	2	17	3	41
	34.2%	12.2%	4.9%	41.5%	7.3%	28.1%
Column Total	103	12	2	19	10	146
	70.6%	8.2%	1.4%	13.0%	6.8%	100.0%

implied by Islamic teachings, or at the very least acceptable according to Islamic teachings (see Table 4.4).

Conversely, among the respondents who favored a socialistic economy, only about 34 percent considered it Islamic or implied by general Islamic teachings. Indeed, a majority of them either considered Islam's politico-economic arrangements reactionary and procapitalist, or they simply refused to describe them, considering them of little interest to a genuine socialist.

ISLAM AND THE FREE MARKET ECONOMY

Radically opposed to the socialistic interpretation of Islam is the view that Islam respects private property, allows no nationalization, and, apart from a few restraints, leaves the economy essentially free. This view, presenting the main ideological opposition to socialism in Pakistan, is espoused by three different social categories: the traditional *ulamā* (see Table 4.1), the Islamic revivalists belonging to the religio-political party Jamaat-i-Islami, and those inclined toward liberal democracy. Of these, the last, though not an inconsiderable number, appear to be least interested in active politics and ideological debate. The second group, Jamaat-i-Islami, is solidly organized and has a highly articulate leadership. Furthermore, unlike the liberals, the members of the Jamaat have strong motivation, equating as they do their political and ideological campaigning with propagation of religious truth. Their numbers are not large, though, and the Jamaat has had a poor showing in attracting votes in most general elections. Indeed, facing the challenge of the growing appeal of socialistic ideas to the Pakistani public and the Pakistani intelligentsia, the Jamaat reevaluated its economic program and ideological stand in 1969. In doing so, it appeared to embrace a part of the economic program it had set out to reject. (The Jamaat's modified position will be considered below in the section on "Islam and the Mixed Economy.")

Unlike both the liberals and the members of the Jamaat are the *ulamā*. Numerous and close to the people, they occupy positions of considerable influence among the masses. Their major shortcoming is their lack of modern education. The *ulamā* constitute a social category that has changed perhaps the least of all the urban groups, despite the century of social change that significantly affected almost all of the rest. As a social category, they have made no effort to learn even the rudiments of the modern sciences. Their ideas and outlook remain overwhelmingly medieval, their understanding of the new realities of life meager, resulting in the *ulamā*'s reduced credibility beyond the essential concerns of religion. Nonetheless, on such political issues as may be considered to be religiously objectionable, the *ulamā* can still considerably, though in most circumstances only temporarily, influence the opinion of the uneducated masses.

THE TRADITIONALIST VIEW OF ISLAM AS A
FREE MARKET ECONOMY

The *ulamā*'s professed opposition to socialism is based, as would be expected, mainly on religious grounds. One of their arguments, gathered through the survey as well as reflected in their published writings, is that private wealth is a prerequisite for the fulfillment of various religious duties. *Hajj, zakāt,* and *sadaqāt* cannot be accomplished, they say, if wealth is solely owned by the state. This, like some other aspects of the *ulamā*'s reasoning, reflects the partial understanding of socialism that they seem to have mustered. Many of them see in the socialist principles a complete denial not only of individual enterprise but also of all individual wealth.

During the 1970 campaign for national elections in Pakistan, a number of *ulamā* issued a *fatwā* (juristic opinion or decision) for the professed purpose of providing general guidance to the Muslim voters there. The *fatwā* denounced socialism as *kufr* (anti-Islam).[30]

Among other things, the *fatwā* contends that socialism is un-Islamic because abolishing private property would render half of the Qur'ān useless; the political parties that consider private property unjust and regard violent dispossession of the rightful owners from their wealth as permissible are rebels against the Qur'ān and the *sunna;* those who hold such convictions are not Muslims even though they recite the *kalima* (formal testimony of God's unity and Muhammad's prophethood) and say their prayers; sharing the activities of such political parties amounts to helping in the destruction of Islam; and voting for them, or aiding them financially is, therefore, *kufr* and *harām* (unbelief and religiously forbidden).[31]

The *fatwā* is far less critical of capitalism, yet it condemns interest, gambling, speculation, hoarding, exploitation of the poor, alcoholism, indecent exposure, and immodesty, all of which it declares to be characteristic features of capitalism.[32] The *fatwā* advised Pakistani Muslims to vote for those political parties that seek to establish an Islamic order in Pakistan by combating the dangers posed by the socialist propaganda, on the one hand, and by eliminating the undesirable features of the capitalist system, on the other.[33]

Despite the obvious political motive and electoral context of this *fatwā*, it is significant that the *fatwā* was endorsed by 230 *ulamā* belonging to both major sects, from the former East Pakistan as well as the former West Pakistan, including some highly respected Sunnī *ulamā* (e.g., Mufti Shafi), as well as Shī'ī *ulamā* (e.g., Ibn Hasan Jarchvi). It reflected the fear and suspicions — common in the late 1960s among many *ulamā* as well as the followers of Jamaat-i-Islami — that Islam in Pakistan was confronted with a new secularist challenge from communists and atheistic socialists who planned to subvert Islam from within under the cover of "Islamic socialism."[34]

The sanctity and importance that the majority of the *ulamā* attribute to the institution of private property are clearly shown in another series of *fatāwā* (pl., juristic opinions) given by some prominent *ulamā* of the Indo-Pakistan subcontinent in 1948.[35] These *fatāwā* were responses to land reforms, notably where the Indian government proposed to restrict landholdings to a maximum acreage and to requisition all land in excess of that ceiling for a price that it would set. The *fatāwā* declare (1) the rights of the owners to their land are inviolable, and to compel them to sell any portion of their property to the government at nominal rates amounts to confiscation; (2) the landlords have a legal and religious right to resist such compulsory sale by all possible means, including the use of physical force, while the rest of the Muslims have the religious obligation to help such resistance according to their capacities; (3) anyone who dies in the course of such resistance attains the status of a martyr.[36]

Despite the commitment to the right of private ownership, the *ulamā* have shown a concern for the plight of the poor. The legal provisions of the traditional *fiqh* concerning institutionalized charity—*zakāt, sadaqāt,* and *awqāf*—make them aware of the "share" that the Qur'ān grants the poor in the riches of the wealthy. Furthermore, the majority of the *ulamā* live on a subsistence level, a condition that must constantly remind them of the sufferings of the poor. Therefore, in their description of the Islamic economic order, the *ulamā* often emphasize the need for economic justice. Indeed, one third of the *ulamā* included in the survey sample would allow major differences in individual incomes only after the basic needs of all members of the society have been satisfied (see Table C.24 in Appendix C). Among the West Pakistani *ulamā* a concern for economic justice was particularly noticeable among the members of Jamiyyat Ulama-i-Islam led by Mawlana Mufti Mahmud.[37]

However, concern for distributive justice is one thing; agreeing to a mechanism adequate to realize it is quite another. The vast majority of the *ulamā* would allow neither nationalization of the economy nor any nontraditional tax (e.g., income tax) that alone could provide enough funds for any kind of comprehensive social security scheme. Instead, the *ulamā* insist that the traditional tax of *zakāt,* if fully paid and supplemented by voluntary gratuities by the rich, will take care of the basic needs of all the poor.[38]

Despite the exhortations of the Qur'ān for social justice, then, and the inclinations of some of the contemporary *ulamā* toward it, the *ulamā*'s progressivism goes, at most, only halfway.

TRADITIONALIST OPPOSITION TO A SOCIALISTIC INTERPRETATION OF ISLAM

Three factors seem most responsible for the *ulamā*'s ardent opposition to socialism. The first is the centuries of recognition of private enterprise by the traditional *fiqh,* which still remains fully authoritative in the opinion of the *ulamā.* This is shown by the *fatāwā* quoted above and needs no further comment.

The second factor is the *ulamā*'s equally old suspicion of the government. The compromise that only insecurely existed between the *ulamā* and the sultan throughout most of Islamic history has been ably commented upon by many scholars.[39] Here one might add that despite their opposition to communism, the *ulamā* paradoxically share one of its fundamental ideas. Short only of accepting the revolutionary implications of their belief, the *ulamā*—at least outside the narrow circle of the establishment *ulamā* patronized by Muslim governments, past or present—conceive the government of actual, historical states, including most Muslim states, almost in Marxist terms, that is, as the executive committee of the rapacious class, the ruling families of the day. The imposition of *mukūs* (technically, taxes that are not sanctioned by the traditional *sharī'a*) by Muslim rulers, for example, was often disapproved of by most *ulamā* as arbitrary and unjust, even in the medieval past.[40] The *ulamā*'s long experience with the secular authority has made them strongly aware of the encroachments over what they regard as the rights of the people and the sphere of the *sharī'a.* Only against an outside non-Muslim threat did most *ulamā* fully recognize the government as the rightful and representative manager of Muslim society. Most other times, because of the indispensable need for law and order, they grudgingly supported the sultan. This uneasy compromise between the *ulamā* and the government of the day turned into virtual hostility during almost 150 years of British rule.

Along with their traditional approach to Islamic religion, then, Pakistan's present *ulamā* have also inherited habits of viewing the government with suspicion and of guarding their autonomy from the government's encroachments. Nationalization of resources becomes an act of confiscation, motivated by greed, in the interests of the ruling class. It is not surprising, therefore, that the *ulamā* see socialism as no better than state capitalism. Indeed, a Pakistani *ālim* compares the socialist government to a huge dragon that swallows the smaller snakes, that is, capitalists.[41] The *ulamā* see nationalization as a move toward authoritarian government that would further reduce both the sphere of the *sharī'a* and the *ulamā*'s own autonomy.

Likely the most potent factor to turn the *ulamā* against a socialist economy, though, was their association of socialism with atheistic, revolutionary communism. The *ulamā* know little about the democratic and evolutionary socialist movements in Western European countries, perhaps due to the imperialist role of some of these countries in the Muslim World, causing the *ulamā* to reject everything Western as part of the imperialist movement, either Christian or atheist.

To the *ulamā*, socialism essentially implies class war and godlessness. Their revulsion to godlessness is too clear to require any comment, and it is not hard to find the explanation of their rejection of class war even as a strategy. Among the foremost ideals of traditional Islam has been the unity of the Islamic community (*umma*). The prime concern of the *ulamā*, therefore, has been to avoid civil strife. Indeed it was for these two reasons that the *ulamā* partly compromised with the secular authority of the sultans. The intensity of their concern may perhaps be realized from Gibb's observation that the efforts of the orthodox religious institution to maintain Islam's universalism against internal and external changes and to realize the widest possible measure of religious, social, and cultural unity throughout the Islamic world dominated the whole of medieval Islamic history.[42] It is no wonder that the *ulamā* reject an ideology that suggests dividing the Muslim community into hostile socioeconomic classes. Conversely, even those few *ulamā* who have been attracted to some halfway socialism have found in it not the message of discord and conflict that may accompany revolutionary war but of peace and solidarity that are expected to result from distributive justice. Since the vast majority of Pakistani *ulamā* are aware only of revolutionary socialism, they recoil from it.

THE REVIVALIST RESTATEMENT OF ISLAM AS A FREE MARKET ECONOMY

The position of Islamic revivalists in Pakistan, led by Jamaat-i-Islami, has been generally similar to that of the traditionalist *ulamā*, in that both essentially support the principles of free market economy, plus a social security scheme financed by *zakāt*. However, the Jamaat's argument has been logically more rigorous and its presentation more systematic than the argument of the *ulamā*. More politically conscious than the *ulamā*, the Jamaat has also shown a greater sense of rivalry and suspicion toward socialistic ideologies. The Jamaat launched in the late 1960s a vigorous campaign to make the *ulamā*, as well as the general public, aware of what it considered the evils of socialism and the deceptive political strategy of the socialists in Pakistan.[43]

A study of the Jamaat's views is important for two reasons: one, the Jamaat has a strong and increasing ideological influence on middle-class Muslims' understanding of Islam; and two, the Jamaat's position generally represents a systematic and rationalized form of traditionalist Islam that has an even larger following.

The position of the Jamaat on economic matters was shaped, as were its views on most other matters, by its founder and late chief, Mawlana Abul Ala Mawdudi (1903–1979).[44] Presenting his view of Islam's economic theory, Mawlana Mawdudi first outlines what he considers to be Islam's objectives in economic life and then describes certain "principles" or features that, he argues, follow from the nature of such objectives.

Mawlana Mawdudi begins by saying that according to Islam every human being is individually accountable to God. In view of this accountability, everyone should be given the fullest possible control over his actions. The first objective of Islam's economic order is to create conditions in which each individual can develop his personality and potentialities according to his own choice and judgment.[45] This means, Mawlana Mawdudi says, that the state should place on the individual only those restrictions truly necessary for the general welfare of mankind, leaving man's freedom of action essentially intact.[46] Important among freedoms of the individual, he argues, is the freedom of economic action, which will be most certainly lost if the state becomes the only entrepreneur.[47] Once individuals lose the freedom of economic action, they lose other freedoms as well; a person who depends for his livelihood on another individual or on the government "possesses no independence, either of expression or of action."[48] Islam, says Mawlana Mawdudi, is, therefore, opposed even to evolutionary socialism that may seek to nationalize through a gradual and constitutional process, because by its very nature socialism kills what is essential to humanity.[49]

The second objective of Islam's economic order, according to Mawlana Mawdudi, is to promote human feelings of generosity and sympathy. Islam, he says, attaches primary importance to faith, worship, education, and moral training, which, in turn, create a strong moral sense in society, moving individuals to be charitable and generous toward the poor and the needy.[50] Simultaneously, Islam seeks to create a strong public opinion capable of informally pressuring those members of the society who despite their capability seek to evade their moral responsibility to contribute their share to meeting the needs of the poor.[51] If neither personal conscience nor public pressure produces results, then, as a last resort, Islam seeks to apply the sanction of the state.[52] But the sanction of the state, he insists, must be limited in accordance with the principles of the Islamic law.[53]

The third objective of Islam's economic order, as described by Mawlana Mawdudi, is to avoid class conflict. Islam, he says, believes in the basic unity and brotherhood of all mankind, but it does not seek to create a classless society, which would be both unnatural and impossible to achieve.[54] Islam distinguishes between two types of social stratification: one type, encouraged by feudalism and Brahmanism, entails special privileges and is anchored permanently in the society; the other type emerges naturally in the course of socioeconomic interaction among men, because of the natural differences in their capabilities and their circumstances in life.[55] This second type of class structure continually changes naturally. Islam aims to destroy class division of the first category but allows class division of the latter type to run its own course.[56] After stating the above three objectives of the Islamic economic system, Mawlana Mawdudi argues that Islam's economic rules are designed to realize these objectives and states the following "basic principles" that characterize Islam's economic system.

The first important principle of the Islamic economic system, says Mawlana Mawdudi, is the recognition of the validity of private ownership of property. He and his colleagues in the Jamaat took pains to emphasize that Islam knew no legal distinction between ownership of the items of consumption and ownership of the means of production, a distinction claimed by some supporters of Islamic socialism.[57] Neither, says he, is the status of agricultural land different from any other means of production, as claimed by those who wish to put a ceiling on landownership.[58]

However, following a concept of traditional Islamic *fiqh,* Mawlana Mawdudi and his colleagues recognize the special status of those natural resources that need no human effort to render them valuable. These resources, among which Mawlana Mawdudi counts rivers, streams, natural forests, meadows, and open mines, are considered common property of mankind.[59] They cannot be owned by anyone, and everyone is entitled to their free use. However, anyone wishing to use them for commercial purposes may be required to pay a tax. Barring such objects, the individual's right to all private property—if the property is acquired in conformity with Islamic regulations—is inviolable.[60]

Islam and nationalization, says Mawlana Mawdudi, are therefore antithetical to each other, and Pakistanis must reject all proposals that either aim at collective ownership of property or take it to be a valid principle.[61] Islam does not even allow anyone to be forced to sell his property to the government.[62]

The second fundamental principle of the Islamic economic order, is, according to Mawlana Mawdudi, the freedom of enterprise and investment, subject only to the limitations imposed by the traditional Islamic *sharī'a*.[63] Mawlana Mawdudi and his colleagues emphatically repudiate the stand of some Islamic socialists that Islam allows one only what one earns with one's personal effort. They point out to the Islamic socialists that the Qur'ānic verse "To a human being belongs only the reward of his or her labor,"[64] which the Islamic socialists consider basic Qur'ānic dictum in support of their socialist position, actually refers to the reward in the next world and not in this.[65] Islam, insist Mawlana Mawdudi and his colleagues, makes absolutely no distinction between earned income and unearned income; it recognizes both capital and labor as valid factors in production, holding both to be entitled to a share in the profit.[66]

Following the traditional Islamic law once again, Mawlana Mawdudi and his colleagues recognize some limitations on free enterprise, some of which are taken for granted by almost all states, Islamic or non-Islamic. Mention of such factors as a ban on all earnings from theft, bribery, and cheating in the context of a discussion of characteristic features of the Islamic economic order seems rather strange. Other features include the impermissibility of prostitution (as well as of all income from it) and the illegality, for all Muslims, of the production and sale of articles of consumption, such as wine and pork, declared *harām* (forbidden) by the Islamic law. Illegal also are the hoarding and cornering of goods by businessmen in an effort to artificially raise their prices. Also illegal are all those activities in which gain or loss depends merely on chance, as in gambling and speculation.[67]

The institution that Mawlana Mawdudi especially rejects, however, as do the *ulamā*, is that of bank interest. Mawlana Mawdudi and the Jamaat would like to replace the modern system of banking by a system of interestless banking.[68] In view of the role of bank interest in the contemporary free economies, one of the survey questions solicited respondents' views about Islamic permissibility of interest given or charged by modern banking institutions in Pakistan in 1969. Another solicited respondents' opinions whether the modern banking systems in Pakistan should be abolished for Islamic reasons. Most *ulamā* favored prohibiting interest charged on bank loans right away, though several of them in the former West Pakistan thought it should not be prohibited until the banking system was reformed overall. Among the professionals, only 27 percent in the former East Pakistan and about 42 percent in the former West Pakistan favored prohibiting bank interest on Islamic grounds (see Table C.27 in Appendix C). All *ulamā* of our sample advocated abolishing Western-style banking and replacing it with a system of interestless banking (see Table C.28 in Appendix C). Those who opposed interest gave one basic reason for their stand, which has been historically upheld by most traditional Muslims: it is essentially unjust for the moneylender to profit from the need of the borrower or, in the case of a business loan, to insist on his specified rate of interest without taking any risk of loss, which the entrepreneur alone has to bear. Reflecting the approach of the traditional Islamic *fiqh*, they consider the interest impermissible.

The third salient feature of Islamic economic order that Mawlana Mawdudi describes is its concern for the circulation of wealth and for the social security of all the citizens of the Islamic state. He points to the two traditional Islamic arrangements designed to ensure the circulation of wealth and social security: the Islamic law of inheritance and *zakāt*. The law of inheritance is expected to effectively disintegrate the large estates and thus prevent perpetuation of wealth in the hands of only a few families.[69] The institution of *zakāt*, in the words of Mawlana Mawdudi, is "the cooperative society of the Muslims, their insurance company, their provident fund."[70] Like many others who understand the Islamic state to be a social welfare state, Mawlana Mawdudi believes that the government must carry a social security scheme that should be financed from the funds collected as *zakāt* and *ushr* (the traditional 10 percent tax on agricultural crops).

Besides these two legal arrangements, Islam, according to Mawlana Mawdudi (and according to the traditional *ulamā*), relies on moral exhortations. It disapproves hoarding of wealth and encourages charity for the sake of the poor and the needy. The Qur'ān, he insists, seeks to promote a sense of sympathy and cooperation among men and thus seeks to achieve social justice on a voluntary basis. The Qur'ān, says Mawlana Mawdudi, also checks waste of money as it teaches its followers to live a simple life, free from expensive luxuries.[71] At the same time, it discourages miserliness and encourages spending money on the simple pleasures of life, so that wealth may circulate and the economy may prosper.[72]

ISLAM VIS-À-VIS CAPITALISM

Mawlana Mawdudi and the Jamaat reject their opponents' charge that their understanding of Islam's economic system differs little from a Western-type capitalist system with a social security scheme. Dr. Khurshid Ahmad, for a long time a member of the Jamaat's central executive committee and now one of the most energetic and influential leaders of Islamic revivalism worldwide, observes that Islam's economic order and capitalism are poles apart.[73] Himself an ex-professor of economics, Ahmad maintains that the two systems differ in several ways. Many of his points were also made, during the interviews conducted for our survey, by several of those respondents who found Islam closer to a free market economy than to a socialist economy.[74]

1. Islam is a complete civilization; capitalism is merely an economic system.

2. Islam seeks to shape human life, including its economic sector, according to moral principles; the outlook of capitalism, on the other hand, is purely materialistic. Therefore, even though Islam recognizes the market economy, it, unlike capitalism, subjects market economy to moral and social considerations.

3. A capitalist system takes no responsibility for "social maintenance," but in Islam it is of basic importance because Islam aims at social justice, capitalism merely at increasing personal profits.

4. Capitalism grants capital central importance in the economy, and interest is its main pillar; Islam gives central importance to labor and inventiveness, and it abolishes interest in order to reform the capitalist bent of mind.

5. Islam seeks to disperse wealth in the society widely; capitalism, on the contrary, rests on the concentration of wealth.

6. Islam's approach to capital-labor relations differs from that of capitalism: Islam values and promotes brotherly relations among all social classes; capitalism, however, allows divisiveness as the economic classes in a capitalist economy selfishly pursue their own economic interests.[75]

7. Equitability of wages is a fundamental principle of Islam, but capitalism will have nothing to do with it. Capitalism lets the factors of supply

and demand play their roles and cares little if that results in equitable wages or not.

8. Islam, unlike capitalism, imposes certain limits on production, commerce, and expenditure. (The reference here is obviously to the production and sale of such Islamically forbidden commodities as wine and the expenditure on such forbidden items of luxury as, for men, gold jewelry.)[76]

ISLAM AND THE MIXED ECONOMY

The survey findings indicated wide support in 1969 for the view that Islamic teachings favor a mixed economy. Almost 40 percent of our sample of the middle-class professionals in the former West Pakistan and about 37 percent of the professionals in the former East Pakistan desired a mixed economy. Even some *ulamā* of West Pakistan (29 percent) approved of it (see Table 4.1 above; see also Tables C.20–C.23 in Appendix C). Overall about 71 percent of those who desired a mixed economy considered it Islamic (see Table 4.4 above).

All supporters of the mixed economy agree, of course, on the basic principle that the economy should be neither absolutely free, leaving all manufacturing and trade in private hands, nor entirely socialistic, allowing ownership of all means of production and their management only to the state. Beyond this basic agreement, however, they differ greatly among themselves on such issues as which means of production should be nationalized; what restrictions should be placed on private ownership and economic activities; and in what circumstances, and for how long, should those restrictions be placed.

Those who support the mixed economy on Islamic grounds generally do not prescribe a fixed extent of state control of the economy; rather, they make the extent of state control dependent on the social needs of each society at a given time. They consider private ownership and free exchange of goods and services the desirable norm, from which one may depart whenever circumstances require.

Among the supporters of this view was Dr. Fazlur Rahman (1919–1988), a former director of the Islamic Research Institute of Pakistan. Dr. Rahman says that "people can and do own wealth and have the right to produce wealth for themselves and for the society at large."[77] He believes that "the nearest form of free enterprise to the teachings of the Qur'ān is undoubtedly a kind of cooperative industry in the form of joint stock companies."[78]

Indeed, he maintains that such cooperative industry could help solve many problems of underdevelopment and economic disparity. He says,

> [It] would liberalize the economic base. It would keep the freedom of the initiative intact, which would, in turn, be a factor in the fast generation of wealth; it would avoid the gross form of capitalistic exploitation symbolized by cartels. The wealth thus generated will partly be distributed among investors and partly through fiscal measures over society as a whole.[79]

Although Dr. Rahman takes the principle of labor to be the keynote of Islam's economic order, he rejects the Islamic socialist view that all income must be earned with one's own labor. Agreeing with the traditionalist understanding of Islam, he insists that Islam has patently allowed a share to capital in production.[80]

The traditionalist Islam, however, has generally refused to accept admissibility of interest in all its forms. Rahman caused quite an uproar in newspapers, periodicals, and mosques in 1966, and again in 1968, with his declaration that bank interest was not against Islam. It is interesting to note that those modernist writers who understand Islam's economic order to be basically socialistic start from the premise of traditionally accepted illegality of interest and then argue that the profit in business, being as much a form of unearned income, is equally illegal.[81] Conversely, from the premise of traditionally accepted dividends, Rahman reasons that "if capital has a share in the production of wealth, bank interest must be allowed."[82] However, qualifying his statement, Rahman insists that the share of capital, whether invested directly in industry or deposited in a bank and thus indirectly invested, is subject to the same two limitations. First, the interest rate as well as the share in the profit should not be disproportionate (i.e., excessive of what the prevailing conditions may determine the demands of social justice to be at a given time); and second, the interest may be charged on capital that is lent only for productive purposes and not for purely consumptive purposes.[83] Rahman thus accepts the permissibility, indeed the desirability, of some characteristic features of the free economy, including the Islamic permissibility of interest for financing business, in normal acceptable social conditions. But Rahman insists that if at a given time inequality and injustice prevail in a society, the state must regulate the economy, implementing whatever measures are necessary to achieve social justice. Along with many other respondents of the survey sample, Rahman

felt that gross and intolerable injustice existed in Pakistan: "Disproportionate exploitation of power—economic, political, spiritual, and social (including the sexual)—has been rampant in our society and our masses are
still bleeding from its consequences. Landlordism, political authoritarian-
ism and spiritual exploitation have left the masses in shambles."[84] He
urges, therefore, that

> if the dilapidated condition of the society can be remedied without
> resorting to wholesale socialization and by keeping the freedom of the
> individual initiative intact, Islam would undoubtedly prefer this. If,
> however, it is found that the state of the society is economically irre-
> mediable in the visible future without the state's taking over direct
> management of industry, Islam would not only forbid this but would
> obviously enjoin this upon the state as a most imperative duty.[85]

As to the extent and degree of the state's regulation and direction of the
economy, Rahman says the Qur'ān's guiding principle dictates that "in the
basic interest of socioeconomic justice, the state shall interfere with private
wealth to the extent that socioeconomic justice demands."[86] This principle
determines not only the extent but also the duration of state interference in
the economy: "As soon as enough wealth is generated in the country, social
and economic justice is established, and people are on the road to intellectual and moral self-awareness and confidence, external reins must be relin-
quished to bring out from within people their best."[87]

Professor Rahman insists that if for a temporary period nationalization of
industries is seen as necessary, it must be accompanied by nationalization
of labor: "To nationalize industries without corresponding mobilization
and regimentation of labor . . . is not only ineffectual but is patently illogical
and absurd."[88] He criticizes those developing countries that have nationalized capital but have stopped short of the regimentation of labor as taking
only a halfway measure that yields little fruit and creates more confusion.[89]

Rahman appears to be the only writer of importance, besides Ghulam
Parwez, who candidly recommends on Islamic grounds—although for a
temporary period—what he calls the "total assumption of direction on the
part of state," that is, of capital and labor. And he does not see it as contrary
to civic liberty: "In a society which may be economically and intellectually
so backward that it is not easy for it even to realize what lies ahead of it, purposefully applied direction is absolutely required and is in no real sense
against the concept of freedom."[90]

In the critical circumstances, therefore, all economic measures—whether they generally characterize a free market economy, a mixed economy, or even a socialistic and regimented economy—are acceptable according to the given circumstances. Presenting the Islamic reasons for his support of the state's regulation of the economy, Rahman says that Islam seeks to create social conditions in which every individual can find maximum facilities for the development and expression of his personality.[91] Islam attaches utmost importance to fulfilling man's economic needs, first because of the obvious fact that humans have material needs that must be fulfilled, and second because Islamic requirements for man's moral development will not be fulfilled without every individual's getting a fair chance.[92] One can have a fair chance, he argues, only when the basic needs—food, clothing, shelter, health, and education for each individual and defense for the community as a whole—are met; only then will it be possible for a society to move toward the greater Islamic ideal.[93] The economy, therefore, "cannot be allowed to run riot and produce what it pleases and as it pleases."[94]

Like modernist thinker Dr. Fazlur Rahman, some Islamic revivalists in Pakistan, led by Jamaat-i-Islami, came to accept some measures that are seen generally as inconsistent with the free market economy. Although the Jamaat's criticism of socialism and "Islamic socialism" continued unabated, as did the understanding of its followers that Islam and socialism are antithetical, at its central executive committee meeting in March 1969 it adopted a resolution that later became the basis of the Jamaat's 1970 election manifesto. Previously the Jamaat supported the view that no landowner could be forced to part with his land against his wishes;[95] now it proposed to impose, by an act of Parliament, a maximum limit of ownership of land in Pakistan (100 or 200 acres, depending on the fertility of the soil) and require landlords to sell to the government all their land in excess of the maximum limit.[96] The Jamaat also recommended that the government assume management of the "key industries," "if a representative national assembly deems it necessary."[97] This, too, represented a radical departure from the Jamaat's earlier position, which totally opposed nationalization.[98]

Pointing to these and other changes, some of the Jamaat's opponents charged that the Jamaat was guilty of hypocrisy and that it had secretly accepted socialism.[99] The Jamaat's own position on these changes was that these were emergency and abnormal measures needed to cope with the abnormal disparity of wealth in Pakistan.[100] The Jamaat insisted that in principle it was still opposed to nationalization and that it still considered putting any ceiling on ownership of land acreage to be against the rules of the *sharī'a.*[101]

Thus, the Jamaat's approach to economic matters came to resemble Rahman's: both prefer a free market economy in normal circumstances but would allow the state's "interference" in unusual conditions to achieve social justice. For Rahman, all steps toward a socialistic or a mixed economy would be as fully Islamic as the measures related to free enterprise, provided that the Islamic goal of social justice is sought and provided that the economic conditions seem to demand such measures. In the case of the Jamaat, however, one notices a realization that nationalization, even in unusual circumstances, would be far less Islamic than free enterprise. The Jamaat insisted in 1970 that after removing the current disparities through the temporary measures of nationalization and limitation of landownership, it would in the future depend only on the law of the *sharī'a.*[102]

Over the past decades, since the great public debate on economic issues in Pakistan in the 1960s, a new Islamic discipline, called "Islamic economics," has emerged. A number of Muslim economists are engaged in developing this new discipline. The underlying assumption of this Islamic discipline is the belief that the teachings of the Qur'ān and the *sunna,* plus the historical example of the early Muslim community, contain most essential economic principles and precedents. These principles and precedents, complemented by appropriate *ijtihād,* can enable one to formulate a comprehensive Islamic economic order. The basic principles accepted by the new discipline derive heavily from the ideas and interpretations of Mawlana Mawdudi of Pakistan and Sayyid Qutb of Egypt. The former's ideas were discussed above. The discipline's objective is to develop a full-fledged economic system that is genuinely Islamic and incorporates the best features of capitalism as well as socialism.[103] The literature associated with this new Islamic discipline covers an expanding range of economic subjects.[104] Some critics have charged that the literature is marred by historical misconceptions and offers impractical proscriptions.[105] Nonetheless, the literature has partially influenced legislation in Pakistan and Saudi Arabia.[106] It is perhaps too early to say whether the ideas associated with "Islamic economics" will have any substantial impact on the actual economies of the Muslim countries.

5 ✤ Conclusion

The dramatic occurrence of the Islamic revolution in Iran in 1979 fired an interest in the study of Islamic reassertion that continues unabated even as we approach the end of the millennium. A bibliographical survey of the literature on Islamic resurgence included over two thousand major articles and books, published between 1981 and 1988, on various aspects of what is called Islamic revivalism or Islamic resurgence.[1] A sequel to the work cataloged another twelve hundred articles and books on the subject, published between 1989 and 1994.[2]

Four issues have figured prominently in scholarly discussions of political Islam since the Irani revolution of 1979: (1) the nature and character of the ideas associated with Islamic reassertion, especially, the question whether political Islam is predominantly "militant" and "fundamentalist" or includes a very significant diversity of approaches; (2) the compatibility, or incompatibility, of political Islam with democracy; (3) the global significance of Islamic resurgence, particularly the question whether it represents a threat to Western political interests and cultural values; and (4) the historical origins and future prospects of political Islam. This work touches upon all these issues except the global significance of political Islam.

THE DEBATE ON "FUNDAMENTALISM"

Although an increasing amount of scholarly literature now recognizes the broad diversity of Islamic political views, the tendency to equate political Islam with "fundamentalism," and fundamentalism with militancy, persists. This tendency is noticeable more often in articles written for popular magazines and newspapers than in academic publications:

> Islamic fundamentalism of the Sunni or Shia variety in Iran, Egypt, Jordan, the West Bank and Gaza, the Maghreb and also Algeria is not

merely resistant to democracy but wholly contemptuous of and hostile to the entire democratic political culture. . . . [It] is an aggressive revolutionary movement as militant and violent as the Bolshevik, Fascist, and Nazi movements of the past.[3]

Thoughtful scholars criticize such indiscriminate characterizations, sometimes equally emphatically:

The phrase 'Muslim fundamentalist' has become a convenient, if misleading, way for the media . . . to identify a wide-ranging array of groups in the Muslim world. . . . For many, 'fundamentalism' conjures up images of mobs shouting death to America, embassies in flames, assassins and hijackers threatening innocent lives, hands lopped off, and women oppressed. The contemporary revival of Islam in Muslim politics is far more multifaceted and significant than these images and slogans communicate. Its presence in and impact upon Muslim societies is more pervasive and nuanced as both a political and a social phenomenon.[4]

Many other observers of Islam have shown their uneasiness with the term *fundamentalism.* Bernard Lewis offers his reason:

The term 'fundamentalism' derives from a series of Protestant tracts, *The Fundamentals,* published in the United States around 1910 . . . to designate certain groups that diverge from the mainstream churches in their rejection of liberal theology and biblical criticism and their insistence on the literal divinity and inerrancy of the biblical text. The use of the term to designate Muslim movements is therefore at best a loose analogy and can be very misleading. Reformist theology has at times in the past been an issue among Muslims; it is not now, and it is very far from the primary concerns of those who are called Muslim fundamentalists. Those concerns are less with scripture and theology than with society, law, and government.[5]

Other analysts defend the use of the term. Bruce Lawrence and, especially, the editors of the multivolume, comparative study published by the Fundamentalism Project at the University of Chicago, argue for the validity of the term and advocate the view that fundamentalism is cross-cultural and multicreedal. To those who restrict the use of the term to certain Protestant Christians in America, Lawrence replies:

Places are incidentally significant, not historically decisive in the development of socioreligious movements. Even though nationalism originated in Western Europe, the nation-state model has become a global transplant; it has pressed into its confines even groups that continue to be antagonistic to virtually everything else that Europe represents.[6]

In a similar vein, Martin Marty and Scott Appleby, editors of the series *Fundamentalisms,* argue: "All words have to come from somewhere and will be more appropriate in some contexts than in others. Words [such as] 'modern,' 'religious,' 'liberal,' and 'secular' are examples."[7] Pointing to the practical need of the term, they say that fundamentalism

> serves to create a distinction against cognate but not fully appropriate words such as "traditionalism," "conservatism," or "orthodoxy" and "orthopraxis." If the term were to be rejected, the public would have to find some other word if it is to make sense of a set of global phenomena which urgently bid to be understood. However diverse the expressions are, they present themselves as movements which demand comparison.[8]

Since "journalists, public officials, scholars, and publics have settled on this term," the editors favor correcting the misuses of it, "rather than seek an idiosyncratic alternative."[9]

Of course, there is nothing wrong in using any term, as long as its denotations are precise and the term is used appropriately. The core problem with "fundamentalism," therefore, does not have do with where the term originated or whether it could be legitimately employed across cultures and creeds. Rather, the problem has to do with an insufficient conceptual discernment of the term from other orientations, on the one hand, and its indiscriminate application, on the other, resulting in a distortion of the reality. Any term conceived as a part of a typology is expected not only to convey faithfully the actual traits associated with a category but also to distinguish it sufficiently from other categories. Indeed, three conditions seem essential for a neat typology: emotional neutrality, specificity and consistency of criteria, and compatibility with the empirical reality. If one meets these conditions stringently, one can employ even the popularly misused and stereotypical expressions that would otherwise pose a great hazard to objective discussion. Regrettably, this is not the case in some writings.

Despite the great merit of the *Fundamentalisms* series, as a treasure trove of factual information and perceptive analyses, the conceptual treatment of "fundamentalism" by its editors and some core authors seems, in places, inappropriate. None of the three conditions mentioned above is met rigorously.

First, the condition of emotional neutrality requires abstaining from sensationalism and gross generalizations. Series editors Marty and Appleby promise to correct the popular misuse of "fundamentalism"; instead, they show signs of having yielded to it. In volume one of the Fundamentalism Project, entitled *Fundamentalisms Observed,* they declare militancy to be a central characteristic of fundamentalism. They characterize fundamentalists as those who "fight back," "fight for," "fight with," "fight against," and so on.[10] Fundamentalists, they argue, fight for their culturally inherited worldview, for their concepts of family norms and gender roles, and, if necessary, they "fight for a change in the civil polity."[11] Fundamentalists fight back, as they "perceive some challenge or threat to their core identity, both social and personal." They fight against "agents of assault on all that is held dear."[12] Fundamentalists fight with a particularly "chosen repository of resources which one might think of as weapons." They fight with words, ideas, ballots, or "in extreme cases, bullets."[13] Although several essays in later volumes recognize some of the differing characteristics of "fundamentalist" movements and distinguish among several types of fundamentalist organizations within the major traditions of the world, the overall association of militancy and "fundamentalism" is occasionally reiterated by the editors in these volumes.

Even some of those who defend the use of the term *fundamentalism* recognize the risk of stereotyping: "Labels do influence how we think about those labeled, and the label 'fundamentalism' runs the risk of becoming just another stereotype. Used uncritically, it summons up a shorthand abstraction that may assist popular discourse but at the expense of damning the target group."[14]

Second, Marty and Appleby do not provide an adequate conceptual framework for religious movements and outlooks that are not fundamentalist—the "cognate" yet different orientations: "traditionalism, conservatism or orthodoxy," and so on—from which fundamentalism could be distinguished, according to some specific and clearly articulated criteria. Individual contributors to the volumes occasionally talk about these other orientations in limited contexts. On a theoretical plane and in the overall

global context, though, they are not systematically compared with "fundamentalism," nor is "fundamentalism" contrasted against them. The lack of
a conceptual framework classifying cognate religious orientations, vis-à-vis
"fundamentalisms," leads the core authors of the concluding volume to a
self-inflicted paucity of terms. In the final volume of the work, some of these
differing orientations are labeled simply as "nonfundamentalist" and "fundamentalistlike" movements. Worse, having failed to recognize the cognate
movements fully and independently, the authors of the concluding chapters
find themselves in the unenviable position of having to subsume some religious movements identified as "nonfundamentalist" and "fundamentalistlike" under the broader category of "fundamentalist" movements.[15]

The third problem with the limited typology employed by the editors of
the *Fundamentalisms* series is that it does not precisely reflect the empirical reality. It lumps together some religious groups that have little in common and implicitly attributes to many what is characteristic of only some.
Groups that pointedly eschew political involvement for religious reasons,
such as the American Amish, as well as those that avowedly seek it for ideological reasons, such as the Jamaat-i-Islami and Muslim Brotherhood, are
all considered fundamentalist.[16] And since militancy is described as a main
characteristic of fundamentalism, the quiet, peaceful, intensely personal,
religious orientation of the Amish could, by implication, be seen potentially
as militant as the religious Zionists among the Israeli settlers or the Takfīr
group in Egypt.

It cannot be too emphatically reiterated that the term *fundamentalism*
has its limitations and should not be overloaded to cover religious movements that differ from one another in substantial and significant ways.

DIVERSITY OF ISLAMIC POLITICAL ORIENTATIONS

The information presented in the preceding chapters demonstrates the
existence of a wide-ranging normative pluralism in predivided Pakistan —
a pluralism of values, ideas, ideals, and visions relating to the civic order; a
pluralism that, in many respects, parallels the current Muslim orientations
in other Muslim countries. The diversity documented in this study is multidimensional: encompassing the old and the new, religious and secular, liberal and authoritarian, as well as many shades in between. It includes assertive ideologies as well as passively held views, total commitment as well
as selective acceptance. This multidimensional diversity cannot be ade-

quately conveyed by such simple dichotomies as "democrats" and "fundamentalists." A broader typology is needed.

Whatever typology of contemporary Islamic orientations one approves of will be meaningful in proportion to the degree that it covers the extent of Islam's desired role in the civic order, as well as the character of Islam's perceived political message. Additionally, a typology will be valid, as noted above, in proportion to the degree that it reflects the empirical reality and covers the issues that are seen as important by those who are committed to them.

Hence, the empirical method employed by this study, and the study's coverage of some central political issues important to contemporary Muslims, will be of interest here. The central concern of this study has been to determine the extent of Islam's role in politics deemed appropriate by contemporary Muslims, especially in matters related to national identity, the state, and the economy. Muslim views on many specific issues related to these three subjects have been discussed in the preceding chapters. Presented here are some of the survey data indicating the overall role that the respondents conceded to Islam in regulating the civic order.

To assess the overall role assigned to Islam, six composite scales — one each on national identity, polity, law, economy, morality, and the extent of guidance expected from the Qur'ān and *sunna*—were constructed from a greater number of variables. These individual scales were then consolidated to achieve a 30-point grand scale, to represent the full range of Islam's sociopolitical demands felt differentially by the respondents.[17] A score of 6 on this grand scale represented the minimum and 30, the maximum. All respondents included on this grand scale were then divided into three categories. Table 5.1 presents the distribution of these three positions among the *ulamā* and professionals of predivided Pakistan.

The first of these categories (scoring 6 to 14) is recognized here as the "Muslim secularists," since they acknowledge no political message in Islam and feel none of its political demands. For the Muslim secularists, Islam, like Christianity in the industrialized West, is a matter of personal conscience, whose proper domain includes mainly spiritual experience, ritual worship, and theological doctrine. If the Muslim secularists find any political angle in Islam at all, they consider it incidental to Islam's historical development and as such an unessential aspect of the Islamic faith.

TABLE 5.1
DISTRIBUTION OF "SECULARISTS," "ISLAMISTS," AND
"ISLAMISTS-CUM-SECULARISTS" AMONG THE *ULAMĀ* AND
THE MODERN-EDUCATED PROFESSIONALS

Social Category	Overall Position on "Secularity-Islamicity" Grand Scale			Row Total
	"Secularist"	"Islamist-cum-Secularist"	"Islamist"	
Ulamā	0	0	29	29
	0.0	0.0	100.0%	17.9%
Professionals, West Pakistan	12	15	43	73
	16.4%	20.5%	63.0%	45.1%
Professionals, East Pakistan	32	18	10	60
	53.3%	30.0%	16.7%	37.0%
Column Total	44	33	85	162
	27.2%	20.4%	52.5%	100.0%

A notable feature of contemporary Muslim secularism, however, is that it does not seek a true separation of state and religion. Muslim secular governments in the twentieth century have often used state resources and institutions to weaken, to mold, and sometimes to eliminate some religious institutions. This has been either through co-option of the religious establishment or through radically restrictive laws. Co-option of the religious establishment in Muslim countries is not new; the Ottoman sultans and other traditional Muslim kings practiced it far more successfully than the contemporary secular Muslim rulers to secure support from the *ulamā* establishment. However, radically antireligious laws such as those implemented in Kemalist Turkey were something new. Few secular Muslim governments can currently decree such laws or the likes of them. Many secular Muslim governments do continue, however, to use the state's power and resources to maintain the dominance of state institutions over religion.

The third category (scoring 22.1 to 30) is the "Islamists." The Islamists acknowledge Islam's sociopolitical teachings and feel Islamic demands in most of the areas mentioned above. For them Islam is a complete way of life, encompassing the personal as well as the civic, the spiritual as well as the material. Those who see in Islam a political message and feel an Islamic compulsion to actualize that message hold views that, as noted in the preceding chapters, differ considerably. Yet there seems to exist among them a general consensus on three points. (1) All concede a role—partial or total—to the Islamic sentiment in their national, and hence political, self-identity. (2) All see Islam actively seeking and supporting a fair judicial system and some democratic ideals, foremost among which are the rule of law and a measure of equality. (3) All insist that Islam makes economic justice a social responsibility, though they differ on the extent of this responsibility as well as on the mechanism to meet this responsibility. This consensus is obviously on generalities rather than specifics and more often on ends than on means.

The second, middle category (scoring 14.1 to 22) is designated as "Islamists-cum-secularists," since they concede either a partial role to Islam in all the sociopolitical areas or a major role in some but a minor role in others.

As one moves from the query "how much politically oriented Islam" to "what kind of politically oriented Islam," one realizes that the situation warrants greater discernment and allows fewer generalizations. As we have seen in the previous chapters, supranational Muslim identity, as well as territorial nationalism, free market economy, as well as socialistic economy, representative government, as well as restricted freedoms are seen by Muslims to be fully consistent with Islam. The question, then, is whether these differing views are neatly associable with any named categories.

Before the recent popular confounding of diverse contemporary Islamic movements with radical "Islamic fundamentalism," many analysts recognized three distinct Islamist orientations: Islamic traditionalism, Islamic modernism, and Islamic revivalism (or Islamic fundamentalism, in the narrower, older use of the term). These three were themselves distinguished from the fourth Muslim approach: Islamic secularism. These older categories reflect the reality more faithfully than the simple dichotomy that has currently overshadowed them, namely, the dichotomy between the "democrats" and the "fundamentalists." The three Islamist orientations have been defined in the literature already.

In his recent essay on "Islamic Movements in the Arab World," for example, John Voll describes the essential character of revivalism. "Islamic fundamentalism," he says, denotes

> the reaffirmation of foundational principles and the effort to reshape society in terms of those reaffirmed fundamentals. . . . those commonly referred to today as 'fundamentalists' adopt . . . an approach marked by an exclusive and literalist interpretation of the fundamentals of Islam and by a rigorist pursuit of sociomoral reconstruction. Islamic fundamentalism is, in other words, a distinctive mode of response to major social and cultural change . . . perceived as threatening to dilute or dissolve the clear lines of Islamic identity, or to overwhelm that identity in a synthesis of many different elements.[18]

The chief attribute that characterizes Muslim modernists is their advocacy of an enhanced role of reason in human affairs, especially in interpreting the Qur'ān. However, it is one thing to interpret the Qur'ān liberally, quite another to look for a liberal message therein: not all Muslim modernists are liberal, in the second sense. Two quite distinct types of Islamic modernism exist, notable for their differing sociopolitical priorities. One, represented by the thought of individuals like Ali Shariati of Iran and Khalifa Abdul Hakim of Pakistan, has emphasized the importance of social justice and supported the ideas associated with "Islamic socialism." This interpretation of Islam now has far less support than in the 1960s or the early 1970s. The other variety, paramount in the writings of persons like Muhammad Asad, recognizes the importance of liberal democratic institutions and assumes that liberal democratic practices will provide the right conditions to meet Islamic goals, including social justice.

Most contemporary Muslim modernists in fact desire liberal democratic institutions. This second variety of Islamic modernism—Islamic liberalism proper—itself includes two distinct approaches:

> The first finds the idea of a liberal Islamic state possible and desirable not only because such a liberal, democratic state [generally] accords with the spirit of Islam, but especially because, in matters political, Islam has few specific requirements. . . . The second form of Islamic liberalism would justify the establishment of liberal institutions (par-

liament, elections, civil rights) . . . on the basis of quite specific Islamic legislation, which they are inclined to deduce from canonical sources and from the available anecdotal histories of the early caliphate.[19]

These statements are confirmed by the present study. The central issues that divide the Islamic orientations surround two major themes: the understanding of Islam's normative, especially political, demands, and the view toward the classical Islamic tradition. I have discussed Muslim attitudes on a relatively large number of issues throughout the preceding chapters. Some of those basic views are summarized here. The situation is too fluid to allow any claim to an absolute categorical association of the individual attitudes with broader Islamic orientations. Nonetheless, views concerning seven variables, mostly related to these two major themes, seem to characterize these orientations. Table 5.2A presents characteristic views concerning the Islamic tradition; Table 5.2B selectively presents some basic views concerning specifically "political" issues.

If one defines Islamic revivalism as a movement that wants to revive the original, pristine form of Islam, then one can describe Islamic traditionalism as an orientation that wants to conserve or rebuild the Islamic tradition, Islamic modernism as an orientation that wants to reform it, and Muslim secularism as a movement that wants to simply cast aside, or at least to benignly ignore, its political teachings.

The recommended means are as significant as the desired Islamic goals. Islamic traditionalism seeks its goal of rebuilding the Islamic tradition through an expanded traditional Islamic educational system and occasionally employs political pressure on the government in power to secure progressive re-Islamization of the law. Revivalism seeks, especially, to assume governmental power, in pursuit of its goal of re-creating what it believes to be the earliest model of the comprehensive Islamic order. Islamic modernists want to accomplish their goal of reforming the Muslim society through intellectual discourse, modern education, and selective legal reform. The Muslim secularists seek to preserve or expand the already existing secular ideas and institutions in their society through diverse means. Secular Muslim governments, in particular, frequently employ territorial or ethnic nationalism, as well as other Western ideologies, as a counterweight to the Islamic tradition. Some patronize the performance of the ritual—as distinct from the political—aspects of Islam. Some secular Muslim governments, as well as the revivalist governments in Iran and Sudan, have used coercion to achieve compliance.

A major difference among the three Islamist positions lies in their approach to the basic Islamic religious texts: the Qur'ān and the *hadīth*. The difference lies, in essence, in their understanding of the relationship between reason and revelation. The issue that divides them is not, however, acknowledging or rejecting scriptural inerrancy. Practically all believing Muslims accept both the divine origin and the binding character of Qur'ānic teachings. The dividing issue for them is the extent of the use of reason permitted in interpreting the essential Qur'ānic teachings, as distinguished from their specific verbal formulations. From a broader perspective, this issue is about interpreting the will of God as contained in the Qur'ān and His creation. As Leonard Binder puts it,

> For Islamic traditionalists, the language of the Quran is the basis for absolute knowledge of the world. For Islamic liberals, the language of the Quran is coordinate with the essence of revelation, but the content and meaning of revelation are not essentially verbal. Since the words of the Quran do not exhaust the meaning of revelation, there is a need for an effort at understanding which is based on the words, but which goes beyond them, seeking that which is represented or revealed by language.[20]

The political views that characterize the contemporary Muslim orientations concern such basic issues as Islamization of the law, the character of the desired state, the concept of the nation, and the character of the desired economy.

All Islamists want to Islamize the law. To the Islamic liberals, this involves a broad-ranging reform and innovation; to the Islamic revivalists and traditionalists, however, it implies mostly a restoration of the classical *shar'ī* norms. All three use the conceptual tools of *ijtihād* and *ijmā,* but their understanding and application of these concepts differ significantly. For the traditionalists, in particular, *ijtihād* is merely a method of research, not a tool for innovation.

The understanding of what constitutes an "Islamic" state also differs significantly. To the Islamic liberal it is a Muslim-majority country that works for the general Islamic goals of justice and equality; to the Islamic

TABLE 5.2A
VIEWS ASSOCIATED WITH CONTEMPORARY ISLAMIC ORIENTATIONS (A) CONCERNING THE ISLAMIC TRADITION

Subject	Orientation			
	Traditionalism	*Revivalism*	*Modernism*	*Secularism*
General goal concerning Islamic tradition	Conservation	"Restoration"	Reformation	Renunciation or neglect; selective support of the purely spiritual or artistic segment of the Islamic tradition when politically expedient
Major recommended means for desired change	Traditional education; limited collaboration with conservative, religiously sympathetic Muslim rulers	Ideological campaigns; political activities, including organizing political parties and mass movements, participation in elections, assumption of governmental power; some small groups condone militant revolutionary means	Intellectual discourse; liberal education; legal reform	Secular education; government propaganda; legal reform; Democratic politics; or forceful assumption of governmental power with military support

| View toward major Islamic texts | Both the Qur'ān and, sound *hadīth* are binding and their standard classical interpretation should be followed | Both the Qur'ān and, sound *hadīth* are binding; standard classical interpretive texts are not binding, though they are good sources of Islamic understanding | The broad, general teachings of the Qur'ān and *sunna* are binding; *sunna* is to be distinguished from *hadīth*; technically, *sunna*, not *hadīth*, is binding. | Religious texts cannot be taken as guides to sociopolitical matters |

TABLE 5.2B
VIEWS ASSOCIATED WITH CONTEMPORARY ISLAMIC ORIENTATIONS (B) CONCERNING SOME "POLITICAL" ISSUES

Subject	Orientation			
	Traditionalism	Revivalism	Modernism	Secularism
Objective concerning the Classical Islamic law (*sharīʿa*)	Preserving the *sharīʿa*; *taqlīd* of established schools; *ijtihād* (reasoning) is understood as a research method, not a tool for innovation	Restoring the *sharīʿa* with limited modification, plus expanding it to cover entirely new developments	Reformulation of the *sharīʿa* through broad-ranging *ijtihād*; *ijtihād* is seen as a primary tool for innovation	Disregard of all restraints placed by Islamic law and jurisprudence; Islamic concepts employed used only for tactical political advantage
Character of the desired state	"Muslim" state (a state having Muslim government and Muslim majority)	"Islamic" state (a state that enforces the Islamic norms of the *sharīʿa*)	"Islamic" state or Muslim state (a state that works for the general Islamic goals of justice and equality)	Secular state (a state that maintains separation between religious institutions and government or one that permits governmental regulation of religious institutions but not vice-versa)

Attitude toward secular nationalism (of territorial or ethnic variety)	Passive and partial acceptance of secular nationalism; yet primacy of Islamic identity is acknowledged	Rejection of nationalism; promotion of universal Islamic identity	Advocacy for cooperation between territorial nationalism and Islamic identity	Promotion of territorial or ethnic nationalism; rejection or disregard of Islamic identity, except for tactical political advantage or in times of national crisis to buttress national defense
Type of preferred economy	Free economy with limited regulation according to Islamic norms	Free economy; welfare state; regulation of the economy in the interests of social justice and Islamic morality	No characteristic view: free, socialist, or regulated economy, with special regard for economic development and social justice	No characteristic view: free, socialist, or regulated economy, with special regard for economic development and social justice

revivalist, however, an indispensable characteristic of the Islamic state is enforcement of the Islamic *sharīʿa*.

Attitudes toward the nation-state and, especially, toward modern nationalism differ as well. Though the Islamic traditionalists theoretically acknowledge the primacy of the Islamic identity, they have, by and large, passively accepted the implications of the nation-state. The revivalists, though willing to accept the boundaries of the contemporary Muslim nation-states, reject strongly the emotional demands of modern territorial and ethnic nationalism. The Islamic modernists often advocate a simultaneous acceptance of both the Islamic national identity and territorial nationalism. This "Islamic-cum-patriotic" approach, described in detail in Chapter 2, aims at reconciling the traditional Islamic view with modern nationalism.

There are fewer characteristic differences among Islamic orientations concerning the desired economic order. Despite some important exceptions, the supporters of an essentially free economy tend to prevail among all Islamist positions. The differences supported by most Islamists have to do with a narrower or broader extent of regulation, recommended in the interests of morality and social justice. The traditionalists are generally concerned more with moral regulation of the economy—a ban against the production of intoxicants, a ban against usury, and so on. The revivalists also advocate such regulation but are equally concerned about meeting the demands of social justice through the *zakāt* system.

Fuller discussions of the Muslim approaches to the issues concerning the above subjects are included in Chapters 1 to 3.

ISLAM AND DEMOCRACY

Two simultaneous yet apparently contradictory developments in the Muslim world over the past decade have drawn considerable attention: democratization of politics in some Muslim countries and escalation of political conflict in some others. In countries such as Jordan, Kuwait, and Malaysia, the "Islamists" have participated, and continue to participate, in the political and electoral process. In others, such as Algeria, Egypt, and Afghanistan, some Islamic revivalist groups have been engaged in violent confrontations against the secular governments or, as in the case of Afghanistan, against rival Islamic groups.

These contradictory developments have led many to explore the wider question whether Islam is compatible with democracy. The question is not new, but the level of interest and the extent of discussion are much greater now than in the middle of the century. The recent coverage of the subject ranges from treating select issues and concepts to examining the political activities and ideas of Islamic movements in major Muslim countries. An example of the former is Bernard Lewis's article "Islam and Liberal Democracy" and of the latter, *Islam and Democracy* by John Esposito and John Voll.[21]

Three different views of the relationship of Islam and democracy are reflected in current scholarship: (1) Islam is incompatible with or opposed to democracy; (2) it is compatible with, in some ways even potentially supportive of, democracy; and (3) it is not inconsistent with democracy.

The arguments given for Islam's incompatibility with democracy often cite the restraints of Islamic religious doctrine and the character of historical Muslim states. "According to Muslim doctrine," says Bernard Lewis,

> there was no legislative function in the Islamic state, and therefore no need for legislative institutions. The Islamic state was in principle a theocracy — not in the Western sense of a state ruled by the Church and the clergy, since neither existed in the Islamic world, but in the more literal sense of a polity ruled by God. For believing Muslims, legitimate authority comes from God alone, and the ruler derives his power not from the people, nor yet from his ancestors, but from God and from the holy law. . . . The history of the Islamic states is one of almost unrelieved autocracy.[22]

Those who consider Islam compatible with democracy often recognize the Islamic insistence on God's ultimate ethical authority. They argue, however, that divine authority does not preclude representative government. Indeed, they say, certain Islamic principles and teachings encourage — some say require — popular participation in the governmental process. Cited often among these principles are the Islamic juristic concepts *ijtihād, ijmā,* and *shūrā* (reasoning, consensus, and consultation, respectively). John Esposito and James Piscatori, for example, point to the current Muslim understanding of the Qur'ānic recommendation for consultation, *shūrā:*

> All [Muslims] would accept that the divine will is supreme and, in theory, that God's law is immutable and cannot be altered by human de-

sire or whim. Yet, at the same time, by the insistence on the need of rulers to consult and to rule on the basis of consensus, they effectively concede that some form of popular participation is required.[23]

Even Bernard Lewis, despite his understanding of the Islamic theological doctrine and the historical Muslim experience as obstacles to democratization, concedes that some elements in the Islamic tradition can, in favorable circumstances, help the development of democracy in Muslim societies. "Of special importance among these elements," says he,

> is the classical Islamic concept of supreme sovereignty—elective, contractual, in a sense even consensual and revocable. The Islamic caliphate, as prescribed and regulated by the holy law, may be an autocracy; it is in no sense a despotism. According to Sunni doctrine, the Caliph was to be elected by those qualified to make a choice. The electorate was never defined, nor was any procedure of election ever devised or operated, but the elective principle remains central to Sunni religious jurisprudence, and that is not unimportant.[24]

As noted in Chapter 3, the view granting Islam's compatibility with democracy was widely held among those in Pakistan who desired an Islamic polity. The middle-class professionals, as well as the *ulamā,* claimed that elected government, equality, and socioeconomic justice were common features of Islam and democracy. There is considerable agreement among the traditionalists, the revivalists, and the modernists concerning these ideals but not on all of their implications. The actual Muslim views of representative institutions and democratic legislation, as well as democratic values, are consequently multiple and differ significantly. (A discussion of these and related topics is included in Chapter 3; see especially "Islam and Democracy," "Equality and Rule of Law," "Freedom as a Democratic Value," "Islamic Government," and "Islamic Law and Legislation.") Perhaps the very question whether Islam is compatible or incompatible with democracy is too broad for a categorical response. Any sweeping answer to it is bound to be only partially correct.

First, it is not Islam in the abstract but Muslim interpretations of it that may or may not be compatible with democracy. And the current Muslim interpretations of Islam, we know, do differ considerably. Some of the same concepts that some Muslims understand as Islamic bases of democracy are understood by others as evidence against it. The concept of *tawhīd*, the supremacy of the one true God, for example, leads some Muslims to emphasize God's legal sovereignty, while other Muslims see in it the Islamic foundation of human equality and democracy. Second, "democracy" itself has multiple connotations. Three distinct elements are subsumed under it even in some scholarly writings: practices and institutions associated with representative government (elections, parliaments, parliamentary discussions), liberal values (freedom of expression, rule of law, governmental accountability), and what are generally considered to be the ideological and epistemological underpinnings of Western democracy (secularism and rationalism). Sometimes all three, often the first two, of these sets are considered part and parcel of each other.

Included in the conceptual understanding of democracy is the assumption that an individual who supports representative institutions will also support liberal values and that one who does not support all liberal values supports, in effect, none. Empirical research does not confirm this association. In our own survey, we found that individual attitudes toward liberal values and representative institutions are uneven. Commitment to some values and institutions seems complete and robust, to others lukewarm, to still others nonexistent. A democratically oriented Muslim, for example, may support civil liberties in some very important matters and yet constrain freedom of expression in some other, equally important matters. Conversely, some individual attitudes which are seen in the West as characteristic of a single ideological orientation can actually be associated in the Muslim world with more than one such orientation. Some democratic values are supported not only by the Western-oriented liberal Muslims but, as noted in Chapter 2, also by most other Muslims, including the so-called fundamentalists, whose thinking is sometimes indiscriminately characterized as fascist or totalitarian.[25]

Much has been made lately of the dictates of ethical monotheism and, particularly, the scriptural character of Islam (and the other Abrahamic traditions). Much has been said about how these strengthen "fundamentalism" and inhibit progressive change. One tends to forget the obvious fact that, in the final analysis, it matters far less what the scriptures say and far more what the believers in those scriptures interpret them to mean. Religious histories are replete with examples of finding new messages in old texts and assigning new meanings to scriptural and traditional concepts.

Major shifts in emphases, even some radical changes in many religious traditions, were often secured through new interpretation of older texts and concepts. The emergence of Protestant Christianity is one example of how even radical changes can take place in this manner. In Islam, particularly in the Sunnī Islamic tradition, where the traditional interpretation of the *ulamā* is granted neither exclusive validity nor backed by the regulatory authority of an organized church, shifts in emphasis as well as popular acceptance of new interpretations can occur without great social upheavals.

Indeed, the old understanding of a concept can, in some circumstances, even facilitate the acceptance of a new idea or institution. The partial accommodation of modern nationalism, as noted in Chapter 2, is a case in point. It can be argued that the classical ideal of the independence of the Muslim community (*umma*) not only provided support for the recent nationalist movements in Muslim countries but has also facilitated partial acceptance of modern nationalism.

The same seems to be the case with the new Muslim understanding of the classical concepts of reasoning, consensus, and consultation (*ijtihād, ijmā,* and *shūrā*). No Muslim scholar (*ālim*) in the eighteenth century or earlier would recognize the meanings and attributes that the contemporary Muslim liberals associate with them today, considering them to be among the Islamic foundations of democracy.

As noted in Chapter 3, the concept *ijmā* was understood by the *ulamā* in the traditional past to be a principle that lends validity to the past agreement on specific legal issues. Now, however, *ijmā* is seen by the contemporary Muslim supporters of democracy as an important mechanism for reaching national consensus for resolving the current issues through legislation by representative bodies. Despite the weight of the Islamic tradition in this respect, it is the newer understanding of this concept that has been gaining acceptance over the past hundred years. Although the Islamic liberals have clearly lost ground in many matters to the revivalist tide during the past quarter century, equally clear is the fact that some Islamic liberal ideas, primarily the new interpretations of *ijmā, ijtihād, shūrā,* have come to be accepted by an increasing number of contemporary Muslims, including even many revivalists. Obviously, much more seems to be at play here than the dictates of the doctrine and the weight of history. Certainly, doctrinal inclinations, traditional concepts, historical experiences all have their consequences, but so do the contemporary social, cultural, and political conditions. New factors are as important as the old, politics is as influential as theology.

Indeed, some observers find the explanation for the differing behavior of Islamic revivalist groups in the current politics of Muslim countries. They argue that the prevailing political conditions in given countries are partly responsible for the ideological rigidity and revolutionary character of some revivalist groups in some Muslim countries and their flexibility in others: confrontation in some countries, participation in the democratic process in others.

Said Arjomand, for example, identifies two explanatory factors for these differences: "the degree of pluralism of the political regime, and the extent of integration of the Islamic fundamentalist movements within it." [26] He argues, "Partial political integration [of fundamentalist movements] tends to give rise to practical fundamentalism and splinter ideological radicalism, while political exclusion fosters radical ideological fundamentalism and revolutionary sectarianism." [27] In a similar vein, John Esposito and John Voll underscore the role of the existing political systems within which the Islamist political movements operate. In their view, the character of that system not only affects the behavior of the Islamist oppositional organizations, but it can also account for their relative power:

> More open political systems, as have existed in Malaysia and at times in Pakistan along with alternative secular and Islamic organizations, have generally made for greater ideological and political flexibility and prevented any one Islamic group from emerging as the dominant opposition party. Conversely, as the recent histories of Algeria, Tunisia, and Egypt demonstrate, Islamist groups are more likely to emerge as the major opposition party when they are "the only game in town," that is, when they function in political environments in which they become the sole credible voice of opposition and thus attract the votes of those who simply wish to vote against the government or system, as well as the votes of their members. [28]

The full impact of the revival of Islamic political values and of the contemporary Islamist political movements on Muslim societies remains to be determined. Given the relative weakness of representative institutions, civic awareness, and national solidarity in the contemporary Muslim world generally, the potential impact of contemporary Islamic ideas, values, and movements within Islamic societies can be unifying as well as divisive, constructive as well as destructive.

The Islamic faith, like all other major religions, can provide intellectual and emotional underpinnings for democracy as well as despotism, universal brotherhood as well as sectarianism. Much depends on the Muslim interpretation of Islam. Interpreted positively, with generosity of mind and spirit, the Islamic values of equality, justice, and compassion can contribute to the harmony of the civil society and thus contribute to the strength of the civic order, in theory infusing both with a sense of moral responsibility and civic virtue. Interpreted narrowly, however, Islam, like any other faith, can be used by zealots, bigots, and despots to justify discrimination, intolerance, and oppression.

So far, the actual impact of the revival of Islamic political culture has been uneven. On the one hand, one may grant that the collection and distribution of *zakāt*, which is part of the Islamization program in some Muslim countries, must be playing a role, albeit a limited role, in ameliorating the suffering of the poor, especially where full-fledged social welfare programs are currently not attainable. Islamic national consciousness must also be playing its role in limiting ethnic tensions and conflicts in countries with multilingual, multiethnic, multicultural populations.

On the other hand, general heightening of the religious sentiment has led to sectarian tensions and senseless violence in some places. The Shī'ī-Sunnī violence as well as the anti-Ahmadi riots in Pakistan took place under conditions that legitimized social distinction based on religious allegiance. Some Islamization measures, particularly introduction of some traditional social norms of the Islamic *sharī'a*, have widened the gulf between the religiously and the secularly oriented Muslims as well as between Islamic revivalists and Islamic modernists. The civil war in Afghanistan that began as an anti-Soviet national movement has continued, due to sectarian intolerance and a power struggle between Islamist groups as well as ethnic interests. The confrontation between the secularist government and some Islamist groups in Algeria deteriorated into indiscriminate and horrible violence, though it is unclear whether the secular government itself or an Islamist group has been responsible for the worst atrocities there.

The dialogue between Muslims of differing political persuasions continues. Even as physical confrontation and civil war in Algeria were taking place, ideological and normative accommodations appeared in Iran. It is, therefore, unclear what shape, or shapes, the emerging political system(s) in the Muslim world will eventually assume.

IDEOLOGICAL DIMENSION OF CONTEMPORARY ISLAM

Just as some interpretations of Islam may be compatible with democracy and others not, some approaches to Islam may resemble political ideologies while others don't.

In the 1960s, at the height of the cold war between the Western and Communist blocs, ideology was a favored subject of scholarly discussion. The treatment of ideology, however, was often confined to investigating secular ideologies, primarily nationalism, communism, and radical socialism. Rare were sociological investigations of "religious ideology." Indeed, the "religious" and the "ideological" were often understood as two contrary approaches to life, the former characteristically passive and otherworldly, the latter dynamic and politically engaged, the former essentially a relic of the past, the latter preeminently modern. "Religion," wrote Daniel Bell in 1968, "symbolized, drained away, dispersed emotional energy from the world onto litany, liturgy, the sacraments, edifices, and the arts. Ideology focuses the energies and channels them into politics." [29] The global reassertion of religion, particularly the recent resurgence of political Islam around the globe, has challenged, indeed shattered, this dichotomy. A number of writers now approach these contemporary religious movements as ideologies. [30]

This work shares the view that examining the ideological manifestation of contemporary Islam is both appropriate and rewarding: appropriate because of the common characteristics of all ideologies, whether religious or secular, rewarding because it enhances our understanding of the assertive character of some important sociopolitical movements in contemporary Islam. This approach to the subject provides a conceptual device to distinguish the activist and assertive religious approaches from predominantly spiritual and devotional ones. It corrects, as Bruce Lawrence argues, some conceptual problems in the study of religious movements:

> [It] removes religion from the garbage heap of history to which early ideologues have consigned it. Religion is no longer separated from the modern world, as something to be linked to prescientific error, the opposite of rational truth. Second, religious ideology suggests the varied forms of expressiveness that are available to institutional religion in

the modern world. Religion is not just individual commitment entailing personal piety nor group loyalty eliciting ecclesiastical membership. It can also be the corporate public action of religiously motivated individuals on behalf of what they perceive to be their deepest spiritual loyalties.[31]

The approach thus provides a conceptual framework that can be validly employed to compare a variety of religious movements across the globe. It is especially useful for studying modern Islamic movements and contemporary Islamic political attitudes, which are examined in this work.

The two main objectives of this study, delineation of Islamic political ideas and an assessment of their relative popularity among some important sections of the Muslim populace in predivided Pakistan, have been treated in the preceding chapters. A third aspect of Islamic political attitudes pertains to their overall consistency, their comprehensiveness, and their potential for mobilization. This can be explored effectively by asking the question: Is contemporary Islam an ideology?

In the sense the term is used here, ideology stands for a set of beliefs and values that, to the minds of their holders, demand that the collective affairs of their society be fashioned in accordance with those beliefs and values, that appear to them to be more or less logically coherent by their own standards, and with which they identify emotionally, claiming that such beliefs are theirs.

The three characteristic features of ideology have been long established in the literature. The first aspect, what David Apter calls "action-in-relation-to-principle," has been stated by Daniel Bell:

> Ideology is the conversion of ideas into social levers. . . . It is the commitment to the consequences of ideas. . . . What gives ideology its force is passion. . . . For the ideologue, the truth arises in action, and meaning is given to experience by the "transforming moment." He comes alive not in contemplation but in deed.[32]

Philip Converse, commenting upon the second characteristic of ideology, the mutual coherence of various ideas and values that make up the fabric of ideology, prefers the term "belief system" to ideology. The "idea-elements" of a belief system, says Converse, are bound together by some form of constraint or functional interdependence. He distinguishes between two aspects of constraint and interdependence: the static and the dynamic. Static constraint "may be taken to mean the success we would have in predicting, given initial knowledge that an individual holds a specified attitude, that he holds certain further ideas and attitudes."[33] The dynamic constraint or interdependence, he says, "refers to the probability that a change in perceived status (truth, desirability and so forth) of one idea-element would psychologically require, from the point of view of the actor, some compensating change(s) in the status of idea-elements elsewhere in the configuration."[34]

The third characteristic of ideology—a sense of identification on the part of its bearer with his ideology—is usually taken for granted by most writers on the subject. But the discussion of a related concept, that ideology reinforces self-identity of its bearer by making reality more meaningful, is most associable with Erik Erikson. In his classic study of Martin Luther, Erikson describes ideology as "an unconscious tendency underlying religious and scientific as well as political thought: a tendency at a given time to make facts amenable to ideas, and ideas to facts, in order to create a world image convincing enough to support the collective and the individual sense of identity."[35]

Finally, an ideology is different from a mere outlook or system of thought. As Edward Shils has noted, "An ideology differs from a prevailing outlook and its creeds through its greater explicitness, its greater internal integration or systemization, its greater comprehensiveness, the greater urgency of its application and its much higher intensity of concentration focused on certain central positions or evaluations."[36]

Is Islam, then, an ideology in the sense that ideology has been defined above? Certainly, when Islam emerged first in seventh-century Arabia it assumed the form of an ideological movement. The Prophet Muhammad himself, and most of those who immediately succeeded him, felt an urgency to take political action not only in defense of the Islamic faith but also in accordance with, and because of, the teachings of Islamic faith. However, what Islam was in the seventh century, according to either the understanding of Muslims then or the understanding of the scholars of the Islamic texts thereafter, cannot be the criterion for whether Islam is or is not an ideology today; only the contemporary understanding of the Muslims can decide that.

The contemporary understanding of the Muslims, as elaborated in this work, is far from uniform. There is no single Islamic interpretation that is accepted by all Muslims; instead there are several approaches to Islam, recognized in this work as "Islamist," "secularist," and "Islamist-cum-secularist," from one perspective and as traditionalist, revivalist, and modernist, from another. Depending on the subjective feelings of their holder, that is, feelings of commitment to and compulsion for actualizing the demands of one's beliefs, any of these orientations can assume the character of an ideology or prove to be a mere outlook.

In the context of predivided Pakistan, the survey conducted for this study found that those Muslims who accept a wide extent of Islam's political message (scoring high on the 30-point "Islamicity-secularity" scale) exhibited a considerable coherence and consistency in their beliefs and values. Table 5.3 presents the strong statistical correlation between respondents' overall "Islamist" position and their acceptance of Islam's specific sociopolitical demands in several individual areas.

Logical coherence and consistency of commitment shown by the "Islamists" of the survey sample are also reflected in the published views of those contemporary Muslims who claim that Islam is an ideology. Their writings underscore their two convictions: that Islam's teachings do not merely constitute a religious doctrine and a set of rituals but include sociopolitical principles as well, and that the social, political, and economic teachings of Islam, as well as its religious and moral doctrines, are both related to its same fundamental principles and share an essential unity of purpose and approach.[37] For many, and particularly for the revivalist supporters of the Jamaat-i-Islami, the accent has been on the blueprint of the desired society. "When we use the term Islamic ideology," wrote Khurshid Ahmad, a leader of the Jamaat-i-Islami, "we mean by it that political and cultural program of action that Islam offers."[38]

Besides consistency and comprehensiveness, the major criteria that distinguish an ideology from an outlook—as also from a school of thought— are mostly psychological in nature. Most of the questions included in the survey were designed to explore mainly the cognitive aspects of the popular attitudes and their relation to Islam. A few follow-up questions, however, sought to assess specifically emotional concomitants of these attitudes. Responses to the following questions indicated the intensity of commitment that the respondent himself professed toward what he described as his ideology:

It appears from your answers that you have a desire to see the fundamental demands of your ideology realized. Which of the following statements seems to express your feelings about such demands?

TABLE 5.3

STRENGTH OF CORRELATION BETWEEN OVERALL
"SECULARITY-ISLAMICITY" WITH "SECULARITY-ISLAMICITY"
IN INDIVIDUAL AREAS OF SOCIOPOLITICAL CONCERN*

Area of Sociopolitical Concern with which Overall "Secularity-Islamicity" Is Correlated	Strength of Statistical Correlation	
	Gamma*	Kendall's Tau B*
National Identity	.81	.66
Political System	.93	.76
Law	.91	.76
Morality	.75	.63
Economy	.87	.69
Expectation for Guidance From the Qur'ān and *sunna*	.94	.75

*On a scale from zero to one: 0 = no association; 1 = perfect association.

    a. Conformity to ideology is necessary. We all should do whatever we
       can to realize its demands.
    b. Conformity to ideology is *desirable* but not imperative.
    c. Conformity to ideology is no less than a matter of life and death.
       (Question 42)

Table 5.4 presents the responses to the question vis-à-vis the overall Islamic secular position on the 30-point grand scale. It is obvious from the table that the majority of the "Islamists" of the survey sample professed a strong commitment to their beliefs and values, while the predominant majority of the "Islamists-cum-secularists" professed a commitment that is character-ized here as "mildly strong" (choice b, in response to the above question). The third characteristic of ideology—holder's personal identification with his beliefs and values—is also most noticeable among the "Islamists."

TABLE 5.4
INTENSITY OF COMMITMENT PROFESSED BY THE "SECULARISTS,"
THE "ISLAMISTS," AND THE "ISLAMISTS-CUM-SECULARISTS" FOR
THEIR RESPECTIVE IDEOLOGIES

| Position on Overall "Secularity-Islamicity" Grand Scale | Intensity of Commitment | | | |
	(B) Weak or None	(A) Mildly Strong	(C) Strong	Row Total
"Secularist"	8 20.5% 72.7%	19 48.7% 28.8%	12 30.8% 21.1%	39 29.1%
"Islamist-cum-Secularist"	3 10% 18.2%	22 73.3% 33.3%	5 16.7% 8.8%	30 22.4%
"Islamist"	0 0.0 0.0	25 38.5% 37.9%	40 61.5% 70.2%	65 48.5%
Column Total	11 8.2%	66 49.3%	57 42.5%	134 100.0%

Indeed, many analysts of contemporary Islam see the need for reasser-tion of Islamic identity as a paramount reason for insistence on the distinc-tiveness, or comprehensiveness, of some Islamic theories. The vast major-ity of those who scored high on the secularity-Islamicity scale not only professed Islam to be their ideology (see Table 5.2 above), but they were also most insistent on the need to realize "in-group" consensus on the es-sentials of Islamic ideology. Responses to the following survey question pointed to the extent of consensus demanded by those who occupy the "Is-lamist" and the "Islamist-cum-secularist" positions on the 30-point grand scale:

To which of the following propositions would you subscribe?
  a. The Muslims in Pakistan must share the fundamentals of our Islamic ideology. The non-Muslims must respect them.

TABLE 5.5

THE DEMAND FOR CONSENSUS ON ISLAMIC IDEOLOGY BY
"ISLAMISTS," "SECULARISTS," AND "ISLAMISTS-CUM-
SECULARISTS"

Position on "Secularity-Islamicity" Scale	The Extent of Demand			
	(B) Not Demanded	(A, B)* Restricted Demand	(A) Demanded	Row Total
"Secularist"	40 95.2% 54.8%	0 0.0 0.0	2 4.8% 2.8%	42 27.8%
"Islamist-cum-Secularist"	21 77.8% 28.8%	1 3.7% 16.7%	5 18.5% 6.9%	27 17.9%
"Islamist"	12 14.6% 16.4%	5 6.1% 83.3%	65 79.3% 90.3%	82 54.3%
Column Total	73 48.3%	6 4.0%	72 47.7%	151 100.0%

Kendalls Tau^b = 0.68213; Gamma = 0.92632.
*Consensus demanded from Muslims, who may not be allowed to criticize Islam, but not demanded from non-Muslims.

b. The citizens of our country, both Muslims and non-Muslims, should be allowed every right to oppose and reject, in good conscience, even what could be regarded by others as the fundamentals of Islamic ideology.

Table 5.5 indicates that those who occupy a high position on the "Islamicity" scale tend to demand consensus, while a vast majority of the "Islamists-cum-secularists" do not.

Despite the understanding of many contemporary Muslims that Islam seeks to regulate sociopolitical life, and despite their commitment to the position that Islam would not be complete without its sociopolitical message, none of the "Islamists" assigned sociopolitical teachings of Islam priority over faith in God and other basic Islamic theological beliefs, not even over Islamic demands of personal morality. This is shown in Table 5.6, which presents the responses to the following question:

> **Every ideology has some concern about the beliefs and actions of its followers. Some give more importance to the desirable kind of beliefs, others to the desirable kind of society. How would you rate the following in importance?**
> *a.* Right kinds of beliefs — in God, the hereafter, and prophethood.
> *b.* Right kinds of morals and personal relations.
> *c.* Right kind of political and economic organization of the society.

For the typical upholder of a secular ideology, sociopolitical doctrine as well as sociopolitical order of his conception would be far more important than questions of religious beliefs and personal piety. Does, then, the fact that none of the Islamists assign priority to the sociopolitical order mean that their conception of Islam constitutes only a religion and not an ideology? As noted above, Daniel Bell and many others who treated the subject in the 1960s consider religion conceptually as well as factually different from ideology.[39] From that perspective, even the question whether Islamic religion is an ideology seems inappropriate.

But the fact, now abundantly clear, is that there are politically oriented religious approaches as well as non–politically oriented ones. It may not be, therefore, quite precise to speak of the differences between religion and ideology; rather, one might speak of two types of religion, politically oriented and non–politically oriented, and two types of ideology, religious and secular.

The variables involved in these dichotomies are two, the first having to do with the view toward the supernatural, and the other having to do with the appropriate domain of political action. Despite the radical philosophical differences between the secular and the religious views of the cosmos, religious experience can be essentially the same as secular ideological experience. It has been long recognized that among the aspects of a religious experience is an intense feeling of loyalty, of utter seriousness, a profound concern and a sense of the imperative. As noted above, these are also some of the elements that characterize, though perhaps to a lesser degree, the feelings of one who is committed to a secular ideology. In view of this

TABLE 5.6

PRIORITY OF FAITH, MORALITY, OR POLITICS IN ISLAM AS PROFESSED BY THE "SECULARISTS," THE "ISLAMISTS," AND THE "ISLAMISTS-CUM-SECULARISTS"

Position on "Secularity-Islamicity" Grand Scale	Understanding of Priorities					Row Total
	Only Faith and Morality Are Important	Faith First, Then Morality, and Last Politics	All Are Equally Important	First Polity and Economy, Then Faith and Morality	"Don't Know" or Refused to Answer	
"Secularist"	11 52.4% 57.9%	5 23.8% 12.8%	1 4.8% 5.0%	0 0.0 0.0	4 19.0% 18.2%	21 21.0%
"Islamist-cum-Secularist"	6 35.3% 31.6%	2 11.8% 5.1%	7 41.2% 35.0%	0 0.0 0.0	2 11.8% 9.1%	17 17.0%
"Islamist"	2 3.2% 10.5%	32 51.6% 82.1%	12 19.4% 60.0%	0 0.0 0.0	16 25.8% 72.7%	62 62.0%
Column Total	19 19.0%	39 39.0%	20 20.0%	0 0.0	22 22.0%	100 100.0%

essential similarity, a religion that is committed to political action is sub-stantially the same as an ideology that claims the existence of a transcen-dental truth. Like a religion, such an ideology seeks its own affirmation by referring to and drawing inspiration from the claimed truth.

Because of the nature of their beliefs, believers in a politically oriented religion cannot assign priority to their political values over their belief in a transcendental reality. They can, however, insist on equal importance of the two, as did some of the Islamists of our sample (see Table 5.6 above). A statement like that of Mawlana Abul Ala Mawdudi, the late founder of the Jamaat-i-Islami, that personal, social, and political aspects of Islam are as organically related to one another and are as important for one another as are the roots, the branches, and the leaves of a tree is a far cry from dispers-ing emotional energy onto litany, liturgy or any sacraments.[40] Even among the traditionalist *ulamā,* there are some who assign great importance to po-litical action. The 1970 *fatāwā* signed by 230 *ulamā* of Pakistan and what is now Bangladesh declared, for example:

> Those political parties which are struggling against both socialism and capitalism, and which have agreed together upon the [necessity of es-tablishing] the pure Islamic order [in Pakistan], are indeed fighting against the greatest threat to Islam. To donate funds to them, to assist them [by any other means] in achieving that goal, and to vote for them [in the general elections] are all aspects of *jihād* as described by the Is-lamic *sharī*ᶜ*a.*[41]

In conclusion, contemporary Muslims understand Islam in multiple and varied ways; some understand Islam in conventional religious terms, con-ceding little political role to it. Many others recognize in Islam important political goals and values, but they either do not take Islam to embody a complete sociopolitical system or do not exhibit any great sense of urgency to actualize Islam's political message. Their approach to Islam may amount simply to an outlook. Still other Muslims pointedly hold Islam to be a com-prehensive way of life and feel a great sense of urgency to realize it in prac-tice. Islamic understanding of this last category of contemporary Muslims — most conspicuous among whom in Pakistan are the revivalist supporters of the Jamaat-i-Islami — includes many characteristics that one appropriately associates with an ideology.

ORIGINS AND PROSPECTS OF POLITICAL ISLAM

Explanations of the recent resurgence of Islam fall, in essence, into two categories. Some scholars find the origins of Islamic political ideas and current movements within the Islamic cultural tradition. For them, Islamic revivalism or "Islamic fundamentalism" represents a recurring theme in Islamic history. For some others, the recent Islamic resurgence is sui generis, a historically unique new development, a result predominantly of modern conditions.

A recent version of the first view is offered by John Voll, who sees a clear paradigm operative in much of Islamic history. He believes that historical Islamic communities evolved through the interaction of some definite "styles of Islamic experience," which he designates as adaptationist, conservative, fundamentalist, and individualist.[42] "These styles," he says, "are identified not so much by the content of ideas espoused as by modes of dealing with historic change and of interpreting the Islamic message."[43] Voll explains major cultural and religious changes in Islamic history almost in terms of a cycle of adaptation, conservation, and renewal:

> As Islamic communities are created or expand adaptation to local conditions is necessary, and such adaptations were the foundations for the great syntheses of Islamic history. . . . With the great successes of Islamic adaptationism came a sense of the need to preserve the achievements, and a conservative style of Islamic action worked to preserve the gains that had been made and became a brake upon conscious changes adaptationists wished to make. However, at various times and in different places, the process of adaptation appeared to introduce such flexibility or so many compromises that the clearly Islamic nature of the community seemed to be threatened. In that situation, the process of renewal would take a fundamentalist form.[44]

Applying this historical paradigm to the modern period, Voll argues that the current resurgence of fundamentalist Islam represents yet another interaction among styles of Islamic experience, yet another response to the modernizing adaptation and secular individualism that had recently become the dominant styles in the Muslim world.[45] As the compromises involved in these styles appeared to threaten the authentic, Islamic nature of the community, fundamentalist pressures began to build, and because of factors like the oil boom of the 1970s, the reassertion of the fundamentalist style became an important force in the Islamic world.[46]

Another version of this view that traces the origins of contemporary Islam within the internal dynamics of Islamic civilization is offered by Ernest Gellner. Like some others before him, Gellner sees a polarization of "High Islam" and "Low Islam" in Islamic history. He describes the high variant as "very 'Protestant,' that is, rule-oriented, individualistic, scripturalist, puritan, and entirely suitable for the tastes of urban scholars and urban bourgeoisie."[47] The low version, characterized by normative laxity and the cult of personality, suited the taste of rural populations. Though the two versions of Islam often coexisted, there existed between them an unspoken tension. Occasionally, this latent tension "bursts out into an internal *jihād*, in which the High version tries to convert the Low version, and a Reformation is attempted. For social reasons, however, this was never successful in the past."[48] In Gellner's opinion, the recent Islamic resurgence represents the final triumph of the scripturalist High Islam over the Low Islam. This triumph of the scripturalist, rule-oriented Islam, he says, was made possible, ironically, by the impact of the Western industrial world.[49] Industrialization and urbanization in Muslim countries weakened the rural societies and, along with them, the Low Islam that had countered the trend toward religio-normative discipline.[50] Thus, "in the last hundred years, the central variant of Islam actually carried out a successful Reformation for the first time in history. But it was only noticed by the West, on the whole, in connection with the somewhat untypical case of Iranian Shi'ism, where it very effectively erupted on the political scene."[51]

Bruce Lawrence argues against all theories that consider the current Islamic resurgence a continuation of a historical paradigm: without modernity and secularization, development of religious fundamentalism could not have taken place. "Fundamentalists seem bifurcated between their cause and their outcome; they are at once the consequence of modernity and the antithesis of modernism. Either way, one cannot speak of premodern fundamentalists."[52]

Gabriel Almond, Emmanuel Sivan, and R. Scott Appleby offer yet a third view. Having examined religious "fundamentalisms" across the world, they declare:

We see fundamentalism neither as a "new religious movement" (in the technical sense of that term) nor as simply a "traditional," "conservative," or "orthodox" expression of ancient or premodern religious faith and practice. Rather, fundamentalism is a hybrid of both kinds of religious modes, and it belongs in a category by itself.[53] Indeed, the contemporary Islamic revivalism has old as well as new elements. In some respects, it is historically familiar, in other respects rather novel. The simultaneous existence of the old and the new elements is made possible by the multidimensional character of social movements. Two distinct dimensions of social movements are readily recognizable. (1) Each movement has an ideology, that is, a set of ideas which, as noted above, are more or less coherent and move their believers to social action. Among the ideas associated specifically with religious ideologies, one can make an additional distinction between the basic religious themes, or moral motifs, on the one hand, and rational arguments, or their articulation, on the other. (2) A social movement is often espoused by a distinct group or a set of groups having a specific organization and strategy for achieving the goals embodied in the ideology. The origins of the four, i.e., the moral motifs, the rational arguments, the organizational structure and the group's strategy, can be quite different.

The crucial religious and moral motifs associated with the contemporary Islamic revivalism resemble closely those of the Islamic *tajdīd* (renewal) movements, which, many scholars have noted, emerged repeatedly in Islamic history. The central themes in contemporary revivalist movements are the same as in these premodern reform movements: purification of the faith, primacy of the Qur'ān and the *sunna,* supremacy of the Islamic law (*sharī'a*), and the modality of the Prophet. The contemporary Islamic revivalism is new, nonetheless, in three respects: in the articulation of its themes, in its organization and strategy, and in its reaction to secularization and modern secular ideologies.

The modernity of its articulation becomes apparent as one realizes that the traditional writings in Arabic, Persian, and Turkish employed, especially just prior to the beginning of the modern age, a literary style that was often either poetic or arcane. The language of Islamic revivalism—as well as the language of Islamic liberalism—is strikingly modern, simple, and straightforward. Its expositions—contained in the writings of Abul Ala Mawdudi, for example—are precise and systematic. It is not surprising, therefore, that both Islamic revivalism and Islamic modernism have considerable following among students in modern colleges in many Muslim countries. The use of modern means of communication and organizational techniques by revivalist movements is evident in their dissemination of ideological literature as well as in their organizational structure. Both have been noted by other observers.[54]

The third historically new dimension of Islamic revivalism is its reaction to secularization and modern secular ideologies. Secularization and secular ideologies have provided a strong impetus to revivalist movements. Almond, Sivan, and Appleby appropriately consider secularization to be one of the most crucial causes of revivalism: "The defining and distinctive structural cause of fundamentalist movements is secularization. As we consider the sweep of fundamentalist movements across nations, cultures, and civilizations, some degree of secularization is present in all of them."[55] Being the chief antagonists of revivalist movements, modern secular ideologies have partially determined the characteristic thrust of contemporary revivalist movements. Bruce Lawrence rightly lays emphasis on this aspect of religious "fundamentalism": "The distinctiveness of fundamentalism as a religious ideology emerges when we contrast it with that secular ideology which has become its principal nemesis."[56] In the case of the Islamic world, reaction to secularization is tied with a larger Muslim quest: how to remedy the cultural and political decline of Muslim societies and reconstruct the cultural foundations of Muslim life.

A predominant theme in Islamic history of the past two hundred years has been the erosion of the traditional institutional and cultural foundations of Muslim life, which had lasted a millennium before the end of the eighteenth century. The classical foundations of Muslim life—the Muslim understanding of communal identity and the *umma,* the Muslim belief in the cultural self-sufficiency of the Islamic tradition, the *madrasa* as an institution for comprehensive and not just religious education, as well as the Islamic political institutions such as the sultanate, the *sharī'a* courts, and the *millet* system, and so on—have been eroding over the past two centuries. In some Muslim countries many traditional Islamic institutions disintegrated due to the forceful intervention of European imperialism; in other countries they were abandoned by the secularly oriented Muslim rulers themselves. Other traditional Islamic institutions and basic views were weakened under the steady impact of secular education and socio-cultural modernization. (The impact of some of these factors on national identity is explored in Chapter 2.)

The current Islamic revivalism is an attempt to reconstruct the Muslim societies. However, it is not the only such attempt, nor is it likely to be the last. Indeed, it is a part of the reformist efforts that began in the Ottoman Empire even before the disintegration of the traditional order in the Muslim world. As soon as it became apparent to the eighteenth-century Ottoman rulers that the Muslim lands under their rule were now an easy prey to European imperialist ambitions, they sought to remedy their weakness first through military and then administrative reforms (*tanzīmāt*). When the weakness persisted, European imperial encroachments increased, and the old order began to disintegrate. Muslim rulers then contemplated more radical reforms, and Muslim intellectuals began to recommend differing alternatives.

Reviving and recasting the traditional institutions and norms as well as reforming or abandoning even those elements of the tradition that survived have been repeatedly advocated by Muslim intellectuals and activists. Islamic revivalism, Islamic liberalism, pan-Islamism, patriotism, secular ethnic nationalism, liberal democracy, as well as the radical state have been alternatively recommended, and elements of some have actually been pursued in the past two hundred years.

Though the relative attraction of each of these ideological approaches to the Muslim societies has ebbed or flowed, none of these approaches has been abandoned completely, nor has any won exclusive approval. Two of these approaches, however, are currently the major contestants: Islamic revivalism and secular nationalism. A third, Islamic liberalism, though currently eclipsed by the other two, continues to play its role in the background as the prime synthesizer of the old and the new.

The recent confrontation between revivalism and secular governments in some Muslim countries has focused scholarly interest on revivalist activism. The confrontation has shifted attention away from Islamic liberalism, which, though overshadowed by the other two, continues to represent an important Muslim orientation and to influence Muslim thinking at large. Over the past century and a half, Islamic liberalism has developed new concepts and interpretations to synthesize elements from classical Islamic and modern Western traditions. Undoubtedly, the style of Islamic liberals has been far less activist and passionate than that of the revivalists. Their influence, however, has been no less significant. Some of their ideas, as noted above, have been quietly but surely accepted by increasing numbers of Muslims, including even many revivalists.

The differing ideological approaches in the Muslim world continue not only to compete against one another, but they also continue to interact upon one another and influence one another. A clear victory of either Islamic revivalism or Muslim secularism is not the only possible outcome expected from this competition and interaction. More likely, in the long run, is a new synthesis that will incorporate elements from several of these ideologies and orientations. The evidence for such a probability is already there. For example, the arguments associated with the "Islamic-cum-patriotic" orientation (discussed in Chapter 2) clearly represent both the desire and the efforts of many Muslims to achieve a rapprochement between Islam and nationalism that could be emotionally satisfying as well as politically workable.

Yet some scholarly analyses have ignored such views and discounted the likelihood of the innovative adaptation that these trends indicate. Specifically, with reference to the issues regarding Islam and secularization, some judgments have been highly tendentious, though the actual assertions contained in them have been quite different over time.

In particular, the social scientific assessment of the prospects of Islam as a cultural and political tradition in the contemporary world has changed substantially during the past half century. In 1958 Daniel Lerner, in his famous work, *The Passing of Traditional Society,* asserted emphatically: "Whether from East or West, modernization poses the same basic challenge—the infusion of 'a rationalist and positivist spirit' against which, scholars seem agreed, 'Islam is absolutely defenseless.'"[57]

Writing recently, however, Ernest Gellner comes to a conclusion diametrically opposed to Lerner's: "Secularization," Gellner insists, "simply has not taken place within Islam. The hold of Islam over both the masses and the elite in Muslim countries is as strong now as it was a hundred years ago, and in some ways it is stronger. Thus, whatever merit there is in the logic of the secularization argument, it does not apply in at least one of the four major culture zones of the Old World."[58] Gellner believes, "So far, there is no indication that it [Islam] will succumb to secularization in the future either."[59]

This swing of the pendulum concerning the understanding of the Islamic tradition has, clearly, as much to do with the differing theoretical approaches as with the actual events that have been unfolding in the Muslim world. The classical secularization theory, now abandoned by many sociologists, overstated the impact of modernization. It brushed aside the uniqueness and resilience of modernizing traditions, including those of the Islamic tradition. The recent activism of Islamic revivalist movements seems now to be leading to an alternate theoretical approach that may overstate the uniqueness of cultural traditions. The new approach, represented here by Gellner's recent thesis, virtually makes the Muslim society altogether immune to secularization. The strength of a cultural tradition is one thing, escaping completely all normal consequences of the powerful societal and cultural processes that are often subsumed under the term modernization is quite another.

Gellner's keen observation of how some aspects of industrialization and urbanization in the Muslim world have strengthened the "High Islam" vis-à-vis the "Low Islam" is well taken. However, the historical reality of the past two centuries contradicts his thesis that secularization has not taken place in Islam. Certainly, more Muslims now live in urban areas than ever before. More Muslims indeed now prefer, to use Gellner's terms, the "rule-oriented," "High Islam" that has been historically associated with Islamic cities over the "Low Islam" associated with the rural areas. But the institutional makeup of the contemporary Muslim cities, as well as the lives of the contemporary Muslim bourgeoisie, bears an imprint of considerable secularization. Many social and political institutions that sustained the traditional Islamic life in the past have, in large measure, disintegrated; the values and ideas that survive now have new rivals to compete against. As noted earlier, the traditional caliphate, the sultanate, the *millet* system, the communal law, the *sharīʿa* court, and the *madrasa* system either exist no more or are mere shadows of their former selves. The traditional elite, consisting of the *umarā* (military commanders) and the *kuttāb* (civil bureaucrats), has given way to new social categories that are more conversant with modern professional skills than with traditional Islamic concepts. The power of the *ulamā* has dwindled in direct proportion to the secularization of education and government.

The classical secularization theory hid from view in the mid twentieth century the evidence for the Islamic sentiment and Islam's cultural resilience. The new approach may now obscure the evidence for the secular institutions, liberal and quasi-secular orientations, as well as the substantial adaptationist inclinations that persist in the Muslim world today.

A ❋ The Questionnaire

Concerning National Identification

1. **Do you agree with the following proposition?**
   Our conscience requires of us that we should assign loyalties in the following order of priorities:
   a. First, to relatives and members of our *birādarī* (i.e., extended kinship group).
   b. Then to persons of our own birthplace.
   c. Next, to all fellow Muslims, in general.
   d. Finally, to citizens of our country, both Muslim and non-Muslim.
   Yes/No
   If not, how would you assign priorities?

2. **With which of the following propositions would you agree?**
   a. We are Muslims first and foremost. Only religion is the true basis of our nationhood. All other kinds of nationalism are unworthy.
   b. Feelings of nationhood are based on common language, shared cultural values, and community of economic interests. Religion should play little role in it.
   c. Our feeling of nationhood is based on our historical experiences in the Indo-Pakistan subcontinent. We share Islam with other Muslims, but as a nation we are separate and distinct.
   d. National unity is a false value. The true basis of unity is class interest.

3. **Which one of the following would you consider to be the golden age of your past?**
   a. The Mughal period.
   b. The age of the "rightly guided" caliphs.
   c. The Abbasid period of Harun al-Rashid and al-Mamun.
   d. Or would you say, "No period of our history can be regarded as the golden age. We should look forward rather than backward."
   e. Any other answer.

4. Of the following, which ought to be the most important basis/bases of Pakistan's political unity?
   a. Islam.
   b. Love of the fatherland.
   c. Expedience.
      i. Political.
      ii. Economic.
      iii. Any other answer.

5. What does the term *umma* mean to you? Does it have any political connotations? Which of the following definitions do you hold to be correct?
   a. It is a purely religious concept—*umma* means the followers of Prophet Muhammad.
   b. The concept of *umma* is nonpolitical, essentially one fellowship. *Umma* means the worldwide Muslim community toward which every Muslim extends a feeling of brotherhood and goodwill.
   c. It is a political concept:
      i. *Umma* means the Pakistani nation.
      ii. It follows from the concept of *umma* that Muslim nations all over the world should cooperate and help each other in solving their problems.
      iii. There should be a Muslim commonwealth—a sort of confederation.
      iv. There should be only one great state of all Muslims, with one government.

6. Which of the following is the most desirable to you?
   a. Muslim nations all over the world should cooperate and help each other.
   b. There should even be a Muslim commonwealth—a sort of confederation.
   c. There should be only one great state of all Muslims, with one government.

Concerning Political and Legal Orientations

7. With which of the following propositions do you agree?
   a. Political organization should be based on expedience and should aim at utilitarian ends.
   b. Political organization is required by Islam and should serve the cause of Islam.
   If you agree with neither or take exception to such a dichotomy, what is your own view on this subject?

8. How would you describe the present constitution of Pakistan, with reference to its Islamic or secular character?
   (Read out the following:)
   a. Fully Islamic.
   b. Sufficiently Islamic.
   c. Islamic in appearance only.
   d. Mainly secular.
   Any other description?

9. To which of the following, in your opinion, is Islam closer in spirit?
   a. Democracy.
   b. Socialism.
   c. Dictatorship.
   d. Fascism.
   Any other?

10. *A.* What features does Islam have in common with democracy?
    B. What principles of Islam differ from those of democracy?

11. *A.* What are the minimum requirements of an Islamic state?
    B. Do you hold the Islamic state desirable?

12. How would you describe the present laws of Pakistan with reference to their Islamic character?
    (Interviewer, tell the respondent that this question is not about the Martial Law regulations that are currently in force in the country. Read out the following:)
    a. Mainly un-Islamic.
    b. Mainly Islamic, for those laws which do not originate from the *shariʿa* are nevertheless based on the Islamic principles of justice and equity.
    c. Totally un-Islamic.

13. Would you like to see the law in Pakistan Islamized?

14. How can the law in Pakistan be Islamized?
    (Read out the following:)
    a. By enforcing the *shariʿa* as it is stated in the traditional books.
    b. By free interpretation of the principles of justice and equity found in the Qurʾān and the *sunna*.
    c. By the exercise of limited *ijtihād*. The provisions of the traditional *fiqh* relating to those social, political, and economic problems that have been dealt with by the four schools of Islamic law should be enforced in their virtually original form, but new solutions for new problems may be attempted.
    Any other comment?

15. In what spheres would you particularly like to see the law Islamized?

16. It is said that the *sharīʿa* gives the relatives of a murdered person the right to accept *diyat* (blood money) from the murderer and to let the murderer go unpunished. Would you like to see this law applied in Pakistan?

17. Who, in your opinion, can properly determine what is Islamically right in the present age?
    (Closed question.)
    a. Ulamā.
    b. The political leaders.
    c. Representatives of the people in the National Assembly.
    d. A mixed body of some *ulamā* and some modern educated persons.
    (If the answer is d, ask further:)
    a. How should such a body be constituted?
       i. Nominated by the government.
       ii. Elected by the people.
    b. Will the decisions of the body be final and binding?
    Yes/No

18. Suppose there was a choice only between the following two alternatives with respect to the implementation of Islamic law in Pakistan. Which one would you prefer?
    a. The laws of marriage, divorce, inheritance, and *waqf* should be enforced as they are found in the respective Sunnī and Shīʿī traditions, but no attempt should be made to Islamize the present criminal and commercial laws.
    b. All laws should be revised so that they are brought closer to the spirit (as against the letter) of the Islamic principles of justice and equity, even though through this revision the new Islamic law might emerge as somewhat different from the traditional Islamic law. *Talāq* (divorce), for example, may be allowed only with the permission of a court, instead of leaving it to the discretion of the husband.

Concerning Economic Orientation

19. Which of the following two statements sounds correct to you?
    a. Islam provides a complete economic system. It prescribes all important principles about economic relations between the state and the individual and among the individuals themselves.
    b. In economic matters, all that Islam requires is that one remain honest in one's dealings with others, pay *zakāt*, and not earn wealth by immoral means or spend it on sinful things (e.g., gambling).

20. *A.* What are the basic principles of the economic system of Islam?

B. What economic arrangements are desirable to you?
(Interviewer, note if there are any differences between what the respondent thinks is desirable and what he holds to be Islamic demands about the following. Read out the following:)
a. About the ownership of property:
    i. Private ownership of property is an essential principle of Islam.
    ii. Private ownership is preferable though not imperative.
    iii. Common ownership of property—all sources of production should be nationalized.
    iv. Any other suggestion.
b. About the production of wealth:
    i. Individual enterprise only. However, certain types of enterprises (e.g., gambling, production and sale of alcoholic beverages) are to be prohibited.
    ii. Both public and individual enterprise.
    iii. Public enterprise only, private enterprise to be restricted to the minimum.
    iv. Any other.
c. About the distribution of wealth:
    i. No limit on individual's income, but he has to pay *zakāt*.
    ii. Equitable distribution of wealth on the basis of need.
    iii. Any other.

21. Do you believe in Islamic socialism?

22. (If "yes," ask:) What are its basic principles?

23. (If "yes," to question 21, ask further:) How is Islamic socialism different from non-Islamic socialism?

24. Which of the following statements sounds correct to you?
a. *Zakāt* is primarily a tax to be collected and spent by the government in an Islamic state.
b. *Zakāt* is primarily a religiously obligatory donation to the poor.
c. Any other comment.

25. Do you hold the interest chargeable by banks on loans to be prohibited by Islam?

26. Are you in favor of abolishing the present system of banking in Pakistan?

Concerning Moral Orientations

27. It seems that people have different considerations when they refrain from a morally bad act like bribery. Often the motives are mixed. But insofar as

the motives are discernible, can you say about yourself whether you refrain from a bad act:

   a.   To avoid displeasing God and, thus, to avoid punishment in the hereafter.

   b.   You just feel repulsed by such an act, without any religious consideration.

   c.   Any other answer.

28. Do you agree with the statement that an act that is permitted or recommended on religious grounds can at the same time be immoral?

29. Preaching on a loudspeaker is considered as good and rewarding in the religious sense. Yet this act may very well cause inconvenience to many outside the mosque by disturbing them in their work or rest. In this respect, with which of the following propositions would you agree?

   a.   Though religiously rewarding, this act remains immoral.

   b.   Such an act is bad neither in the religious sense nor in the moral sense.

   c.   Such an act is not only unethical but also sinful according to right Islamic values.

30. Do you agree with the statement that an act that is declared to be forbidden or repulsive by the *sharīʿa* can at the same time be morally neutral?

31. Drinking and dancing are generally regarded as forbidden by the *sharīʿa.* Yet many would hold such acts to be morally neutral insofar as these acts cause no inconvenience to others. In this respect, with which of the following propositions would you agree?

   a.   Such acts are sinful, but from the moral point of view they are neither good nor bad.

   b.   Such acts are neither morally bad nor sinful, according to Islam, if Islam is rightly understood.

   c.   Such acts are not only sinful but also morally bad.

32. Some people hold that certain acts that have been declared to be crimes by the present state law of Pakistan are neither sinful according to the *sharīʿa* nor morally bad. It is said, for example, that apart from a few commodities (such as alcoholic beverages and pork), the *sharīʿa* does not prohibit the importation of goods legally purchased in a foreign country into one's own country for purposes of trade. Yet the State of Pakistan prohibits the importation of numerous articles and punishes violators of these trade restrictions under the law against smuggling.

   a.   Such people say, "Smuggling is a crime only according to state law. But it is neither sinful nor morally bad."

   b.   According to some other people, "Smuggling is morally bad but not sinful."

    c.   According to yet another view, "Smuggling is sinful as well as morally bad, because the law against smuggling is made for the general welfare of the country."

    With which of these views would you agree?

33. Would you like the following things, or any one of them, to be prohibited by law?

    a.   Drinking.

    b.   Mixed dancing in public places.

    c.   Cinema and theater.

    d.   Coeducation.

Concerning Islamic Commitment and Expectations, Generally

34. Do you think the majority of those living in Pakistan hold any particular ideology?

35. (If "yes" to question 34, ask further:) What is that ideology?

36. Do you yourself believe in an ideology?
(If "yes," ask further:) What is your ideology?

37. What are the implications of Islamic ideology?
(Read out the following:)

    a.   Believing in God, the Prophet, and the hereafter.

    b.   Performing the requirements of the other four "pillars" of Islam (*namāz* [daily prayers], *rōza* [fasting], *zakāt*, and *hajj*).

    c.   Observing the Islamic rules of social ethics against drinking, etc.

    d.   Observing the Islamic laws of marriage, divorce, etc.

    e.   Establishing an Islamic state.

    f.   All aspects of life—political, legal, social—should be completely Islamized.

    g.   Any other answer.

38. Every ideology has some concern about the beliefs and actions of its followers. Some give more importance to the desirable kind of beliefs; others, to the desirable kind of society. How would you rank the following in importance?

    a.   Right kind of beliefs—in God, the hereafter, and prophecy.

    b.   Right kind of morals and personal relations.

    c.   Right kind of political and economic organization of the society.

39. With which of the following statements would you agree?

    a.   Islam is the solution for all of our problems. Once we become true Muslims, success will be sure.

    b.   Practice of Islamic values will hurt the cause of economic progress and social reform.

    c.   Islam is largely irrelevant to most of our modern problems. It neither helps nor hurts to be true Muslims.

    d.   Any other answer.

40. Do you think the Qur'ān is a code for the whole life, social, political, economic, that basic principles are all given in the Qur'ān and the *sunna?*
Yes/No
Any other answer.

41. To which of the following propositions would you subscribe?

    a.   The Muslims in Pakistan must share the fundamentals of our Islamic ideology. The non-Muslims must respect them.

    b.   The citizens of our country, both Muslims and non-Muslims, should be allowed every right to oppose and reject, in good conscience, even what could be regarded by others as the fundamentals of Islamic ideology.

42. (If relevant:) It appears from your answers that you have a desire to see the fundamental demands of your ideology realized. Which of the following statements seems to express your feelings about the realization of such demands?

    a.   Conformity to ideology is necessary. We all should do whatever we can to realize its demands.

    b.   Conformity to ideology is desirable but not imperative.

    c.   Conformity to ideology is no less than a matter of life and death.

Concerning Morale

43. Which of the following is/are a correct description(s) of the high government officials in Pakistan?

    a.   Capable people of our nation managing the public affairs well.

    b.   Too much steeped in Western culture, almost outsiders to the rest of the nation.

    c.   Reactionaries, hindering progress.

    d.   Selfish and hypocritical.

    e.   Any other description.

44. Which of the following descriptions is/are true of lawyers, university professors, and journalists?

    a.   Capable people of our nation managing the public affairs well.

    b.   Too much steeped in Western culture, almost outsiders to the rest of the nation.

    c.   Reactionaries, hindering progress.

    d.   Selfish and hypocritical.

    e.   Any other description.

45. Which of the following descriptions is/are true of *ulamā?*
    a.   Capable people of our nation managing the public affairs well.
    b.   Too much steeped in the medieval tradition.
    c.   Reactionaries, hindering progress.
    d.   Selfish and hypocritical.
    e.   Any other description.

46. How would you describe the future of Pakistan, so far as it can be guessed in the light of present developments?
    a.   Politically:
        i.   Healthy.
        ii.   Dubious.
    b.   Economically:
        i.   Considerably improved.
        ii.   No great hope.
    c.   Religiously:
        i.   Satisfactory.
        ii.   Deteriorating.

Concerning Personal and Social Background

47. Age: _____ years

48. Sex:

49. Marital status:

50. Occupation:

51. Grade:

52. Where did you pass your childhood?
In a city, town, or village?

53. Did you migrate from India? Yes_____ No_____

54. Mother tongue:

55. Elementary school education:

56. Secondary school education:
Where:
Medium:

57. Higher education:
Where:
Medium:

58. Father's education:

59. Mother's education:

60. Father's occupation:

61. How would you classify your father's family in terms of economic status?

62. Size of your own family:

63. What is the total monthly income of your own family?
Rupees _____

64. Are you a believing Muslim?
(Read out the following:)
a.   Yes.
b.   No.
c.   Between belief and unbelief.
d.   Believing, but not in the traditional sense.
e.   Any other description.

65. Now, in order to assess the extent of social change that has occurred in a generation's time, I would like to ask these last questions both about yourself and your father. Incidentally, may I ask whether your father is living?
Yes_____
No_____
(Interviewer, phrase the following questions accordingly.)
First, some questions about certain personal and social practices:

66. *A.*   In what language do you habitually read?
B.   In what language did your father (does your father) read?

67. *A.*   What do you usually wear outdoors?
B.   Your father?

68. *A.*   Do your sisters or wife observe *purdah?*
B.   Your paternal aunts and your mother?
Now, about some social institutions.

69. Are you related to a *birādarī* (extended kinship group)?

70. Is that *birādarī* formally organized?

71. *A.*   Do you take part in any of its activities?
B.   Your father?

72. *A.*   Do you feel a sense of belonging to the *birādarī?*
    B.   Your father?

73. *A.*   Do you and your parents and your married brothers share the same house; that is to say, are you living under a joint family system?
    B.   Did your father live under a joint family system?

74. *A.*   Do you use:
      i.   *Darī, chāndnī, qālīn, chārpāī* (traditional furniture and floor coverings), etc., at home.
      ii.   Sofas and chairs.
      iii.   Both.
    B.   Your father?

75. *A.*   Are the meals at your house served on a table or a *dastar khwān* (a traditional mat or covering for serving food)?
    B.   At your father's house?

B ⊛ Primary Variables: Label Information

Every question in the questionnaire (which is reproduced in Appendix A) sought information on one or more variables. Altogether, the seventy-five questions included 239 variables. These 239 "primary" variables were given names for identification, from "VAR001" to "VAR239." Every one of the variables was also assigned a caption or "label" that briefly described its subject matter. Information received on every one of these variables was found classifiable into two or more categories. To facilitate mathematical computation, each category of the responses — or, in the jargon of computer programming, each "value"— of every variable was coded, mostly from one to ten, and each value was assigned a label to describe the contents of its responses. The following table lists only those primary variables and their values that were directly or indirectly employed in this study (labels for 90–91, 96–130, 175–184, and 211–212 not included). Next to each variable in the left margin is the number of the question that is associated with that specific variable.

Primary Variables: Label Information

Question Number	Variable Number	Labels Describing Variables and Their Values
	VAR001.......	Case number
	VAR002.......	Record number
	VAR003.......	Province of residence
	1.	East Pakistan
	2.	West Pakistan
	VAR004.......	City of residence
	1.	Dacca
	2.	Lahore
	3.	Karachi
54	VAR005.......	Province of mother tongue
	1.	East Pakistan
	2.	West Pakistan

54	VAR006.......	Mother tongue
	1.	Bengali
	2.	Punjabi
	3.	Urdu
	4.	Sindhi
	5.	Pushto
	6.	Baluchi
	7.	Other
54	VAR007.......	Broader category of respondent
	1.	Members, Jamaat-i-Islami
	2.	*Ulamā*
	3.	Middle-class professionals
	4.	Intellectuals
54	VAR008.......	Category of respondent
	1.	*Ulamā*
	2.	Teachers
	3.	Lawyers
	4.	Journalists
	5.	Civil servants
	6.	Members, council of Islamic ideology
47	VAR009.......	Age in decades
48	VAR010.......	Sex
	1.	Male
	2.	Female
49	VAR011.......	Marital status
	1.	Married
	2.	Bachelor
	3.	Divorced
	4.	Widowed
50	VAR012.......	Traditionality of occupation
	1.	Traditional
	2.	Semitraditional
	3.	Modern
50	VAR013.......	Occupation
50	VAR014.......	Traditionality of father's occupation
	1.	Traditional
	2.	Semitraditional
	3.	Modern
	VAR015.......	Father's occupation
52	VAR016.......	Community of residence in childhood
	1.	Village
	2.	Town
	3.	City

53	VAR017.......	Cross-country migration
	0.	Missing value
	1.	Migrated
	5.	Did not migrate
57	VAR018.......	Type of education
	1.	Traditional
	2.	Mixed
	3.	Modern
	0.	Missing value
57	VAR019.......	Degree of highest education
	1.	None or primary
	2.	High school or considerable traditional
	3.	College graduate or traditional *sanad* (certificate)
57	VAR020.......	Degree of traditional education
	1.	None
	2.	Reading knowledge
	3.	Considerable, informal
	4.	*Sanad*
	5.	Post-*sanad*
57	VAR021.......	Degree of modern education
	1.	None
	2.	Primary school
	3.	High school
	4.	Bachelor's degree
	5.	Master's degree or higher
58	VAR022.......	Type of father's education
	1.	Traditional
	2.	Mixed
	3.	Modern
	0.	Missing value
58	VAR023.......	Degree of father's highest education
	1.	None or primary
	2.	High school or considerable traditional
	3.	College graduate or traditional *sanad*
58	VAR024.......	Degree of father's traditional education
	1.	None
	2.	Reading knowledge
	3.	Considerable, informal
	4.	*Sanad*
	5.	Post-*sanad*
58	VAR025.......	Degree of father's modern education
	1.	None

		2.	Primary school
		3.	High school
		4.	Bachelor's degree
		5.	Master's degree or higher
60	VAR026......		Type of mother's education
		1.	Traditional
		2.	Mixed
		3.	Modern
		0.	Missing value
60	VAR027......		Degree of mother's highest education
		1.	None or primary
		2.	High school or considerable traditional
		3.	College graduate or traditional *sanad*
60	VAR028......		Degree of mother's traditional education
		1.	None
		2.	Reading knowledge
		3.	Considerable informal
		4.	*Sanad*
		5.	Post-*sanad*
60	VAR029......		Degree of mother's modern education
		1.	None
		2.	Primary school
		3.	High school
		4.	Bachelor's degree
		5.	Master's degree or higher
55	VAR030......		Type of elementary education
		1.	English medium school
		2.	Primary school, native language
		3.	*Maktab* (traditional school)
56	VAR031......		Medium in secondary school education
		1.	English
		2.	Bengali
		3.	Urdu
		4.	Regional language
57	VAR032......		Medium in college education
		1.	English
		2.	Bengali
		3.	Urdu
		4.	Regional language
61	VAR033......		Economic status—3-point scale
62		1.	Poor
63		2.	Middle class

		3.	Rich
61	VAR034......		Economic status—5-point scale
62		1.	Poor
63		2.	Low-middle
		3.	Middle-middle
		4.	High-middle
		5.	Rich
59	VAR035......		Father's economic status—3-point scale
		1.	Poor
		2.	Middle class
		3.	Rich
59	VAR036......		Father's economic status—5-point scale
		1.	Poor
		2.	Low-middle
		3.	Middle-middle
		4.	High-middle
		5.	Rich
64	VAR037......		Degree of belief in Islam
		1.	Belief
		2.	Nontraditional belief
		3.	Between belief and unbelief
		5.	Unbelief
		6.	Refused to answer for reading
66a	VAR038......		Traditionality of language medium
		1.	Traditional
		2.	Both
		3.	Modern
66a	VAR039......		Specific language medium for reading
66a	VAR040......		Traditionality of father's specific language medium
		1.	Traditional
		2.	Both
		3.	Modern
66b	VAR041......		Father's language medium for reading
67a	VAR042......		Traditionality of dress
		1.	Traditional
		2.	Mixed
		3.	Modern
		0.	Missing value
67a	VAR043......		Specific dress—read with preceding column
67b	VAR044......		Traditionality of father's dress
		1.	Traditional

		2.	Mixed
		3.	Modern
		0.	Missing value
67b	VAR045......		Father's specific dress—read with preceding column
68a	VAR046......		*Purdah* observance: score for computation
		1.	Both wife and sister
		2.	Either wife or sister
		3.	None = 3
68a	VAR047......		*Purdah* observance
		1.	Only sister
		2.	Only wife
		3.	Both
		4.	None
68b	VAR048......		*Purdah* observance by mother: score for computation
		1.	Both mother and aunt = 1
		2.	Either aunt or mother = 2
		3.	None = 3
68b	VAR049......		*Purdah* observance by mother, etc.
		1.	Only aunts
		2.	Only mother
		3.	Both
		4.	None
69	VAR050......		Kinship group affiliation
		1.	Yes
		5.	No
		8.	I do not know
		9.	Refused to answer
		0.	Missing value
70	VAR051......		Kinship group formally organized
		1.	Yes
		5.	No
		8.	I do not know
		9.	Refused to answer
		0.	Missing value
71a	VAR052......		Taking part in kinship group activities
		1.	Yes
		5.	No
		8.	I do not know
		9.	Refused to answer
		0.	Missing value
71b	VAR053......		Father's taking part in kinship group activity

		1.	Yes
		5.	No
		8.	I do not know
		9.	Refused to answer
		0.	Missing value
72a	VAR054......		Identification with kinship group
		1.	Yes
		5.	No
		8.	I do not know
		9.	Refused to answer
		0.	Missing value
72b	VAR055......		Father's identification with kinship group
		1.	Yes
		5.	No
		8.	I do not know
		9.	Refused to answer
		0.	Missing value
73a	VAR056......		Family structure
		1.	Joint-family
		3.	Single-family
		2.	Both systems
73b	VAR057		Father's family structure
		1.	Joint-family
		3.	Single-family
		2.	Both systems
74a	VAR058......		Type of furniture in house
		1.	Traditional
		3.	Modern
		2.	Both
	VAR059......		Type of furniture in father's house
		1.	Traditional
		3.	Modern
		2.	Both
75	VAR060......		Manner of serving meals at home
		1.	On *dastar khwān*, etc.
		3.	On table
		2.	On both
75	VAR061......		Manner of serving meals at father's house
		1.	On *dastar khwān*, etc.
		3.	On table
		2.	On both
	VAR062......		Demands of Islamic ideology: summary
		1.	Described

		8.	I don't know
		9.	Refused to answer
34	VAR063.......		Do Pakistanis hold an ideology?
		1.	Yes
		2.	Yes, but without a clear conception
		3.	Yes, but without seriousness
		5.	No
		8.	I don't know
		9.	Refused to answer
		0.	Missing value
35	VAR064.......		Assumed ideologies of Pakistanis: Islamic
		1.	Islam
		2.	Islamic democracy
		3.	Islamic socialism
		4.	Different ideologies
		5.	Islam as religion, plus socialism
		6.	Islam as religion, plus democracy
		7.	None
		8.	I don't know
		9.	Islam not mentioned
35	VAR065.......		Assumed ideology of Pakistanis: Non-Islamic
		1.	Humanism
		2.	Democracy
		3.	Socialism
		4.	Social justice
		5.	Democratic socialism
		6.	Communism or Marxism
		7.	Pragmatism
		8.	Welfare state
		9.	No extra-Islamic ideology mentioned
		0.	Missing value
36	VAR066.......		Respondent's ideology: Islamic
		1.	Islam
		2.	Islamic democracy
		3.	Islamic socialism
		4.	Different ideologies
		5.	Islam as religion, plus socialism
		6.	Islam as religion, plus democracy
		7.	None
		8.	I don't know
		9.	Islam not mentioned
36	VARO67		Respondent's ideology: Non-Islamic
		1.	Humanism

		2.	Democracy
		3.	Socialism
		4.	Social justice
		5.	Democratic socialism
		6.	Communism or Marxism
		7.	Pragmatism
		8.	Welfare state
		9.	No extra-Islamic ideology mentioned
		0.	Missing
37	VAR068.......		Demands of Islamic ideology: (*a*) basic religious beliefs?
		1.	Yes
		2.	In essence; in part
		3.	Indifferent
		4.	Not essential
		5.	No
		8.	I don't know
		9.	Refused to answer
		0.	Missing
37	VAR069.......		Demands of Islamic ideology: (*b*) the standard acts of worship?
		1.	Yes
		2.	In essence; in part
		3.	Indifferent
		4.	Not essential
		5.	No
		8.	I don't know
		9.	Refused to answer
		0.	Missing
37	VAR070.......		Demands of Islamic ideology: (*c*) social ethic?
		1.	Yes
		2.	In essence; in part
		3.	Indifferent
		4.	Not essential
		5.	No
		8.	I don't know
		9.	Refused to answer
		0.	Missing
37	VAR071.......		Demands of Islamic ideology: (*d*) family law?
		1.	Yes
		2.	In essence; in part
		3.	Indifferent
		4.	Not essential

		5.	No
		8.	I don't know
		9.	Refused to answer
		0.	Missing
37	VAR072......		Demands of Islamic ideology: (*e*) Islamic state?
		1.	Yes
		2.	To some extent
		3.	Indifferent
		4.	Not essential
		5.	No
		8.	I don't know
		9.	Refused to answer
		0.	Missing
37	VAR073......		Demands of Islamic ideology: (*f*) total Islamization?
		1.	Yes
		2.	In essence; in part
		3.	Indifferent
		4.	Not essential
		5.	No
		8.	I don't know
		9.	Refused to answer
		0.	Missing
37	VAR074......		Demands of Islamic ideology: other responses
		2.	Separating state and religion
		3.	Abolishing imperialism, feudalism
		4.	Social justice
		5.	Socialist program
		9.	No extra item mentioned
		0.	Missing value
37	VAR075......		Demands of Islamic ideology rejected
		1.	Religious beliefs
		2.	Standard worship
		3.	Social ethic
		4.	Family law
		5.	Islamic state
		9.	None
		0.	Not applicable or missing
37	VAR076......		Demands of Islamic ideology rejected
		1.	Religious beliefs
		2.	Standard worship
		3.	Social ethic

		4. Family law
		5. Islamic state
		9. None
		0. Not applicable or missing
38	VAR077.	Order of priority of faith, morals in Islam and politics
		1. Faith, morals, politics
		2. Only faith counts
		3. Only faith and morals are important
		4. Only morals and politics are important
		5. Only morals count
		6. Politics, morals, faith
		7. Equal importance, etc.
		8. I don't know
		9. Refused to answer
		0. Missing value
39	VAR078.	Islam as the solution of all problems
		1. (a) Islam is total solution
		2. (b) Islam is detrimental
		3. (c) Islam is irrelevant
		4. Islam provides guidelines only
		5. Islam is not opposed to progress
		6. Islam provides comprehensive guidelines
		7. Islam is either irrelevant or detrimental
		9. Refused to answer
40	VAR079.	Qur'ān and Sunna as code of life
		1. Yes
		2. Yes, they provide most guidelines
		3. They provide only moral teachings
		4. They barely provide guidelines
		5. No
		8. I don't know
		9. Refused to answer
1	VARO80	Objects of loyalty: the first loyalty
		1. (a) Relatives and birādarī
		2. (b) Birthplace
		3. (c) Fellow Muslims
		4. (d) Citizens
		5. Working class
		6. Priorities relative to situations
		7. God or one's principles
		8. Humanity
		9. None

1	VAR081.......	Objects of loyalty: the second loyalty
	1.	(*a*) Relatives and *Birādarī*
	2.	(*b*) Birthplace
	3.	(*c*) Fellow Muslims
	4.	(*d*) Citizens
	5.	Working class
	6.	Priorities relative to situations
	7.	God or one's principles
	8.	Humanity
	9.	None
1	VAR082.......	Objects of loyalty: the third loyalty
	1.	(*a*) Relatives and *birādarī*
	2.	(*b*) Birthplace
	3.	(*c*) Fellow Muslims
	4.	(*d*) Citizens
	5.	Working class
	6.	Priorities relative to situations
	7.	God or one's principles
	8.	Humanity
	9.	None
1	VAR083.......	Objects of loyalty: the fourth loyalty
	1.	(*a*) Relatives and *birādarī*
	2.	(*b*) Birthplace
	3.	(*c*) Fellow Muslims
	4.	(*d*) Citizens
	5.	Working class
	6.	Priorities relative to situations
	7.	God or one's principles
	8.	Humanity
	9.	None
2	VAR084.......	Desired bases of Pakistani nationhood—1
	1.	(*a*) Religion
	2.	(*b*) Culture
	3.	(*c*) Indo-Muslim history
	4.	(*d*) Class interest
	5.	Territory
	9.	None
2	VAR085.......	Desired bases of Pakistani nationhood—2
	1.	(*a*) Religion
	2.	(*b*) Culture
	3.	(*c*) Indo-Muslim history
	4.	(*d*) Class interest
	5.	Territory
	9.	None

3	VAR086.......	Historical period for national inspiration—1
	1.	(a) Mughal period
	2.	(b) Khilafa Rashida
	3.	(c) Abbasid period
	4.	(d) No period
	5.	Regional history
	6.	Socialist history
	8.	I don't know
	9.	Refused to answer
	0.	Missing
3	VAR087.......	Historical period for national inspiration—2
	1.	(a) Mughal period
	2.	(b) Khilafa Rashida
	3.	(c) Abbasid period
	4.	(d) No period
	5.	Regional history
	6.	Socialist history
	8.	I don't know
	9.	Refused to answer
	0.	Missing
4	VAR088.......	Desired bases of Pakistan's political unity—1
	1.	(a) Islam
	2.	(b) Fatherland
	3.	(c) Expedience
	4.	(d) Socialism
	5.	Social justice
	6.	Islam, plus expedience
	7.	Islam, fatherland, expedience
	8.	Democracy
4	VAR089.......	Desired bases of Pakistan's political unity—2
	1.	(a) Islam
	2.	(b) Fatherland
	3.	(c) Expedience
	4.	(d) Socialism
	5.	Social justice
	6.	Islam, plus expedience
	7.	Islam, fatherland, expedience
	8.	Democracy
5	VAR092.......	Meaning of the *umma*
	1.	(a) Followers of Muhammad
	2.	(b) Muslim brotherhood
	3.	(c) A political concept
	4.	a + b
	5.	c + b

		8.	I do not know
		9.	Refused to answer
5	VAR093.......		Political connotations of the *umma*
		1.	Pakistani nation
		2.	Muslim world cooperation
		3.	Muslim commonwealth
		4.	One Muslim state
		5.	Cooperation and commonwealth
		6.	One state and cooperation
		9.	Refused to answer
		0.	Not applicable or missing
6	VAR094.......		The desired goal of Muslim unity, etc.
		1.	None
		2.	Muslim world cooperation
		3.	Muslim commonwealth
		4.	One Muslim state
		5.	Cooperation and commonwealth
		6.	One state and cooperation
		9.	Refused to answer
		0.	Not applicable or missing
41	VAR095.......		Demand for consensus on ideology
		1.	(*a*) Demanded
		2.	(*b*) Not demanded
		3.	a + b = demanded in some matters, not demanded in other matters
		8.	I do not know
		9.	Refused to answer
		0.	Missing
7	VAR131.......		The aim of political organization—1
		1.	(*a*) Utility
		2.	(*b*) Islam
		3.	(*c*) Interests of the working classes
		4.	a + b + c
		5.	None
		6.	Social justice
		7.	Human brotherhood and social justice
		8.	I don't know
		9.	Refused to answer
		0.	Not applicable or missing
7	VAR132.......		The aim of political organization—2
		1.	(*a*) Utility
		2.	(*b*) Islam
		3.	(*c*) Interests of the working classes

		4.	a + b + c
		5.	None
		6.	Social justice
		7.	Human brotherhood and social justice
		8.	I don't know
		9.	Refused to answer
		0.	Not applicable or missing

8 VAR133....... Pakistan's constitution—incidental remarks

1. The 1956 constitution was secular
2. I have not read much of it
4. Concept of Islamic constitution is vague
5. 1956 constitution more Islamic
6. 1956 constitution more Islamic due to Islamic provisions
7. 1956 constitution more Islamic due to democratic provisions
0. No remark or missing value

8 VAR134....... Islamic character of Pakistan's 1962 constitution

1. Fully Islamic
2. Sufficiently Islamic
3. Islamic in appearance only
4. Mainly secular
5. Partly Islamic
6. Frustrates people's aspirations
7. Is not constitutional at all
8. I don't know
9. Refused to answer
0. Missing value

8 VAR135....... Approval of Islamic character of the 1962 constitution

1. Approved
5. Not approved
8. I don't know
9. Refused to answer
0. Missing value

9 VAR136....... Similarity of Islam with other political systems—1

1. Democracy
2. Socialism
3. Dictatorship
4. Fascism
5. Similar to none

		6.	Islam is not a political system
		7.	True Islam is democratic; historic Islam, dictatorship
		8.	I don't know
		9.	Refused to answer
		0.	Not applicable or missing
9	VAR137......		Similarity of Islam with other political systems—2
		1.	Democracy
		2.	Socialism
		3.	Dictatorship
		4.	Fascism
		5.	Similar to none
		6.	Islam is not a political system
		7.	True Islam is democratic; historic Islam, dictatorship
		8.	I don't know
		9.	Refused to answer
		0.	Not applicable or missing
10a	VAR138......		Similarity of Islam with democracy: summary
		1.	Yes, similar
		5.	Nothing is similar
		8.	I don't know
		9.	Refused to answer
		0.	Missing value
10a	VAR139......		Features of Islam in common with democracy: egalitarianism
		1.	Human equality, rule of law
		5.	No class distinctions
		9.	No equality item mentioned
		0.	Not applicable or missing
10a	VAR140......		Features of Islam in common with democracy: economic freedom
		1.	Freedom of occupation
		2.	Right to property
		3.	Welfare state
		4.	Equitable distribution of wealth
		9.	No economic item mentioned
		0.	Not applicable or missing
10a	VAR141......		Features of Islam in common with democracy: civil liberties
		1.	Individual's rights
		3.	Freedom of expression

		4.	Autonomous institutions
		9.	No civil liberties mentioned
		0.	Not applicable or missing
10a	VAR142......		Features of Islam common with democracy: form of government—1
		1.	Right to remove ruler
		2.	Majority ruler
		3.	Electoral principle
		4.	People's supremacy
		5.	Consultation principle
		6.	Elected *khalīfa*
		7.	Responsible government
		8.	Division of powers
		9.	No form of government mentioned
		0.	Not applicable or missing
10a	VAR143......		Features of Islam in common with democracy: form of government—2
		1.	Right to remove ruler
		2.	Majority rule
		3.	Electoral principle
		4.	People's supremacy
		5.	Consultation principle
		6.	Elected *khalīfa*
		7.	Responsible government
		8.	Division of powers
		9.	No form of government mentioned
		0.	Not applicable or missing
10a	VAR144......		Features of Islam in common with democracy: miscellaneous—1
		1.	Merit counts
		2.	Respect for man
		4.	Universal education
		6.	Maximum good of all
		9.	No miscellaneous items mentioned
		0.	Not applicable or missing
10a	VAR145......		Features of Islam in common with democracy: miscellaneous—2
		1.	Merit counts
		2.	Respect for man
		4.	Universal education
		6.	Maximum good of all
		9.	No miscellaneous items mentioned
		0.	Not applicable or missing

10b	VAR146.......	Features of Islam different from democracy: summary
	1.	Yes, different
	5.	Nothing is different
	8.	I don't know
	9.	Refused to answer
	0.	Missing value
10b	VAR147.......	Features of Islam different from democracy: citizenship
	1.	Only Muslims are full citizens
	2.	Communal law
	9.	No citizenship item mentioned
	0.	Not applicable or missing
10b	VAR148.......	Features of Islam different from democracy: social justice, etc.
	1.	Government provides basic needs
	2.	Complete social justice
	4.	Welfare state
	5.	Islamic economic system is impractical
	9.	No economic item is mentioned
	0.	Not applicable or missing
10b	VAR149.......	Features of Islam different from democracy: limited civil liberties
	1.	Opposing Islam is prohibited
	2.	Only one political party allowed
	3.	Individual freedom is restricted
	4.	Rule of Muslim elite
	5.	Islamic political system impractical
	9.	No civil-liberty item mentioned
	0.	Not applicable or missing
10B	VAR150.......	Features of Islam different from democracy: government and sovereignty—1
	1.	Sovereignty of God
	2.	Election of the pious
	3.	Wider powers of ruler
	4.	Presidium type of rule
	5.	Election by the pious
	6.	Opinions of only the pious count
	9.	Government item mentioned
	0.	Not applicable or missing
10b	VAR151.......	Features of Islam different from democracy: government and sovereignty—2
	1.	Sovereignty of God

	2.	Election of the pious
	3.	Wider powers of ruler
	4.	Presidium type of rule
	5.	Election by the pious
	6.	Opinions of only the pious count
	9.	No government item mentioned
	0.	Not applicable or missing
10b	VAR152......	Features of Islam different from democracy: spiritual character
	1.	Moral policy, etc.
	2.	Islam is against nationalism
	3.	Religion, moral purpose of the state
	6.	Islam is simply a religion
	9.	No spiritual characteristic mentioned
	0.	Not applicable or missing
10b	VAR153......	Features of Islam different from democracy: miscellaneous
	1.	Islam is more than a political system
	2.	Islam recognizes no class privileges
	4.	Islam represses thinking
	5.	Islam demands total submission
	9.	No miscellaneous item mentioned
	0.	Not applicable or missing
10b	VAR154......	Desirable political system
	1.	Islamic state desirable
	2.	Muslim state desirable
	3.	Concept of Islamic state is vague
	4.	Secular democratic state desirable
	5.	Islamic state undesirable
	6.	Secular socialist state desirable
	8.	I don't know
	9.	Refused to answer
	0.	Missing value
10b	VAR155......	Minimum requirements of Islamic state: summary
	1.	Islamic state described
	2.	Described, adding "the concept is vague"
	3.	Not described, saying "the concept is vague"
	8.	I don't know
	9.	Refused to answer
	0.	Missing value
10b	VAR156......	Minimum requirements of Islamic state: Muslim majority, etc.

	1.	Muslim majority
	2.	Supremacy of Islam
	3.	Either Muslim majority or supremacy of Islam
	4.	Muslims of right beliefs
	9.	No "Muslim supremacy" item mentioned
	0.	Not applicable or missing
10b	VAR157.....	Minimum requirements of Islamic state: Muslim head of state
	1.	Muslim head of state
	2.	Practicing Muslim
	3.	Muslim ruler capable to defend state boundaries
	9.	Muslim ruler not mentioned
	0.	Not applicable or missing
10b	VAR158.....	Minimum requirements of Islamic state: equality, democracy, etc.
	1.	Islamic democracy, equality
	2.	Equality of all citizens
	3.	Justice
	4.	Rule of law
	7.	Brotherhood of man
	9.	Equality, etc., not mentioned
	0.	Not applicable or missing
10b	VAR159.....	Minimum requirements of Islamic state: implementing *sharīʿa*
	1.	Implementing *sharīʿa*
	2.	Prohibiting drinking and immorality
	3.	*Sharīʿa* and prohibiting, etc.
	4.	Enforcing *hudud* (Qurʾānic punishments)
	5.	Enforcing Islamic *tazirat* (punishments)
	6.	Islamizing laws
	7.	No law repugnant to Islam
	9.	No legal item mentioned
	0.	Not applicable or missing
11a	VAR160.....	Minimum requirements of Islamic state: *ulamā* leadership
	1.	*Ulamā* to be authorized to interpret law
	9.	*Ulamā* item not mentioned
	0.	Not applicable or missing
11a	VAR161.....	Minimum requirements of Islamic state: ruler's qualities
	1.	Just, righteous ruler
	2.	*Ālim* and just, righteous

		3.	Bold and just, righteous
		9.	Ruler's qualities not mentioned
		0.	Not applicable or missing
11a	VAR162....		Minimum requirements of Islamic state: social justice, etc.
		1.	Social justice, etc.
		2.	*Zakāt* system
		3.	*Sharī'a* defines state's role in social justice
		4.	Equitable distribution of wealth
		5.	Socialist program
		6.	Interest-free economy
		7.	*Zakāt* and interest-free economy
		9.	No economic item mentioned
		0.	Not applicable or missing
11a	VAR163....		Minimum requirements of Islamic state miscellaneous political—1
		1.	Division of powers
		2.	Separating state and religion
		3.	Democratic government, public good
		4.	Welfare state
		5.	Modernization, etc.
		6.	*Shūrā* (i.e., consultative) system
		7.	Claim to be Islamic
		8.	Quick and fair justice
		9.	No miscellaneous item mentioned
		0.	Not applicable or missing
11A	VAR164....		Minimum requirements of Islamic state: miscellaneous political—2
		1.	Division of powers
		2.	Separating state and religion
		3.	Democratic government
		4.	Welfare state
		5.	Modernization, etc.
		6.	*Shūrā*
		7.	Claim to be Islamic
		8.	Quick and fair justice
		9.	No miscellaneous item mentioned
		0.	Not applicable or missing
11a	VAR165....		Minimum requirements of Islamic state: moral, religious—1
		1.	Honest officials
		2.	Honest officials and society
		3.	People morally and religiously sensitive

	4.	People morally modest
	5.	Enforcing five pillars of Islam
	6.	Practicing Muslims
	7.	Congenial atmosphere for religious practices
	8.	Humanitarianism; public good
	9.	No religious, moral item mentioned
	0.	Not applicable or missing
11a	VAR166......	Minimum requirements of Islamic state: moral, religious—2
	1.	Honest officials
	2.	Honest officials and society
	3.	People morally, religiously sensitive
	4.	People morally honest
	5.	Enforcing five pillars of Islam
	6.	Practicing Muslims
	7.	Congenial atmosphere for religious practices
	8.	Public good: humanitarianism
	9.	No religious, moral item mentioned
	0.	Not applicable or missing
12	VAR167......	Islamic character of law in Pakistan
	1.	Mainly un-Islamic
	2.	Mainly Islamic, etc.
	3.	Totally un-Islamic
	4.	Partly Islamic
	5.	Islamic character unclear
	7.	Not repugnant to Islam
	8.	I don't know
	9.	Refused to answer
	0.	Missing value
13	VAR168......	Desirability of Islamizing law in Pakistan
	1.	Desirable
	2.	No harm in Islamizing
	3.	To the extent of making law just
	4.	Only personal law to be religious
	5.	Undesirable
	6.	Can't say: concept of Islamic law is unclear
	7.	No law is un-Islamic
	8.	I don't know
	9.	Refused to answer
	0.	Missing value
14	VAR169......	Method of Islamizing law in Pakistan
	1.	(a) Enforcing authentic Islamic *sharī'a*

2.   (*b*) Free interpretation of Qur'ān and *sunna*
3.   (*c*) Limited *ijtihād*
5.   Authentic *sharīʿa,* plus limited *ijtihād*
8.   I don't know
9.   Refused to answer
0.   Missing value

15   VAR170....... Spheres of law to be particularly Islamized: piety

1.   Social morality
2.   Enforcing *salāt, siyām*
3.   Social morality, plus *salāt* and *siyām*
4.   Specially, personal law
5.   Social morality, plus personal law
6.   Only personal law
9.   No piety, personal law, etc. mentioned
0.   Not applicable or missing

15   VAR171....... Spheres of law to be particularly Islamized: criminal law, etc.

1.   Criminal law, generally
3.   Administration of justice
4.   Criminal law, plus administration of justice
9.   No criminal law item mentioned
0.   Not applicable or missing

15   VAR172....... Spheres of law to be particularly Islamized: economic

1.   Economic matters generally
2.   State administration of *zakāt*
4.   Trade
5.   Social justice
6.   Interest-free economy
7.   Interest-free economy, plus state administration of *zakāt*
9.   No economic item mentioned
0.   Not applicable or missing

15   VAR173....... Spheres of law to be particularly Islamized: government, constitution, etc.

1.   Honest government officials
2.   No special privileges of officials
3.   Honest officials, no privileges
4.   Fundamental rights of the people
5.   Fair use of political power
6.   Public good, plus honest officials

		8.	Administration of *awqāf*
		9.	No government item mentioned
		0.	Not applicable or missing
16	VAR174.......		Application of *sharī'a* law of blood money
		1.	Yes
		3.	Reinterpretation needed
		4.	Statement is wrong
		5.	No
		6.	Government can punish
		8.	I don't know
		9.	Refused to answer
		0.	Missing value
17	VAR185.......		People to be authorized to determine relevant Islamic law
		1.	*Ulamā*
		2.	Political leaders
		3.	National assembly
		4.	Body of *ulamā,* plus modern educated people
		5.	Modern educated people having Islam knowledge
		6.	General public through referendum
		7.	Practicing jurists
		8.	None exclusively
		9.	Refused to answer
		0.	Missing value
17	VAR186.......		Official body to help the legislating authority
		1.	*Ulamā*
		2.	Political leaders
		3.	National assembly itself
		4.	Body of *ulamā* and modern educated persons
		5.	Modern educated persons who are morally virtuous
		6.	*Ulamā,* plus modern educated persons having Islamic knowledge
		9.	None
		0.	Missing value
17a	VAR187.......		Constitution of the mixed body of *ulamā* and others
		1.	Nominated by government
		2.	Elected by the people
		3.	Government nominated, plus elected by the people
		4.	Elected by the national assembly

		5.	*Ulamā* to elect their own representative
		6.	By competitive exams
		7.	Elected by educated people
		8.	I don't know
		9.	Constituted by none
		0.	Not applicable or missing
17b	VAR188....		Binding character of decisions by the mixed body
		1.	Binding
		2.	Almost binding
		3.	Binding, if not opposed to the Qur'ān and *hadīth*
		5.	Not binding
		7.	If decisions respond to people's needs
		8.	I don't know
		9.	Refused to answer
		0.	Missing value
18	VAR189....		Restricted, traditional Islamic law vs. total liberty
		1.	(*a*) Traditional law be enforced
		2.	(*b*) All law be revised
		3.	All laws should literally conform to Qur'ān and *sunna*
		4.	Present law is just
		5.	Both alternatives are unacceptable
		8.	I don't know
		9.	Refused to answer
		0.	Missing value
18	VAR190....		Uneasiness of respondent with choice
		1.	Uneasiness was apparent
		9.	No uneasiness
		0.	Missing value
18	VAR191....		Islamic character of contemporary Pakistan: incidental remarks
		1.	Islamic
		2.	Dār al-Islām, without *sultān ādil*
		0.	Not described or missing
20a	VAR192....		Islam's economic system: moral, religious character
		1.	Moral behavior in economic pursuits
		2.	Interest-free economy
		3.	Complete Islamic order
		4.	*Zakāt* system

		5.	Property is a trust, not an object of ownership
		6.	Interest-free economy = 2
		7.	Circulation of wealth
		8.	Austerity, etc.
		9.	No additional character mentioned
		0.	Not applicable or missing
19	VAR193.......		Islam provides a complete economic system
		1.	(a) Complete economic system
		2.	(b) Limited economic requirements
		3.	(c) Islam is only a religion: no economic requirements
		4.	Only for social justice
		5.	Islam's economic system is impractical
		6.	a and b are the same
		8.	I don't know
		9.	Refused to answer
		0.	Missing
20	VAR194.......		Islam's economic system: summary
		1.	System described
		3.	I am not sure
		4.	No rigid rules, only a concern for social justice
		5.	System not described
		8.	I don't know
		9.	Refused to answer
20	VAR195.......		Islam's economic system: ownership of property
		1.	Private property is essential
		2.	Private property is preferred, but public property is permitted
		3.	Mostly common property
		4.	Only common property is allowed
		8.	I don't know
		0.	Not applicable or missing
20	VAR196.......		Islam's economic system: production of wealth
		1.	Private enterprise only
		2.	Private enterprise is preferred
		3.	Basic industries should be nationalized
		4.	Collective enterprise only
		8.	I don't know
		0.	Not applicable or missing

20	VAR197.......		Islam's economic system: distribution of wealth
		1.	All differences in income are permitted
		2.	After basic needs of all are fulfilled, inequity in income is permitted
		3.	Equitable distribution
		8.	I don't know
		0.	Missing value
21	VAR198.......		Attitude toward Islamic socialism
		1.	Belief
		2.	Complete Islam includes socialism
		3.	Concept is ambiguous
		4.	No, but in Islamic social justice
		5.	Does not believe
		6.	No, but in scientific socialism
		7.	No, but in democratic socialism
		8.	I don't know
		9.	Refused to answer
		0.	Missing value
22	VAR199.......		Nature of Islamic socialism: moral, religious
		1.	Moral behavior in economic activities
		2.	Interest-free economy
		3.	Complete Islamic order
		4.	*Zakāt* system
		5.	Property is trust, not ownership
		6.	Equal economic rights
		7.	Circulation of wealth
		8.	Austerity
		9.	No general character described
		0.	Missing value
22	VAR200.......		Nature of Islamic socialism: ownership of property
		1.	Equal opportunity
		2.	Minimum nationalization with compensation
		3.	Big industries to be nationalized
		5.	All productive forces to be nationalized
		9.	No ownership item mentioned
		0.	Missing value
22	VAR201.......		Nature of Islamic socialism: production of wealth
		1.	Individual enterprise
		2.	Both private and public enterprises

		3.	Predominantly collective enterprises
		9.	No production-of-wealth item mentioned
		0.	Missing value
22	VAR202......		Nature of Islamic socialism: distribution of wealth
		1.	Social and economic justice
		2.	Social security program
		3.	Equitable distribution of wealth
		4.	Social justice
		6.	Distribution of *zakāt*
		9.	No distribution item mentioned
		0.	Missing value
23	VAR203......		Differences between Islamic and non-Islamic socialisms: summary
		1.	Differences described
		4.	Not much of a difference
		5.	None
		8.	I don't know
		9.	Refused to answer
		0.	Not applicable or missing
23	VAR204......		Differences between Islamic and non-Islamic socialisms: religious, spiritual—1
		1.	(*a*) Islamic socialism is theistic
		2.	(*b*) Islamic socialism is based on spiritual values
		3.	(*c*) Islamic socialism is against no social class
		4.	a + c
		5.	Islamic socialism is unscientific
		9.	No religious, spiritual item mentioned
		0.	Not applicable or missing
23	VAR205......		Differences between Islamic and non-Islamic socialisms: religious, spiritual—2
		1.	(*a*) Islamic socialism is theistic
		2.	Islamic socialism is based on spiritual value
		3.	(*c*) Islam is against no social class
		4.	a + c
		5.	Islamic socialism is unscientific
		9.	No religious, spiritual item mentioned
		0.	Not applicable or missing
23	VAR206......		Differences between Islamic and non-Islamic socialisms: economic freedom
		1.	Islamic socialism allows more individual property

2. Islamic socialism retains individual enterprise

3. After basic needs of all are met, any disparity in income is allowed

4. 1 + 3

5. 2 + 3

6. 1 + 2

7. 1 + 2 + 3

9. No economic item is mentioned

0. Not applicable or missing

23 VAR207....... Differences between Islamic and non-Islamic socialisms: civil liberties

1. Freedom of expression and of opposing government

3. Democratic government

9. No civil liberty item mentioned

0. Not applicable or missing

24 VAR208....... Method of distributing *zakāt*

1. (*a*) Distribution by state

2. (*b*) By individuals

3. Either way

4. None should be so poor as to need *zakāt*

5. *Zakāt* system will not help today

8. I don't know

9. Refused to answer

0. Missing value

25 VAR209....... Bank interest prohibited by Islam?

1. Prohibited

2. Difficult to decide

4. Not in the present system

5. Not prohibited

6. Only if charged by private banks

8. I don't know

9. Refused to answer

0. Missing value

26 VAR210....... Abolishing the present system of banking

1. Should be abolished

2. Interest-free banking should be developed

3. Difficult to decide

4. Only modification of banking needed

5. Should not be abolished

6. Yes, but state can change interest

8. I don't know

		9.	Refused to answer
		0.	Not applicable or missing
27	VAR213.......		Motivation of moral action
		1.	(*a*) Religious
		2.	(*b*) Nonreligious
		3.	(*c*) Both religious and nonreligious
		8.	I don't know
		9.	Refused to answer
		0.	Missing value
28	VAR214.......		Moral quality of religiously recommended act
		1.	Can be immoral
		5.	Cannot be immoral
		3.	Ideally can't, but under the present system may be
		8.	I don't know
		9.	Refused to answer
		0.	Missing value
29	VAR215.......		Moral quality of preaching on loudspeaker
		1.	(*a*) Religiously rewarding, but immoral
		2.	(*b*) Neither sinful, nor immoral
		3.	(*c*) Both immoral and sinful
		4.	Not sinful, but immoral
		5.	Undesirable, but not immoral or sinful
		6.	Immoral and sinful, if untimely
		7.	Immoral, but if don't know of sin
		8.	I don't know
		9.	Refused to answer
		0.	Missing value
30	VAR216.......		Moral quality of religiously forbidden acts
		1.	Morally neutral
		2.	Morally not neutral
		8.	I don't know
		9.	Refused to answer
		0.	Missing value
31	VAR217.......		Moral quality of drinking and dancing
		1.	(*a*) Sinful, but morally neutral
		2.	(*b*) Neither sinful nor immoral
		3.	(*c*) Sinful and immoral
		4.	Dance is neither sinful nor immoral; drinking is both sinful and immoral
		7.	Morally okay, I don't know about sinfulness
		8.	I don't know
		9.	Refused to answer
		0.	Missing value

32	VAR218.......	Civil morality vs. religious morality: smuggling
	1.	(*a*) Crime, not sinful or immoral
	2.	(*b*) Immoral, but not sinful
	3.	(*c*) Sinful as well as immoral
	4.	Currently, a, in true Islamic state c
	6.	Difficult to decide
	7.	Immoral, I don't know of sin
	8.	I don't know
	9.	Refused to answer
	0.	Missing value
33	VAR219.......	Enforcing religious morality with state sanctions: summary
	1.	Yes
	2.	Only in a completely Islamic state
	3.	I don't care
	4.	Controlled, restrained, and not quite because of religion
	5.	No
	8.	I don't know
	9.	Refused to answer
	0.	Missing value
33	VAR220.......	Enforcing religious morality with state sanctions: drinking
	1.	Yes
	3.	I don't care
	4.	Controlled, restrained, and not quite because of religion
	5.	No
	8.	I don't know
	9.	Refused to answer
	0.	Not applicable or missing
33	VAR221.......	Enforcing religious morality with state sanctions: dancing
	1.	Yes
	3.	I don't care
	4.	Controlled, restrained, and not quite because of religion
	5.	No
	8.	I don't know
	9.	Refused to answer
	0.	Not applicable or missing
33	VAR222.......	Enforcing religious morality with state sanctions: cinema and theater

		1.	Yes
		3.	I don't care
		4.	Controlled, restrained, and not quite because of religion
		5.	No
		8.	I don't know
		9.	Refused to answer
		0.	Not applicable or missing
33	VAR223......		Enforcing religious morality with state sanctions: coeducation
		1.	Yes
		3.	I don't care
		4.	Controlled, restrained, and not quite because of religion
		5.	No
		8.	I don't know
		9.	Refused to answer
		0.	Not applicable or missing
43	VAR224......		Evaluation of the civil servants: positive
		1.	(a) Capable people
		3.	Mixed, both good and bad
		9.	No totally positive opinion
		0.	Not applicable or missing
43	VAR225......		Evaluation of the civil servants: negative
		2.	(b) Steeped in Western culture
		3.	(c) Reactionaries
		4.	(d) Selfish, hypocrite
		5.	b + c
		1.	b + c + d
		9.	No totally negative opinion
		0.	Not applicable or missing
44	VAR226......		Evaluation of teachers, lawyers, journalists: positive
		1.	(a) Capable people
		3.	Mixed, both good and bad
		9.	No totally positive opinion
		0.	Not applicable or missing
44	VAR227......		Evaluation of teachers, lawyers, journalists: negative
		2.	(b) Steeped in Western culture
		3.	(c) Reactionaries
		4.	(d) Selfish, hypocrites
		5.	b + c

		1.	b + c + d
		9.	No negative judgment
		0.	Not applicable or missing
45	VAR228.......		Evaluation of the *lamā:* positive
		1.	(*a*) Capable people
		3.	Mixed, both good and bad
		9.	No totally positive opinion
		0.	Not applicable or missing
45	VAR229.......		Evaluation of the *ulamā:* negative
		2.	(*b*) Steeped in medieval culture
		3.	(*c*) Reactionaries
		4.	(*d*) Selfish, hypocrites
		5.	b + c
		1.	b + c + d
		6.	No negative opinion
		0.	Not applicable or missing
46	VAR230.......		Future expectations: summary
		1.	Described
		8.	I don't know
		9.	Did not describe
		0.	Missing value
46	VAR231.......		Future expectations: politics
		1.	Healthy
		2.	Dubious
		3.	Neither very good nor very bad
		4.	Uncertain
		5.	I don't care
		8.	I don't know
		9.	Did not describe
		0.	Not applicable or missing
46	VAR232.......		Future expectations: the economy
		1.	Healthy
		2.	Dubious
		3.	Neither very good nor very bad
		4.	Uncertain
		5.	I don't care
		8.	I don't know
		9.	Did not describe
		0.	Not applicable or missing
46	VAR233.......		Future expectations: religion
		1.	Healthy
		2.	Dubious
		3.	Neither very good nor very bad

	4.	Uncertain
	5.	I don't care
	8.	I don't know
	9.	Did not describe
	0.	Not applicable or missing
42	VAR234.......	Intensity of ideological commitment
	1.	(*a*) Strong
	2.	(*b*) Moderate
	3.	(*c*) Very strong
	4.	Weak, we should be pragmatic
	5.	Weak, dogmatism is undesirable
	8.	I don't know
	9.	Refused to answer
	0.	Missing value
20b	VAR235.......	Desirable economic system: summary
	1.	Same as Islamic economic system
	3.	Only desirable system described
	5.	Described differently from Islamic economic system
	8.	I don't know
	9.	Refused to describe
	0.	Missing value
20B	VAR236.......	Desirable economic system: ownership of property
	1.	Private property is essential
	2.	Private property is preferred, but public property is permitted
	3.	Mostly common property
	4.	Only common property is allowed
	8.	I don't know
	0.	Not applicable or missing
20B	VAR237.......	Desirable economic system: production of wealth
	1.	Private enterprise only
	2.	Private enterprise is preferred
	3.	Basic industries should be nationalized
	4.	Collective enterprise only
	8.	I don't know
	0.	Not applicable or missing
20B	VAR238.......	Desirable economic system: distribution of wealth
	1.	All differences in income are permitted

2. After basic needs of all are fulfilled, inequity in income is permitted
3. Equitable distribution
8. I don't know
0. Missing value

20B   VAR239....... Islamic quality of the desirable economic system
1. Islamic
2. Implied by general Islamic teachings
3. Not against Islam
4. Islam is impractical, etc.
5. Opposed to Islam
8. I don't know
9. Refused to answer
0. Missing value

C ❋ *Select Repository Tables*

TABLES C.1 – C.4
CATEGORY OF RESPONDENT BY THE OBJECT OF "NATIONAL" IDENTITY

TABLE C.1
THE OBJECT OF FIRST LOYALTY*

Category of Respondent	Relatives and Birādarī (a)	Birthplace (b)	Fellow Muslims (c)	Fellow Citizens (d)	Working Class	Priorities Relative to Subject Matter	God	Humanity	None	Row Total
Ulamā, East Pakistan	8 66.7%	0 0.0	4 33.3%	0 0.0	0 0.0	0 0.0	0 0.0	0 0.0	0 0.0	12 7.7%
Ulamā, West Pakistan	15 88.2%	0 0.0	1 5.9%	0 0.0	0 0.0	1 5.9%	0 0.0	0 0.0	0 0.0	17 10.9%
Professionals, East Pakistan	22 39.3%	8 14.3%	0 0.0	14 25.0%	6 10.7%	0 0.0	4 7.1%	2 3.6%	0 0.0	56 33.9%
Professionals, West Pakistan	30 42.3%	1 1.4%	19 26.8%	9 12.7%	4 5.6%	1 1.4%	3 4.2%	4 5.6%	0 0.0	71 45.5%
Column Total	75 48.1%	9 3.8%	24 15.4%	23 14.7%	10 6.4%	2 1.3%	7 4.5%	6 3.8%	0 0.0	154 100.0%

*Responses to Question No. 1 (variable: VAR080).

TABLE C.2
THE OBJECT OF SECOND LOYALTY*

Category of Respondent	The Object of Second Loyalty									
	Relatives and Birādarī (a)	Birthplace (b)	Fellow Muslims (c)	Fellow Citizens (d)	Working Class	Priorities Relative to Subject Matter	God	Humanity	None	Row Total
Ulamā, East Pakistan	0 0.0	8 66.7%	0 0.0	0 0.0	0 0.0	4 33.3%	0 0.0	0 0.0	0 0.0	12 7.8%
Ulamā, West Pakistan	1 5.9%	12 70.6%	2 11.8%	1 5.9%	0 0.0	1 5.9%	0 0.0	0 0.0	0 0.0	17 11.0%
Professionals, East Pakistan	2 3.6%	20 36.4%	10 18.2%	6 10.9%	6 10.9%	0 0.0	0 0.0	0 0.0	11 20.0%	55 35.7%
Professionals, West Pakistan	9 12.9%	26 37.1%	8 11.4%	13 18.6%	0 0.0	1 1.4%	0 0.0	2 2.9%	11 15.7%	70 45.5%
Column Total	12 7.8%	66 42.9%	20 13.0%	20 13.0%	6 3.9%	6 3.9%	0 0.0	2 1.3%	22 14.3%	154 100.0%

*Responses to Question No. 1 (variable: VAR081).

TABLE C.3
THE OBJECT OF THIRD LOYALTY*

Category of Respondent	The Object of Third Loyalty								Row Total
	Relatives and Birādarī (a)	Birthplace (b)	Fellow Muslims (c)	Fellow Citizens (d)	Working Class	Priorities Relative to Subject Matter	Humanity	None	
Ulamā, East Pakistan	0 0.0	0 0.0	8 66.7%	0 0.0	0 0.0	4 33.3%	0 0.0	0 0.0	12 7.8%
Ulamā, West Pakistan	0 0.0	2 11.8%	11 64.7%	2 11.8%	0 0.0	1 5.9%	1 5.9%	0 0.0	17 11.1%
Professionals, East Pakistan	4 7.3%	4 7.3%	12 21.8%	8 14.5%	4 7.3%	0 0.0	0 0.0	23 41.8%	55 35.9%
Professionals, West Pakistan	6 8.7%	8 11.6%	20 29.0%	12 17.4%	1 0.0	1 1.4%	2 2.9%	19 27.5%	69 45.1%
Column Total	10 6.5%	14 9.2%	51 33.3%	22 14.4%	5 3.3%	6 3.9%	3 2.0%	42 27.5%	153 100.0%

*Responses to Question No. 1 (variable: VAR082).

TABLE C.4
THE OBJECT OF FOURTH LOYALTY*

| Category of Respondent | The Object of Fourth Loyalty | | | | | | | | Row Total |
	Relatives and Birādarī (a)	Birthplace (b)	Fellow Muslims (c)	Fellow Citizens (d)	Working Class	Priorities Relative to Subject Matter	Humanity	None	
East Pakistan	0	0	0	8	0	4	0	0	12
	0.0	0.0	0.0	66.7%	0.0	33.3%	0.0	0.0	7.8%
West Pakistan	1	2	1	8	0	1	0	4	17
	5.9%	11.8%	5.9%	47.1%	0.0	5.9%	0.0	23.5%	11.1%
Professionals, East Pakistan	0	0	8	20	0	0	0	27	55
	0.0	0.0	14.5%	36.4%	0.0	0.0	0.0	49.1%	35.9%
Professionals, West Pakistan	4	11	8	21	0	1	2	22	69
	5.8%	15.9%	11.6%	30.4%	0.0	1.4%	2.9%	31.9%	45.1%
Column *Total	5	13	17	57	0	6	2	53	153
	3.3%	8.5%	11.1%	37.3%	0.0	3.9%	1.3%	34.6%	100.0%

*Responses to Question No. 1 (variable: VAR083).

TABLE C.5
THE DESIRED BASIS OF PAKISTANI NATIONHOOD AS SEEN BY THE *ULAMĀ*
AND THE MIDDLE-CLASS PROFESSIONALS*

	Desired Basis of Pakistani Nationhood						
Category of Respondent	*Class Interest (d)*	*Secular Culture & Class Interest (b) + (d)*	*Secular Culture (b)*	*Islam & Class Interest (a) + (d)*	*Provincial Culture (a) + (b)*	*Islam (a)*	*Row Total*
Ulamā, East Pakistan	0 0.0	0 0.0	0 0.0	0 0.0	0 0.0	10 100.0%	10 6.8%
Ulamā, West Pakistan	0 0.0	0 0.0	0 0.0	1 5.9%	2 11.8%	14 28.0%	17 11.6%
Professionals, East Pakistan	0 0.0	2 4.0%	28 56.0%	0 0.0	14 28.0%	5 12.0%	50 34.2%
Professionals, West Pakistan	3 4.3%	2 2.9%	6 8.7%	2 2.9%	19 27.5%	37 53.6%	69 47.3%
Column Total	3 2.1%	4 2.7%	34 23.3%	3 2.1%	35 40.0%	67 45.9%	146 100.0%

*Responses to Question No. 2.
Number of Missing Observations = 16.

TABLE C.6

THE HISTORIC SOURCE OF "NATIONAL" INSPIRATION AND
IDENTITY AS SEEN BY THE *ULAMĀ* AND THE MIDDLE-CLASS
PROFESSIONALS *

Category of Respondent	Source of Inspiration				Row Total
	None	Indo-Muslim History	Indo-Muslim History and Khilāfa Rāshida	Khilāfa Rāshida	
Ulamā, East Pakistan	0 0.0	0 0.0	0 0.0	12 100.0%	12 8.0%
Ulamā, West Pakistan	0 0.0	0 0.0	0 0.0	17 100.0%	17 11.3%
Professionals, East Pakistan	30 60.0%	0 0.0	0 0.0	20 40.0%	50 33.3%
Professionals, West Pakistan	17 23.9%	4 5.6%	1 1.4%	49 69.0%	71 47.3%
Column Total	47 31.3%	4 2.7%	1 0.7%	98 65.3%	150 100.0%

*Responses to Question No. 3.

Category of Respondent	Desired Basis of Pakistan's Political Unity								Row Total
	Socialism	Democracy and Social Justice	Expedience	Fatherland	Islam and Fatherland	Islam, Justice, & Socialism	Islam and Expedience	Islam	
Ulamā, East Pakistan	0 0.0	0 0.0	0 0.0	0 0.0	0 0.0	0 0.0	4 33.3%	8 66.7%	12 7.8%
Ulamā, West Pakistan	0 0.0	0 0.0	0 0.0	0 0.0	2 12.5%	0 0.0	0 0.0	14 87.5%	15 10.4%
Professionals, East Pakistan	0 0.0	2 3.4%	20 34.5%	20 34.5%	4 6.9%	0 0.0	8 13.8%	4 6.9%	58 37.7%
Professionals, West Pakistan	4 5.9%	2 2.9%	6 8.8%	8 11.8%	4 5.9%	5 7.4%	3 4.4%	36 52.9%	68 44.2%
Column Total	4 2.6%	4 2.6%	26 16.9%	28 18.2%	10 6.5%	5 3.2%	15 9.7%	62 40.3%	154 100.0%

*Responses to Question No. 4.

TABLE C.8
CONCEPTIONS OF THE TERM *UMMA**

Category of Respondent	Conceived Meaning of Umma					
	Followers of Muhammad (a)	Worldwide Muslim Brother- hood (b)	Political Community (c)	(a) As Well As (c)	Refused to Answer	Row Total
Ulamā, East Pakistan	0 0.0	0 0.0	12 100.0%	0 0.0	0 0.0	12 7.5%
Ulamā, West Pakistan	1 6.3%	2 12.5%	11 68.8%	2 12.5%	0 0.0	16 10.1%
Professionals, East Pakistan	30 50.0%	6 10.0%	24 40.0%	0 0.0	0 0.0	60 37.7%
Professionals, West Pakistan	21 29.6%	0 0.0	47 66.2%	0 0.0	3 4.2%	71 44.7%
Column Total	52 32.7%	8 5.0%	94 59.1%	2 1.3%	3 1.9%	159 100.0%

*Responses to Question No. 5.

TABLE C.9

THE EXTENT OF MUSLIM UNITY DESIRED BY THE *ULAMĀ* AND THE MIDDLE-CLASS PROFESSIONALS*

Category of Respondent		*Desirable Muslim Unity*			
	None	*Muslim World Cooperation (ii)*	*Muslim Common-wealth (i)*	*One Muslim State (iii)*	*Row Total*
Ulamā, East Pakistan	0 0.0	7 58.3%	5 41.7%	0 0.0	12 8.2%
Ulamā, West Pakistan	0 0.0	3 21.4	7 50.0%	4 28.6%	14 9.6%
Professionals, East Pakistan	36 60.0%	16 26.7%	8 13.3%	0 0.0	60 41.1%
Professionals, West Pakistan	19 31.7%	15 25.0%	25 41.7%	1 1.7%	60 41.1%
Column Total	55 37.7%	41 28.1%	45 30.8%	5 3.4%	146 100.0%

*Responses to Question No. 6.

TABLE C.10

ASSESSED ISLAMIC CHARACTER OF THE 1962 PAKISTAN CONSTITUTION*

Category of Respondent	Assessment of the Constitution					Row Total
	Un-Islamic	Un-acceptable	Partly Islamic	Fully or Sufficiently Islamic	Don't Know or Refused to Answer	
Ulamā, East and West Pakistan	21 72.4%	0 0.0	0 0.0	2 6.9%	6 20.7%	29 19.7%
Professionals, East Pakistan	35 74.5%	6 12.8%	2 4.3%	4 8.5%	0 0.0	47 32.0%
Professionals, West Pakistan	44 64.0%	0 0.0	1 1.4%	8 11.3%	18 25.4%	71 48.3%
Column Total	100 68.0%	6 4.1%	3 2.0%	14 9.5%	24 16.3%	147 100.0%

*Responses to Question No. 8.

TABLE C.11
SIMILARITY OF ISLAM TO OTHER POLITICAL SYSTEMS AS SEEN BY THE *ULAMĀ* AND THE PROFESSIONALS*

The Political System that Islam Resembles

Social Category	Democracy	Socialism	Democracy and Socialism	Dictatorship and/or Fascism	"True Islam Democratic, Actual Islam Dictatorship"	Islam Is Similar to None	Islam Is Not a Political System	Refused to Answer	Row Total
Ulamā, East and West Pakistan	24	0	0	0	0	4	0	0	28
	85.7%	0.0	0.0	0.0	0.0	14.3%	0.0	0.0	18.4%
Professionals, East Pakistan	12	4	24	4	4	0	4	2	54
	22.2%	7.4%	44.4%	7.4%	7.4%	0.0	7.4%	3.7%	35.5%
Professionals, West Pakistan	43	9	8	5	0	3	0	2	70
	61.4%	12.9%	11.4%	7.1%	0.0	4.3%	0.0	2.9%	46.1%
Column Total	79	13	32	9	4	7	4	4	152
	52.0%	18.6%	21.1%	5.9%	2.6%	4.6%	2.6%	2.6%	100.0%

*Responses to Question No. 9.

TABLE C.12

THE EXTENT OF SIMILARITY BETWEEN ISLAM AND DEMOCRACY AS
SEEN BY THE *ULAMĀ* AND THE PROFESSIONALS*

Social Category	The Extent of Similarity/Difference				
	Both Differences and Agreement	Nothing Different	No Agreement	Refused to Answer	Row Total
Ulamā, East and West Pakistan	23 88.5%	3 11.5%	0 0.0	0 0.0	26 19.8%
Professionals, East Pakistan	18 42.9%	22 52.4%	0 0.0	2 4.8%	42 32.1%
Professionals, West Pakistan	31 49.2%	26 41.3%	3 4.8%	3 4.8%	63 48.1%
Column Total	72 55.0%	51 38.9%	3 2.3%	5 3.8%	131 100.0%

*Responses to Question No. 10A.

TABLE C.13
DESIRABILITY OF ISLAMIC LAW IN PAKISTAN *

Social Category	*Desirability of Islamic Law*					
	Undesirable	*No Law Is Un- Islamic*	*Partly Desirable*	*Desirable*	*Don't Know*	*Row Total*
Ulamā, East and West Pakistan	0 0.0	0 0.0	0 0.0	27 96.4%	1 3.6%	28 17.8%
Professionals, East Pakistan	20 33.3%	2 3.3%	28 46.7%	10 16.7%	0 0.0	60 38.2%
Professionals, West Pakistan	9 13.0%	3 4.4%	7 10.1%	47 68.1%	3 4.3%	69 43.9%
Column Total	29 18.5%	5 3.2%	35 22.3%	84 53.5%	4 2.5%	157 100.0%

*Responses to Question No. 13.

TABLE C.14

DESIRABLE METHOD OF ISLAMIZING THE LAW IN PAKISTAN, ACCORDING TO
THOSE *ULAMĀ* AND PROFESSIONALS WHO WANT TO ISLAMIZE THE LAW*

	Method of Islamizing the Law					
Category of Respondent	*Enforcing Sharī'a[a]*	*Free Inter- pretation[b]*	*Limited Ijtihād[c]*	*Sharī'a, Plus Limited Ijtihād[d]*	*Don't Know or Refused to Answer*	*Row Total*
Ulamā, East and West Pakistan	10 38.5%	0 0.0	16 61.5%	0 0.0	0 0.0	26 30.2%
Professionals, East Pakistan	4 66.7%	2 33.3%	0 0.0	0 0.0	0 0.0	5 7.0%
Professionals, West Pakistan	9 16.7%	23 42.6%	16 29.6%	3 5.6%	3 5.6%	54 62.8%
Column Total	23 26.7%	25 29.1%	32 37.2%	3 3.5%	3 3.5%	86 100.0%

*Responses to Question No. 14.
[a] By enforcing traditional *sharī'a*.
[b] By free interpretation of principles found in the Qur'ān and *sunna*.
[c] By the exercise of limited *ijtihād*.
[d] By traditional *sharī'a* plus limited *ijtihād*.

TABLE C.15*

VIEWS ABOUT APPLYING THE *SHARĪ'A* LAW CONCERNING BLOOD MONEY

Category of Respondent	Views about Applying the Law						Row Total
	"Yes"[a]	"Reinterpret"[b]	"Wrong"[c]	"No"[d]	Refused to Answer[e]	"Govt. Can Punish"	
Ulamā, East and West Pakistan	23 85.2%	0 0.0	2 7.4%	0 0.0	2 7.4%	0 0.0	27 22.3%
Professionals, East Pakistan	4 11.8%	2 5.9%	0 0.0	25 73.5%	0 0.0	3 8.3%	34 28.1%
Professionals, West Pakistan	32 53.3%	7 11.7%	1 1.7%	16 28.4%	0 0.0	3 5.0%	60 49.6%
Column Total	59 48.8%	9 7.4%	3 2.5%	42 34.7%	2 1.7%	1 0.8%	121 100.0%

* Responses to Question No. 16.
[a] The law should be applied.
[b] Reinterpretation is needed.
[c] "The statement is wrong; the *sharī'a* has no such provision."
[d] The law should not be enforced.
[e] Don't know.

TABLE C.16
RESPONSES TO THE QUESTION: WHO CAN PROPERLY DETERMINE WHAT IS ISLAMICALLY RIGHT IN THE PRESENT AGE?*

Category of Respondent	Persons or Institutional Body Responsible to Islamize the Law							
	Ulamā	National Assembly	Modern Educated People[a]	Body of Ulamā Plus Modern Educ.[b]	"People, through Referendum"	None Exclusively[c]	Refused to Answer	Row Total
Ulamā, East and West Pakistan	21 80.8%	0 0.0	0 0.0	5 19.8%	0 0.0	0 0.0	0 0.0	26 18.8%
Professionals, East Pakistan	1 2.1%	34 70.8%	2 4.2%	5 10.4%	4 8.3%	0 0.0	2 4.2%	48 34.8%
Professionals, West Pakistan	13 20.3%	15 23.4%	3 4.7%	26 40.6%	0 0.0	3 4.8%	4 6.3%	64 46.4%
Column Total	35 25.4%	49 35.5%	5 3.6%	36 26.1%	4 2.9%	3 2.1%	6 4.3%	138 100.0%

*Responses to Question No. 17.

[a] Modern educated persons having knowledge of Islamic sciences.

[b] Body of *ulamā* plus modern educated persons having knowledge of Islamic sciences.

[c] Practicing jurists; political leaders; "none exclusively."

TABLE C.17

THE CHOICE BETWEEN MODERNIST REINTERPRETATION OF ALL ISLAMIC
LAW AND PARTIAL APPLICATION OF TRADITIONAL ISLAMIC LAW*

			The Choice			
			Conform with			
Category of Respondent	Traditional Law[a]	Revise the Law[b]	Qur'ān and Sunna	Both Alternatives Unacceptable	Refused to Answer	Row Total
Ulamā, East Pakistan	6 50.0%	0 0.0	6 50.0%	0 0.0	0 0.0	12 8.4%
Ulamā, West Pakistan	5 35.7%	1 7.1%	8 57.1%	0 0.0	0 0.0	14 9.8%
Professionals, East Pakistan	31 56.4%	23 41.8%	0 0.0	0 0.0	1 1.8%	55 38.5%
Professionals, West Pakistan	11 17.7%	38 61.3%	6 9.7%	2 3.2%	5 8.1%	62 43.4%
Column Total	53 37.1%	62 43.4%	20 14.0%	1 0.7%	5 4.2%	143 100.0%

*Responses to Question No. 18.
[a] Traditional Islamic law should be enforced.
[b] All law should be revised.
[c] All law should conform with the Qur'ān and *sunna.*
[d] "Both alternatives are unacceptable," or don't know.

TABLE C.18

VIEWS ON WHETHER ISLAM PROVIDES A COMPLETE ECONOMIC SYSTEM*

					(A) and (B)		
		(B)			*Are*		
Category of	*(A)*	*Limited*	*(C)*	*Im-*	*the*	*Refused to*	*Row*
Respondent	*Yes[a]*	*Demands[b]*	*No[c]*	*practicable[d]*	*Same*	*Answer[e]*	*Total*
Ulamā,	4	0	0	0	8	0	12
East Pakistan	33.3%	0.0	0.0	0.0	66.7%	0.0	7.6%
Ulamā,	16	0	0	0	1	0	17
West Pakistan	94.1%	0.0	0.0	0.0	5.9%	0.0	10.8%
Professionals,	12	28	16	2	2	0	60
East Pakistan	20.0%	46.7%	26.7%	3.3%	3.3%	0.0	38.2%
Professionals,	30	23	4	2	6	3	68
West Pakistan	44.1%	33.8%	5.9%	2.9%	8.8%	4.4%	43.3%
Column	62	51	20	4	17	3	157
Total	39.5%	32.5%	12.7%	2.5%	10.8%	1.9%	100.0%

*Responses to Question No. 19.
[a]"Yes, Islam provides a complete economic system."
[b]"Islam makes limited economic demands."
[c]"No, Islam is only a religion."
[d]"Islam's economic teachings are impracticable."
[e]"Islam's concern is only for social justice."

TABLE C.19

INTERPRETATION OF ISLAMIC TEACHINGS ABOUT OWNERSHIP
OF PROPERTY*

Category of Respondent	Ownership of Property				
	Private Ownership[a]	Private Ownership Preferred[b]	Major Industry Publicly Owned[c]	Only Collective Ownership[d]	Row Total
Ulamā, East Pakistan	11 91.7%	1 8.3%	0 0.0	0 0.0	12 8.6%
Ulamā, West Pakistan	11 64.7%	6 35.3%	0 0.0	0 0.0	17 12.2%
Professionals, East Pakistan	16 30.8%	20 38.5%	14 26.9%	2 3.8%	52 37.4%
Professionals, West Pakistan	20 34.5%	28 48.3%	10 17.2%	0 0.0	58 41.7%
Column Total	58 41.7%	55 39.6%	24 17.3%	2 1.4%	139 100.0%

*Responses to Question No. 20A.
[a] Islam favors only private ownership.
[b] Public ownership of major industries is preferred but not required.
[c] Major industries should be nationalized and publicly owned.
[d] All means of production should be nationalized and collectively owned.

TABLE C.20

INTERPRETATION OF ISLAMIC TEACHINGS ABOUT PRODUCTION
OF WEALTH*

Category of Respondent	Public or Private Enterprise					Row Total
	Private Enterprise Only	Private Enterprise Preferred[a]	Mixed[b]	Total Public Enterprise[c]	Don't Know	
Ulamā, East Pakistan	0 0.0	12 100.0%	0 0.0	0 0.0	0 0.0	12 8.6%
Ulamā, West Pakistan	1 5.9%	16 94.1%	0 0.0	0 0.0	0 0.0	17 12.2%
Professionals, East Pakistan	10 19.2%	22 42.3%	14 26.9%	2 3.8%	4 7.7%	52 37.4%
Professionals, West Pakistan	6 10.3%	46 79.3%	5 8.6%	0 0.0	1 1.7%	58 41.7%
Column Total	17 12.2%	96 69.1%	19 13.7%	2 1.4%	5 3.6%	139 100.0%

*Responses to Question No. 20A.

[a] Private enterprise is preferred, though not absolutely required.

[b] Basic industries should be managed by the state.

[c] All means of production should be managed by the state.

TABLE C.21

INTERPRETATION OF ISLAMIC TEACHING ABOUT DISTRIBUTION OF
WEALTH AND DISPARITY IN INCOME*

	Distribution of Wealth				
Category of Respondent	*Any Income Disparity Acceptable*[a]	*Basic Necessities First*[b]	*Equitable Distribution*[c]	*Don't Know*	*Row Total*
Ulamā, East Pakistan	11 91.7%	1 8.3%	0 0.0	0 0.0	12 8.6%
Ulamā, West Pakistan	7 41.2%	10 58.8%	0 0.0	0 0.0	17 12.2%
Professionals, East Pakistan	28 53.8%	10 19.2%	14 26.9%	0 0.0	52 37.4%
Professionals, West Pakistan	29 50.0%	22 37.9%	6 10.3%	1 1.7%	58 41.7%
Column Total	75 54.0%	43 30.9%	20 14.4%	1 0.7%	139 100.0%

*Responses to Question No. 20A.

[a] All differences in income are legally acceptable.

[b] Income disparity can be allowed only after the basic needs of all members of the society are satisfied.

[c] Equitable distribution according to need and merit.

TABLE C.22

DESIRABLE ECONOMIC SYSTEMS

	Ownership of Property *				
Category of Respondent	Only Private Ownership[a]	Private Ownership Preferred[b]	Major Industries Should Be Publicly Owned[c]	Only Collective Ownership[d]	Row Total
Ulamā, East Pakistan	11 91.7%	1 8.3%	0 0.0	0 0.0	12 7.8%
Ulamā, West Pakistan	12 70.6%	5 29.4%	0 0.0	0 0.0	17 11.1%
Professionals, East Pakistan	4 6.7%	16 26.7%	37 61.7%	3 5.0%	60 39.2%
Professionals, West Pakistan	19 29.7%	25 39.1%	20 31.2%	0 0.0	64 41.8%
Column Total	46 30.1%	47 30.7%	57 37.3%	2 1.3%	153 100.0%

*Responses to Question No. 20B.
[a] Only private ownership is desirable.
[b] Public ownership of major industries is preferred but not required.
[c] Major industries should be nationalized and publicly owned.
[d] All means of production should be nationalized and collectively owned.

TABLE C.23

DESIRABLE ECONOMIC SYSTEM: PRODUCTION OF WEALTH *

| Category of Respondent | Type of Enterprise | | | | Row Total |
	Private Enterprise Only	Private Enterprise Preferred[a]	Mixed[b]	Total Public Enterprise[c]	
Ulamā, East Pakistan	0 0.0	12 100.0%	0 0.0	0 0.0	12 7.8%
Ulamā, West Pakistan	1 5.9%	16 94.1%	0 0.0	0 0.0	17 11.0%
Professionals, East Pakistan	0 0.0	24 40.0%	34 56.7%	2 3.3%	60 39.0%
Professionals, West Pakistan	5 7.7%	48 73.8%	12 18.5%	0 0.0	65 42.2%
Column Total	6 3.9%	100 64.9%	46 29.9%	2 1.3%	154 100.0%

* Responses to Question No. 20B.
[a] Private enterprise is preferred, though not absolutely required.
[b] Basic industries should be managed by the state.
[c] All means of production should be managed by the state.

TABLE C.24
DESIRABLE ECONOMIC SYSTEM: DISTRIBUTION OF WEALTH*

Category of Respondent	Distribution of Wealth			Row Total
	Any Income Disparity Acceptable[a]	Basic Necessities First[b]	Equitable Distribution[c]	
Ulamā, East Pakistan	11	1	0	12
	91.7%	8.3%	0.0	7.8%
Ulamā, West Pakistan	7	10	0	17
	41.2%	58.8%	0.0	11.0%
Professionals, East Pakistan	4	18	38	60
	6.7%	30.0%	63.3%	39.0%
Professionals, West Pakistan	24	26	15	65
	36.9%	40.0%	23.1%	42.2%
Column Total	46	55	53	154
	29.9%	35.7%	34.4%	100.0%

*Responses to Question No. 20B.

[a] All differences in income are legally acceptable.

[b] Income disparity can be allowed only after the basic needs of all members of the society are satisfied.

[c] Equitable distribution must be according to needs and merit.

TABLE C.25

BELIEF IN "ISLAMIC SOCIALISM"*

Category of Respondent	Belief in "Islamic Socialism"								
	Belief	Complete Islam Includes Socialism	Concept Is Ambiguous	No, but Islam Has Its Arrangement for Social Justice	Unbelief	No, but in Scientific Socialism	No, but in Democratic Socialism	Don't Know or Refused to Answer	Row Total
Ulamā, East Pakistan	0 0.0	0 0.0	0 0.0	0 0.0	12 100.0%	0 0.0	0 0.0	0 0.0	12 7.6%
Ulamā, West Pakistan	0 0.0	0 0.0	0 0.0	1 5.9%	16 94.1%	0 0.0	0 0.0	0 0.0	17 10.8%
Professionals, East Pakistan	18 30.5%	2 3.4%	2 3.4%	4 6.8%	20 33.9%	6 10.2%	7 11.9%	0 0.0	59 37.6%
Professionals, West Pakistan	14 20.3%	1 1.4%	1 1.4%	7 10.1%	41 59.4%	1 1.4%	0 0.0	4 5.7%	69 43.9%
Column Total	32 20.4%	3 1.9%	3 1.9%	12 7.6%	89 56.7%	7 4.5%	7 4.5%	4 2.5%	157 100.0%

*Responses to Question No. 21.

TABLE C.26
PREFERRED METHOD OF DISTRIBUTING ZAKĀT*

Category of Respondent	Method of Distribution						Row Total
	(a) Tax to Be Distributed by the State	(b) Tax to Be Distributed by Individuals	Either Way	Society Should Be So Egalitarian that No One Should Have to Pay Zakāt	"Zakāt Will Not Help Today"	Don't Know or Refused to Answer	
Ulamā, East Pakistan	0 0.0	4 33.3%	8 66.7%	0 0.0	0 0.0	0 0.0	12 9.8
Ulamā, West Pakistan	1 7.7%	1 7.7%	11 84.6%	0 0.0	0 0.0	0 0.0	13 10.7%
Professionals, East Pakistan	16 36.1%	18 42.9%	2 4.8%	2 4.8%	2 4.8%	2 4.8%	42 34.4%
Professionals, West Pakistan	17 30.9%	21 38.2%	11 20.0%	0 0.0	2 3.6%	4 7.3%	55 45.1%
Column Total	34 27.9%	44 36.1%	32 26.2%	2 1.6%	4 3.3%	6 4.9%	122 100.0%

*Responses to Question No. 24.

TABLE C.27
VIEWS ON PROHIBITION OF BANK INTEREST ON ISLAMIC GROUNDS*

Category of Respondent	Attitude toward Bank Interest							
	"Should Be Prohibited"	"Difficult to Decide"	"Not in Present System of Banking"	"Should Not Be Prohibited"	"Should Be Prohibited Only for Private Banks"	Don't Know or Refused to Answer	Row Total	
Ulamā, East Pakistan	10 100.0%	0 0.0	0 0.0	0 0.0	0 0.0	0 0.0	10 8.3%	
Ulamā, West Pakistan	5 45.5%	0 0.0	3 27.3%	3 27.3%	0 0.0	0 0.0	11 9.2%	
Professionals, East Pakistan	12 27.3%	0 0.0	2 4.5%	18 40.9%	0 0.0	12 27.3%	44 36.7%	
Professionals, West Pakistan	23 41.6	2 3.6%	1 1.8%	14 25.5%	3 5.5%	12 21.9%	55 45.8%	
Column Total	50 41.6%	2 1.7%	6 5.0%	35 29.2%	3 2.5%	24 20.0%	120 100.0%	

*Responses to Question No. 25.

TABLE C.28
VIEWS ON ABOLISHING THE MODERN SYSTEM OF BANKING*

Category of Respondent	Views on Abolition of the Modern Banking System							Row Total
	"Should Be Abolished"	"Interest-free Banking Should Replace It"	"Difficult to Decide"	"Only Some Modifications Are Needed"	"Should Not Be Abolished"	"Yes, but State Can Charge Interest"	Don't Know or Refused to Answer	
Ulamā, East Pakistan	10 100.0%	0 0.0	0 0.0	0 0.0	0 0.0	0 0.0	0 0.0	10 8.5%
Ulamā, West Pakistan	11 100.0%	0 0.0	0 0.0	0 0.0	0 0.0	0 0.0	0 0.0	11 9.4%
Professionals, East Pakistan	0 0.0	2 4.5%	0 0.0	2 4.5%	32 72.7%	0 0.0	8 18.2%	44 37.6%
Professionals, West Pakistan	11 21.2%	2 3.8%	2 3.8%	4 7.7%	21 40.4%	3 5.8%	9 17.3%	52 44.4%
Column Total	32 27.4%	4 3.4	2 1.7%	6 5.1%	53 45.3%	3 2.6%	17 14.5%	117 100.0%

*Responses to Question No. 26.

TABLE C.29
VIEWS ON WHETHER PAKISTANIS HOLD AN IDEOLOGY*

Category of Respondent	Response to the Question: Do Pakistanis Hold an Ideology?					
	"Yes"	"Yes, but with Some Confusion"	"Yes, but Not Seriously"	"No"	Don't Know	Row Total
Ulamā, East Pakistan	12	0	0	0	0	12
	100.0%	0.0	0.0	0.0	0.0	7.4%
Ulamā, West Pakistan	17	0	0	0	0	17
	100.0%	0.0	0.0	0.0	0.0	10.5%
Professionals, East Pakistan	36	2	0	21	0	59
	61.0%	3.4%	0.0	35.6%	0.0	36.4%
Professionals, West Pakistan	56	2	3	11	2	74
	75.7%	2.7%	4.1%	14.9%	2.7%	45.7%
Column Total	121	4	3	32	2	162
	74.7%	2.5%	1.9%	19.8%	1.2%	100.0%

*Responses to Question No. 34.

TABLE C.30
ASSUMED IDEOLOGIES OF PAKISTANIS*

	Assumed Ideology					
Category of Respondent	"Islam"	"Different People Have Different Ideologies"	"Islam Is a Religion"	"None"	Don't Know	Row Total
Ulamā, East Pakistan	8 66.7%	4 33.3%	0 0.0	0 0.0	0 0.0	12 7.5%
Ulamā, West Pakistan	12 70.6%	5 29.4%	0 0.0	0 0.0	0 0.0	17 10.6%
Professionals, East Pakistan	30 50.8%	6 10.2%	2 3.4%	21 35.6%	0 0.0	59 36.6%
Professionals, West Pakistan	56 76.7%	3 4.1%	2 2.7%	10 13.7%	2 2.7%	73 45.3%
Column Total	106 65.8%	18 11.2%	4 2.5%	31 19.3%	2 1.2%	161 100.0%

*Responses to Question No. 35.

TABLE C.31

RESPONDENT'S PROFESSED "IDEOLOGY"*

Category of Respondent	Ideology Professed by the Respondent									Row Total
	Islam	Islamic Democracy	Islamic Socialism	Humanism	Democracy	Democratic Socialism	Socialism	Communism, Marxism	No Ideology	
Ulamā, East and West Pakistan	28	0	0	0	0	0	0	0	0	28
	100.0%	0.0	0.0	0.0	0.0	0.0	0.0	0.0	0.0	17.5%
Professionals, East Pakistan	15	11	11	0	4	6	8	2	2	59
	25.4%	18.6%	18.6%	0.0	6.8%	10.2%	13.6%	3.4%	3.4%	36.9%
Professionals, West Pakistan	52	0	6	2	1	5	5	0	2	73
	71.2%	0.0	8.2%	2.7%	1.4%	6.8%	6.8%	0.0	2.7%	45.6%
Column Total	95	11	17	2	5	11	13	2	4	160
	59.4%	6.9%	10.6%	1.2%	3.1%	6.9%	8.1%	1.2%	2.5%	100.0%

*Responses to Question No. 36.

TABLE C.32
DEMANDS OF ISLAMIC IDEOLOGY*

Category of Respondent	Demands of Islamic Ideology						Row Total
	Beliefs Only[a]	Belief and Ibādat[b]	Socio-ethical Concern[c]	Traditional Islamic Laws[d]	Islamic State	Total Life[e]	
Ulamā, East and West Pakistan	0 0.0	0 0.0	0 0.0	0 0.0	1 3.4%	28 96.6%	29 20.4%
Professionals, East Pakistan	2 4.3%	4 8.7%	3 6.5%	25 54.3%	4 8.7%	8 17.4%	46 32.4%
Professionals, West Pakistan	0 0.0	3 4.5%	7 10.4%	9 13.4%	7 10.4%	41 61.2%	67 47.2%
Column Total	2 1.4%	7 4.9%	10 7.0%	34 23.9%	12 8.5%	77 54.2%	142 100.0%

*Responses to Question No. 37.
[a] Belief in God, the Prophet, and the hereafter.
[b] Belief and performing *namāz, rōza, zakāt,* and *hajj.*
[c] Observing the Islamic rules of social ethics against drinking, etc.
[d] Observing the traditional legal Islamic laws about marriage, divorce, etc.
[e] Islamization of all aspects of life: political, legal, social.

TABLE C.33

PRIORITY OF FAITH, MORALITY, OR POLITICS IN ISLAM ACCORDING
TO THE *ULAMĀ* AND THE MIDDLE-CLASS PROFESSIONALS*

Category of Respondent	*Understanding of Priorities*				
	Only Faith and Morality Are Important	*Faith First, Then Morality, and Last Politics*	*All Are Equally Important*	*Don't Know or Refused to Answer*	*Row Total*
Ulamā, East and West Pakistan	0 0.0	13 65.0%	1 5.0%	6 30.0%	20 20.0%
Professionals, East Pakistan	10 41.7%	8 33.3%	4 16.7%	2 8.3%	24 24.0%
Professionals, West Pakistan	9 16.1%	18 32.1%	15 26.8%	14 25.0%	56 56.0%
Column Total	19 19.0%	39 39.0%	20 20.0%	22 22.0%	100 100.0%

*Responses to Question No. 38.

TABLE C.34

VIEWS ON WHETHER ISLAM PROVIDES A SOLUTION TO ALL PROBLEMS*

	View				
Category of Respondent	Islam Is Irrelevant or Detrimental[a]	Islam Is Not Opposed to Progress	Islam Provides Considerable Guidelines	Islam Provides a Total Solution to All Problems[b]	Row Total
Ulamā, East and West Pakistan	0 0.0	2 6.9%	1 3.4%	26 89.7%	29 18.5%
Professionals, East Pakistan	13 21.7%	1 1.7%	32 53.3%	14 23.3%	60 38.2%
Professionals, West Pakistan	11 16.2%	0 0.0	7 10.3%	50 73.5%	68 43.4%
Column Total	24 15.3%	3 1.9%	40 25.5%	90 57.3%	156 100.0%

*Responses to Question No. 39.

[a]"Islam is largely irrelevant to most of our modern problems, or practice of Islamic values will hurt the cause of economic progress and social reform."

[b]"Islam is the solution to all our problems. Once we become true Muslims, success will be sure."

TABLE C.35

VIEWS ON WHETHER THE QUR'ĀN AND THE *SUNNA* PROVIDE A COMPLETE CODE OF LIFE*

		View			
Category of Respondent	"No"	"No, Only Moral Teachings"	"Yes, but Mostly Guidelines"	"Yes"	Row Total
Ulamā, East and West Pakistan	1 3.8%	0 0.0	0 0.0	25 96.2%	26 17.7%
Professionals, East Pakistan	7 10.4%	2 3.0%	7 10.4%	51 76.1%	67 45.6%
Professionals, West Pakistan	24 44.3%	8 14.8%	0 0.0	22 40.7%	54 36.7%
Column Total	32 21.8%	10 6.8%	7 4.8%	98 66.7%	147 100.0%

*Responses to Question No. 40.

TABLE C.36

THE DEMAND FOR CONSENSUS ON FUNDAMENTALS OF ISLAMIC
IDEOLOGY ACCORDING TO THE *ULAMĀ* AND THE
MIDDLE-CLASS PROFESSIONALS*

Category of Respondent	(B) Not Demanded	(A, B) ** Restricted Demand	(A) Demanded	Row Total
Ulamā, East and	0	3	25	28
West Pakistan	0.0	10.7%	89.3%	18.5%
Professionals,	48	0	10	58
East Pakistan	82.8%	0.0	17.2%	38.4%
Professionals,	25	3	37	65
West Pakistan	38.5%	4.6%	56.9%	43.0%
Column	73	6	72	151
Total	48.3%	4.0%	47.7%	100.0%

*Responses to Question No. 41.

**Consensus demanded from Muslims, who may not be allowed to criticize Islam, but not demanded from non-Muslims.

TABLE C.37

INTENSITY OF RESPONDENT'S COMMITMENT TO HIS "IDEOLOGY" *

	Intensity of Commitment				
Category of Respondent	*None ("Dogma Is Undesirable")*	*(B) Weak*	*(A) Mildly Strong*	*(C) Strong*	*Row Total*
Ulamā, East and West Pakistan	0 0.0	0 0.0	3 16.7%	15 83.3%	18 13.4%
Professionals, East Pakistan	1 1.8%	7 12.5%	32 57.1%	16 28.6%	56 41.8%
Professionals, West Pakistan	1 1.7%	2 3.3%	31 51.7%	26 43.4%	60 44.8%
Column Total	2 1.5%	9 6.7%	66 49.3%	57 42.5%	134 100.0%

*Responses to Question No. 42.

Notes

1. INTRODUCTION

1. Sir Muhammad Iqbal, *The Reconstruction of Religious Thought in Islam* (Lahore: Sh. Muhammad Ashraf, 1962), 154.

2. Bernard Lewis, "Muslims, Christians, and Jews: The Dream of Coexistence," *New York Review of Books,* March 26, 1992, 49.

3. For a comprehensive bibliography of the works dealing with current Islamic resurgence, see Yvonne Haddad, John Voll, and John Esposito, eds., *The Contemporary Islamic Revival: A Critical Survey and Bibliography* (New York: Greenwood Press, 1991).

4. For an objective and judicious treatment of political Islam that challenges sensationalism, see John L. Esposito, *The Islamic Threat: Myth or Reality,* 2nd ed. (New York: Oxford University Press), 1995.

5. See, for example, *The New Encyclopaedia Britannica: Macropaedia,* 1994 ed., s.v. "Fundamentalism"; *Columbia Encyclopedia,* 1993 ed., s.v. "Fundamentalism."

6. For some analyses of the legal and institutional "Islamization" in Pakistan under President Zia-ul-Haq, see Anita Weiss, ed., *Islamic Reassertion in Pakistan* (Syracuse, N.Y.: Syracuse University Press, 1986).

7. See, for example, Hamza Alavi, "Ethnicity, Muslim Society, and the Pakistan Ideology," in Weiss, ed., *Islamic Reassertion,* 21–47; Ann Elizabeth Mayer, "The Fundamentalist Impact on Law, Politics, and Constitution in Iran, Pakistan, and the Sudan," in Martin E. Marty and Scott R. Appleby, eds., *Fundamentalisms and the State: Remaking Polities, Economies, and Militance* (Chicago: University of Chicago Press, 1993), 123–28.

8. Weiss, ed., *Islamic Reassertion,* xv.

2. ISLAM AND NATIONAL IDENTIFICATION

1. Cf. *The New Encyclopaedia Britannica: Macropaedia,* 1994 ed., s.v. "Nationalism"; Louis Snyder, "Introduction," *Encyclopedia of Nationalism* (Saint Paul, Minn.: Paragon House Publishers, 1990); Ernest Gellner, *Nations and Nationalism* (Ithaca, N.Y.: Cornell University Press, 1989), 1.

2. Benedict Anderson, *Imagined Communities: Reflections on the Origins and Spread of Nationalism,* rev. ed. (London: Verso, 1983; repr., 1991), 4.

3. Six major questions in the survey questionnaire sought to determine respondents' attitudes toward nationalism and Islamic identity (see the section on national identity in Appendix A: The Questionnaire). The specific answers received to those six questions are given in tabular form in Appendix C.

4. These three categories were achieved by combining and collating answers to questions number 1 and 2 (VAR080, VAR081, VAR084, VAR085). See Appendix A: The Questionnaire and Appendix B: Primary Variables.

5. Bureau of National Reconstruction, East Pakistan, *Pakistani Nationhood: A Collection of Papers Read at the National Seminar Held at Dacca from Nov. 5–9, 1961* (Dacca: Government of East Pakistan, 1962), 47.

6. Shariful Mujahid, "Basis of Pakistani Nationhood," in *Pakistani Nationhood: A Collection of Papers Read at the National Seminar, at Dacca, in 1961* (Dacca: Bureau of National Reconstruction, 1963), 19–20.

7. Muhammad Shafi Akhtar, "Hamārā Thaqāfatī Wirtha," in Waheeduz Zaman, ed., *The Quest for Identity* (Islamabad: Islamabad University Press, 1974), 132–33.

8. Yusuf Abbas Hashimi, "The Quest for Identity," in ibid., 59.

9. Ibid., 63.

10. Government of West Pakistan, *Report of the Seminar on Greater National Integration Held from Sept. 18–22, 1961* (Lahore: Bureau of National Reconstruction, West Pakistan, 1963), 17.

11. Allama Allauddin Siddiqui, "Islam and National Outlook in Pakistan," in ibid., 110–11.

12. Zaman, ed., *The Quest,* v–vi.

13. For a wealth of similar *hadīth,* see the chapter on *fitna* in standard *hadīth* collections.

14. Pakistan is among the countries having such restrictions.

15. Perhaps the clearest indication of this is the number of books published on religious topics. In *Qāmūs al-Kutub-i-Urdū* one finds ten times as many works on Islamic topics as on all other religions combined. The same is true about the faith of their authors.

16. Punjabi as the historical origin of Urdu is not accepted by all scholars of Urdu language and literature; philological affinity between Urdu and Punjabi is, however, recognized by all.

17. Bureau of National Reconstruction, East Pakistan, "How to Achieve Cultural Homogeneity in Pakistan," in Bureau of National Reconstruction, East Pakistan, *Pakistani Nationhood,* 78.

18. For some recent studies on the role of Islam in Bangladeshi national identity and economic development, see David Abecassis, *Identity, Islam, and Human Development in Rural Bangladesh* (Dhaka, Bangladesh: University Press, 1990); Razia Akter Banu, *Islam in Bangladesh* (Leiden and New York: Brill, 1992);

Muhammad Abdul Mannan, *Economic Development and Social Peace in an Analytical Study of the Process of Economic Development in the Muslim Community of Today (with an Account of Real-life Experiments in Bangladesh)* (London: Ta Ha Publishers; Dhaka: Bangladesh Social Peace Foundation, 1990).

19. Dr. Mahmud Hussain, "Welcoming Address," in Bureau of National Reconstruction, East Pakistan, *Pakistani Nationhood*, 6.

20. Muhammad Iqbal, *Speeches and Statements of Iqbal*, comp. Shamloo, 2nd ed. (Lahore, 1948), 225.

21. See Hafeez Malik, *Moslem Nationalism in India and Pakistan* (Washington, D.C.: Public Affairs Press, 1963), 272–73.

22. *Mukālama al-Sadarayn* (Lahore: Hashimi Book Depot, [1945]), 6–40.

23. Shaikh al-Islam Allama Shabbir Ahmad Uthmani, *Payghām* (Lahore: Hashimi Book Depot, [1945]), 12–25.

24. See, for example, a series of articles on Islamic ideology and secularism in *Outlook* (Karachi), issues of March 16 and April 13, 1963.

25. Ibid., 200.

26. Dr. Mahmud Hussain, "Address," in Bureau of National Reconstruction, East Pakistan, *Pakistani Nationhood*, 3.

27. Ibid., 9.

28. Ibid.

29. Syed Moizuddin Ahmad, "The Quest for Identity," in Waheed-uz-Zaman, ed., *Quest for Identity* (Islamabad: University of Islamabad Press, 1974), 74.

30. Qudratullah Fatimi, "The Territorial Basis of the Two Nation Theory," in ibid., 37–38.

31. Ibid., 39.

32. Ibid., 40.

33. Cf. Roy Wallis and Steve Bruce, "Secularization: The Orthodox Model," in Steve Bruce, ed., *Religion and Modernization* (New York: Oxford University Press, 1992), 8–28.

34. Ernest Gellner, *Nations and Nationalism* (Ithaca, N.Y.: Cornell University Press, 1989).

35. Ernest Gellner, *Postmodernism, Reason and Religion* (London: Routledge, 1992), 4–5.

36. Ibid., 5–6.

37. Ibid., 18.

38. For recent critiques of the orthodox secularization theory, see Callum Brown, "A Revisionist Approach to Religious Change," in Bruce, ed., *Religion and Modernization*, 31–56; Peter Van Der Veer, *Religious Nationalism: Hindus and Muslims in India* (Berkeley: University of California Press, 1994), 13–18.

39. The classical statement of this view is contained in Karl Mannheim, *Man and Society in an Age of Reconstruction* (New York: Harcourt Brace, 1951), 125–43; for a restatement of this view, see Ernest Gellner, *Nations and Nationalism* (Ithaca, N.Y.: Cornell University Press, 1989).

3. THE ISLAMIC STATE

1. Gabriel Almond, Emmanuel Sivan, and Scott Appleby, "Fundamentalism: Genus and Species," in Martin E. Marty and Scott R. Appleby, eds., *Fundamentalisms Comprehended* (Chicago: University of Chicago Press, 1995), 399-424.

2. Gabriel Almond, Emmanuel Sivan, and Scott Appleby, "Examining the Cases," in ibid., 447-78.

3. As defined in the previous chapter.

4. Iqbal, presidential address, 1930, delivered to the annual All-India Session of the Muslim League, in Syed Abdul Vahid, ed., *Thoughts and Reflections of Iqbal* (Lahore: Sh. Muhammad Ashraf, 1964), 173.

5. Jinnah, presidential address, March 1940, in G. Allana, *Pakistan Movement: Historic Documents,* 2nd ed. (Karachi: Paradise Subscription Agency, 1968), 244.

6. Cf., for example, Jamalud Din Ahmad, *Muslim India and Its Goal,* Muslim League Publication no. 8 (Aligarh: Muslim University, 1940), 40.

7. Abul Ala Mawdudi, *al-Jihād fi'l-Islām,* 2nd ed. (1948), 89-90, translated in Aziz Ahmad and Gustave E. von Grunebaum, *Muslim Self-Statement in India and Pakistan* (Wiesbaden: Otto Harrowitz, 1970), 156.

8. Mawdudi, *Tahrīk-i-Islam kī Akhlāqī Bunyāden,* 5th ed. (1954), translated in ibid., 157.

9. Interviews.

10. Interviews.

11. Khalifa Abdul Hakim, *Islamic Ideology* (Lahore: Institute of Islamic Culture, 1965), 191-92.

12. Hakim, *Islamic Ideology,* 195.

13. Cf. Fazlur Rahman, "Some Reflections on the Reconstruction of Muslim Society in Pakistan," *Islamic Studies* (June 1967): 103.

14. Cf. Fazlur Rahman, "Economic Principles of Islam," *Islamic Studies* (March 1969): 1.

15. Interviews.

16. Mufti Muhammad Shafi, *Basic Principles of the Qur'ānic Constitution of the State* (Karachi: Dar al-Ulum, 1953), 3.

17. Al-Mawardi, *Ahkām al-Sultāniyya,* excerpt in John Alden Williams, *Themes of Islamic Civilization* (Berkeley: University of California Press, 1971), 86-87, and Ibn Jamaa, *Tahrīr al-Ahkām fi Tadbīr ahl al-Islām,* excerpt in ibid., 93.

18. Translated in ibid., 86-87.

19. Ibn Jamaa, *Tahrīr al-Ahkām,* excerpt translated in ibid., 93.

20. Shafi, *Qur'ānic Constitution,* 13.

21. See Abida Sultana, *Ahmadiyyat kiyā Hay awr Ahmadiyyūn ko Aqalliyyat kiyūn Qarār Diyā Jāe?* (Lahore: 1974), 38, 39.

22. The analysis of this paragraph has been generally influenced by Hamilton Gibb's "An Interpretation of Islamic History," in *Studies on the Civilization of Islam* (Boston: Beacon Press, 1962).

23. Shafi, *Qur'ānic Constitution,* 3.

24. Fazlur Rahman, "Implementation of the Islamic Concept of State in the Pakistan Milieu," *Islamic Studies* (September 1967): 215.

25. Ibid.

26. Fazlur Rahman, "Some Reflections on the Reconstruction of Muslim Society in Pakistan," *Islamic Studies* (June 1967): 116.

27. Muhammad Idris Kandhalwi, *Dastūr-i-Islām* (Lahore: Talimi Press, n.d.), 34.

28. Ibn Jamaa, *Tahrīr al-Ahkām,* excerpt translated in Williams, *Themes,* 93.

29. Excerpt translated in ibid., 87.

30. *Islāmī Manshūr* (Lahore: Kul Pakistan Jamiyyat Ulama-i-Islam, [1970]), 53.

31. Ibid.

32. See, for example, Government of West Pakistan, *The Constitution,* article 25.

33. Government of West Pakistan, *Report of the Commission on National Education* (Pakistan: Ministry of Education, January–August 1959), 10.

34. Cf. article 40 of the 1973 constitution with article 15 of the 1956 constitution.

35. Preamble to the 1956 constitution.

36. "Basic Principles of an Islamic State" (the resolution passed by the 1951 convention of the *ulamā* at Karachi), translated in William Theodore de Bary, ed., *Sources of Indian Tradition* (New York: Columbia University Press, 1958), 2:310.

37. Ibid.

38. Cf. Shafi, *Qurʾānic Constitution,* 12.

39. Cf. the Qurʾān (49:13).

40. Kandhalwi, *Dastūr-i-Islām,* 80–81.

41. Ibid.

42. Bernard Lewis, "Muslims, Christians, and Jews: The Dream of Coexistence," *New York Review of Books,* March 26, 1992, 49–50.

43. Article 18 of the 1956 constitution. Similar provisions are included in the 1962 and 1973 constitutions.

44. Hakim, *Islamic Ideology,* 205–6.

45. Interviews.

46. Shafi, *Rights of Non-Muslims,* 9; and Abul Ala Mawdudi, *Islamic Law and Constitution,* 2nd ed. (Karachi: Islamic Publications, 1960), 312–13.

47. "Basic Principles of an Islamic State," translated in de Bary, *Sources,* 2:309–12.

48. Cf. Mawdudi, *Islamic Law and Constitution,* 265.

49. Mawlana Shabbir Ahmad Uthmani, speaking to the Pakistan Constitutional Assembly, quoted by E. I. J. Rosenthal, *Islam in the Modern National State* (Cambridge: Cambridge University Press, 1965), 211.

50. Article 17 in the 1956 constitution. Similar provisions are included in the 1962 and 1973 constitutions.

51. Our interviews indicated that such an exception represents the sentiments of many modernist Muslims in Pakistan.

52. "Basic Principles of an Islamic State," translated in de Bary, *Sources,* 2:310–11.

53. See, for example, Shafi, *Rights of Non-Muslim Citizens,* 8.

54. Ghulam Ahmad Parwez, *Islam: A Challenge to Religion* (Lahore: 1968), 265.

55. Franz Rosenthal, *The Muslim Concept of Freedom* (Leiden: 1960), 122.

56. "Basic Principles of an Islamic State," translated in de Bary, *Sources,* 2:131.

57. Interviews.

58. Fazlur Rahman, "Some Reflections on the Reconstruction of Muslim Society in Pakistan," *Islamic Studies* (June 1967): 103.

59. Interviews; see also, for example, Kandhalwi, *Dastūr-i-Islām,* 23-30.

60. Kandhalwi, *Dastūr-i-Islām,* 25-30; cf. al-Mawardi, *Ahkām al-Sultāniyya,* excerpt translated in Williams, *Themes,* 85.

61. See the "Views," reproduced in Leonard Binder, *Religion and Politics in Pakistan* (Berkeley: University of California Press, 1963), appendixes A and B.

62. See "Views," in Binder, *Religion and Politics,* appendix A, 387-89.

63. Kandhalwi, *Dastūr-i-Islām,* 23-24.

64. Cf. ibid.

65. Ibid., 25-26.

66. Ibid., 29-30.

67. Mawdudi, *Islamic Law and Constitution,* 260-61.

68. Interviews.

69. Shafi, *Qur'ānic Constitution.*

70. See "Views," in Binder, *Religion and Politics,* appendix A, 391-92.

71. "Principles of an Islamic State," translated in de Bary, *Sources,* 2:311.

72. Al-Mawardi, *Ahkām al-Sultāniyya,* translated in Williams, *Themes,* 84-86.

73. See, for example, Dr. Qureshi's speech (1950) in de Bary, *Sources,* 2:317.

74. Cf. Ibn Jamaa, *Tahrīr al-Ahkām fī ahl al-Islām,* excerpt translated in Williams, *Themes,* 90.

75. Ibid.

76. Ibid., 90.

77. Interviews.

78. "Basic Principles of an Islamic State," translated in de Bary, *Sources,* 2:311.

79. Ibid.

80. Interview; cf. Kandhalwi, *Dastūr-i-Islam,* 69.

81. *Islāmī Manshūr,* Kul Pakistan Jamiyyat Ulama-i-Islam (1969), 45-46; cf. Mawdudi, *Islamic Law and Constitution,* 242-43.

82. Mawdudi, *Islamic Law and Constitution,* 242-43.

83. Interview.

84. Interviews.

85. Interviews.

86. Cf. Shafi, *Qur'ānic Constitution,* 9-10.

87. See, for example, Abul Ala Mawdudi, "Pakistan men Islāmī Qānūn kī Amalī Tadābīr," *Chirāgh-i-Rāh Islāmī* (Qānūn number, 1958): 254-57.

88. Kandhalwi, *Dastūr,* 80-81.

89. Interviews.

90. Cf., for example, Mufti Muhammad Shafi, "Bahth wa Nazar: Islāmī Qānūn awr Tamīr-i-Nau," *Chirāgh-i-Rāh* (July–August 1958): 272–73.

91. For example, Qureshi, "Bahth wa Nazar," ibid., 290.

92. Mufti Muhammad Shafi, "Bahth wa Nazar," ibid., 273.

93. Ibid.

94. See, for example, Mawlana Amin Ahsan Islahi, "Bahth wa Nazar," ibid., 283.

95. Ibid., 286.

96. Shah Waliallah, "Iqd al-Jīd fī Ahkām al-Ijtihād w' al-Taqlīd," trans. M. Daud Rahbar in *Muslim World* (October 1955): 347.

97. Ibid., 350.

98. Cf. Mawlana Zafar Ahmad Ansari, "Bahth wa Nazar," *Chirāgh-i-Rāh,* 296; Amin Ahsan Islahi, "Bahth wa Nazar," ibid., 284; Abul Ala Mawdudi, "Bahth wa Nazar," ibid., 303.

99. Mufti Muhammad Shafi, "Bahth wa Nazar," ibid., 271–73; Ansari, "Bahth wa Nazar," ibid., 298; and Mawdudi, *Islamic Law and Constitution,* 80–81.

100. Interviews.

101. Interviews.

102. Interviews.

103. Reproduced in "Views," Binder, *Religion and Politics,* appendix A, 396; cf. Shafi, *Qur'ānic Constitution,* 5.

104. See, for example, Shafi, "Bahth wa Nazar," *Chirāgh-i-Rāh,* 273.

105. Interviews.

106. Interviews.

107. See Appendix C, Table C.17.

108. See, for example, articles 6 and 199–205 of the 1962 constitution.

109. Sir Muhammad Iqbal, *The Reconstruction of Religious Thought in Islam* (Lahore: Sh. Muhammad Ashraf, 1962), 173–74.

110. Ibid., 176.

111. Interviews.

112. Ishtiaq Husayn Qureshi (from the second All-Pakistan Political Science Conference Proceedings, 1951), reproduced in de Bary, *Sources,* 2:321.

113. Interviews.

114. Interviews.

115. Shafi, *Qur'ānic Constitution,* 6.

116. Rahman, "Implementation of the Islamic Concept of State in the Pakistani Milieu," *Islamic Studies* (September 1967): 206. Italics are Dr. Rahman's.

117. John L. Esposito and John O. Voll, *Islam and Democracy* (New York: Oxford University Press, 1996), 6–7.

4. ISLAM AND ECONOMIC ORIENTATIONS

1. For an assessment of the role of Islamic banking, see Clement H. Moore, "Islamic Banks: Financial and Political Intermediation in Arab Countries," *Orient* 29 (1988): 45–57.

2. Shah Aziz-ur-Rahman speaking in the National Assembly on June 24, 1965; see *Pakistan Times*, June 25, 1965.

3. These three categories were achieved by combining and collating answers to question 20 (VAR236, VAR237, and VAR238). See Appendixes A and B.

4. Muhammad Ismail Azad, "Islāmī Socialism awr A. K. Sumar," *Nusrat*, March 8, 1970, 15.

5. Ibid.

6. Muhammad Hanif Ramey, "Islāmī Socialism," *Nusrat* (September-October 1966): 3.

7. Ibid., 8; see also Faqir M. Bugti, "Islām kā Maʿāshī Nizām," *Nusrat* (October 1966): 135-36.

8. Cf. Ramey, "Islāmī Socialism," 1; Bugti, "Islām kā Maʿāshī Nizām," 131-32.

9. Muhammad Uthman Siddiqi, "Islāmī Socialism," a lecture delivered at the Pakistan Council, Rawalpindi, on September 24, 1966, published in *Nusrat* (October 1966): 7.

10. Bugti, "Islām kā Maʿāshī Nizām," 149; cf. Ghulam Ahmad Parwez, *Islam: A Challenge to Religion* (Lahore: 1968), 28-29.

11. Parwez, *Islam*, 28-29.

12. Ibid.

13. Ibid., 35.

14. Bugti, "Islām kā Maʿāshī Nizām," 132.

15. Ibid., 142, 145.

16. Ibid., 145.

17. For some examples of the argument, see Sami Hanna, *Arab Socialism* (Salt Lake City: University of Utah Press, 1969).

18. Ramey, "Islāmī Socialism," 2.

19. Ibid., 1-3.

20. Cf. Ghulam Dastgir Rashid, *Islāmī Ishtrākiyyat* (Lahore: Al-Bayan, n.d.), 8.

21. Shaikh Iftikhar Ahmad, "Islām, Sarmāyadārī, Yā Socialism," *Nusrat* (October 1966): 212-213.

22. For example, Siddiqi, "Islāmī Socialism," *Chatān,* September 12, 1966, reprinted in *Nusrat* (October 1966): 77.

23. Cf. Rashid, *Islāmī Ishtrākiyyat*, 7-8.

24. Parwez, "Islāmī Socialism," *Nusrat* (September 1966): 75.

25. For example, Mawlana Ubaydullah Sindhi and the poet Hasrat Mohani.

26. For example, Prime Minister Liaqat Ali Khan and Professor Khalifa Abdul Hakim.

27. Cf., for example, Ramey, "Islāmī Socialism," 4-7.

28. Ibid.

29. Government of West Pakistan, *Statistical Pocketbook of Pakistan* (Karachi: Manager of Publications, 1969), 200-201.

30. Ibid., 94-97.

31. *Socialism Kufr Hay: Akābir Ulamā kā Muttafiqa Faysla* (Karachi: Nazim Dawat al-Haq, [1970]).

32. Ibid.

33. Ibid., 6.

34. Cf. ibid.

35. See, for example, twelve leading *ulamā's* advice to the Muslims to hold aloof from secular ideologies in *Dawn*, February 10, 1969; for the Jamaat's view, see the next section.

36. Mawlana Abdul Hamid Badayuni, comp., *Ishtrākiyyat awr Zirāatī Musāwāt* (Karachi: Muhammad Abid al-Qadiri, Nazim Dar al-Tasnif, 1949).

37. Ibid., 38-49.

38. The Jamiyyat is one of the two major associations of the *ulamā* in Pakistan. Both of these associations bear the same name, and both also act as political parties.

39. This was one of the frequent answers that the *ulamā* gave during our survey.

40. See, for example, M. Halpern, *Politics of Social Change in the Middle East and North Africa* (Princeton, N.J.: Princeton University Press, 1964), 5-8.

41. See *makāis* in the *Encyclopedia of Islam*.

42. Mawlana M. Idris Kandhalwi, *Dastūr-i-Islām* (Lahore: Talimi Press, [1968]), 176.

43. H. A. R. Gibb, "An Interpretation of Islamic History," *Studies on the Civilization of Islam* (Boston: Beacon Press, 1962), 4.

44. One aspect of the campaign was publication of numerous booklets, pamphlets, and magazine articles criticizing socialism, designed for circulation among working students as well as the general public.

45. Although Abul Ala Mawdudi was not formally educated at any institution of traditional Islamic learning, his followers honored him with the traditional title Mawlānā, "Our Master," reserved generally for respected traditional *ulamā* with *madrasa* credentials.

46. Abul Ala Mawdudi, *Islāmī Nazm-i-Maʿīshat ke Usūl awr Maqāsid* (Lahore: Islamic Publishers, Ltd., n.d.), 6; and Mawdudi, *Islām awr Jadīd Maāshī Nazariyyāt* (Lahore: Islamic Publishers, Ltd., 1959), 119-21.

47. Mawdudi, *Islām awr Jadīd Maāshī Nazariyyāt*, 119-121.

48. Ibid., 121-22.

49. Ibid.

50. Ibid.

51. Mawdudi, *Islāmī Nazm-i-Maʿīshat*, 7-8.

52. Ibid.

53. Ibid.

54. Ibid.

55. Ibid.

56. Ibid.

57. Ibid.

58. Ibid., 10.

59. Mawdudi, *Masala Milkiyyāt-i-Zamīn* (Lahore: Islamic Publishers, Ltd., 1950), 90.

60. Mawdudi, *Islām kā Iqtisādī Nizām* (Karachi: Idara Matbuat Mudafat, n.d.), 3-4.

61. Mawdudi, *Masala Milkiyyat-i-Zamīn*, 107-8.

62. Ibid., 105-6.

63. Ibid.

64. Mawdudi, *Islām awr Jadīd Maāshī Nazariyyāt*, 123.

65. Qur'ān (53:39).

66. Naim Siddiqi, *Islām awr Shakhsī Milkiyyat* (Karachi: Maktaba Chiragh-i-Rah, 1953), 47-54.

67. Mawdudi, *Islāmī Nazm-i-Ma'īshat*, 9, 23.

68. Ibid., 12-13.

69. Ibid., 25-27.

70. Ibid., 111.

71. Ibid., 110.

72. Ibid., 99-118.

73. Ibid.

74. Khurshid Ahmad, "Socialism Yā Islām," *Chirāgh-i-Rāh* (December 1967): 158.

75. Ibid., 158-59.

76. Cf. Mufti Muhammad Shafi, *Islām kā Nizām-i-Taqsīm-i-Dawlat* (East Pakistan: Anjuman Ishaat Islam, n.d.), 39-44.

77. Mawdudi, *Islāmī Nazm-i-Ma'īshat*, 12-15.

78. Fazlur Rahman, "Economic Principles of Islam," *Islamic Studies* (March 1969): 7.

79. Ibid., 6.

80. Ibid.

81. Ibid., 7.

82. See, for example, the views of Hanif Ramey and Faqir Bugti, discussed above.

83. Rahman, "Economic Principles," *Islamic Studies* (March 1969): 7.

84. Ibid.

85. Ibid., 4-5.

86. Ibid., 5.

87. Ibid., 6.

88. Ibid., 5.

89. Ibid.

90. Ibid., 6.

91. Ibid., 1.

92. Ibid., 3.

93. Ibid., 3-4.

94. Ibid., 3.

95. Mawdudi, *Masala Milkiyyat-i-Zamīn*, 109; Siddiqi, *Islām awr Shakhsī Milkiyyat*, 4-45, 75-79.

96. Cf. "Jamaat-i-Islami kā Maʿāshī Progrām," *Asia* (March 1969): 12; Mawlana Mawdudi's televised address, *Dawn*, November 4, 1970.

97. "Jamaat-i-Islami kā Maʿāshī Progrām," 13; Mawdudi's televised address.

98. See, for example, Mawdudi, *Masala Milkiyyat-i-Zamīn*, 101-8.

99. Muhammad Ismail Azad, "Jamaat-i-Islami kā Tāza Dastūr," *Nusrat*, March 25, 1970, 25-34.

100. "Jamaat-i-Islami kā Maʿāshī Progrām," 12.

101. Mawdudi's address; "Jamaat-i-Islami kā Maʿāshī Progrām," 12-13.

102. Mawdudi's address.

103. Timur Kuran, "Islamic Economics and the Islamic Subeconomy," *Journal of Economic Perspectives* 9, no. 4 (Fall 1995): 155.

104. For a sample of writings by the exponents of Islamic economics, see Khurshid Ahmad, ed., *Studies in Islamic Economics* (Ann Arbor, Mich.: New Era Publications, 1980); Muhammad Abdul Mannan, *Islamic Economics: Theory and Practice* (Boulder, Colo.: Westview Press, 1987).

105. See especially Timur Kuran, "The Economic Impact of Islamic Fundamentalism," in Martin E. Marty and Scott R. Appleby, eds., *Fundamentalisms and the State: Remaking Polities, Economies, and Militance* (Chicago: University of Chicago Press, 1993), 302-42; Timur Kuran, "The Discontents of Islamic Economic Morality," *American Economists Review* 86, no. 2 (May 1996): 438.

106. See, for example, Michel G. Nehme, "Saudi Development Plans between Capitalist and Islamic Values," *Middle Eastern Studies* 30, no. 3 (July 1994): 632.

5. CONCLUSION

1. Yvonne Haddad, John Voll, and John Esposito, eds., *The Contemporary Islamic Revival: A Critical Survey and Bibliography* (New York: Greenwood Press, 1991).

2. Yvonne Haddad and John Esposito, eds., *The Islamic Revival since 1988: A Critical Survey and Bibliography* (Westport, Conn.: Greenwood Press, 1997).

3. Amos Perlmutter, "Wishful Thinking about Islamic Fundamentalism," *Washington Post*, January 22, 1992, C7.

4. John L. Esposito, *The Islamic Threat: Myth or Reality*, 2nd ed. (New York: Oxford University Press, 1995), 77.

5. Bernard Lewis, "Islam and Liberal Democracy," *Atlantic Monthly* (February 1993): 90-91.

6. Bruce Lawrence, *Defenders of God* (San Francisco: Harper and Row, 1989), 93.

7. Martin E. Marty and Scott R. Appleby, eds., *Fundamentalisms Observed* (Chicago: University of Chicago Press, 1991), viii.

8. Ibid.

9. Ibid.

10. Ibid., ix-x.

11. Ibid., ix.

12. Ibid., x.

13. Ibid., xi.

14. Lawrence, *Defenders of God*, 91.

15. Gabriel A. Almond, Emmanuel Sivan, and R. Scott Appleby, "Fundamentalism: Genus and Species," in Martin E. Marty and Scott R. Appleby, eds., *Fundamentalisms Comprehended* (Chicago: University of Chicago Press, 1995). See, for example, the charts on pages 410 and 414.

16. Gabriel A. Almond, Emmanuel Sivan, and R. Scott Appleby, "Explaining Fundamentalisms," in ibid., 426.

17. Of these six scales, the scale on national identity was based on two questions (see Appendix A: The Questionnaire, questions 1 and 2); the scale on politics was based on two (questions 7 and 11); the scale on law was based on one (question 13); the scale on economy was based on one (question 20); the scale on morality was based on three (questions 27, 28, and 33); and the scale on the extent of expectation for guidance from the Qur'ān and *sunna* was based on one (question 40).

18. John Voll, "Fundamentalism in the Sunni Arab World," in Marty and Appleby, eds., *Fundamentalisms Observed*, 347.

19. Leonard Binder, *Islamic Liberalism* (Chicago: University of Chicago Press, 1988), 243-44.

20. Ibid., 4.

21. Lewis, "Islam and Liberal Democracy," 89-98; John L. Esposito and John O. Voll, *Islam and Democracy* (New York: Oxford University Press, 1996).

22. Lewis, "Islam and Liberal Democracy," 96.

23. John L. Esposito and James P. Piscatori, "Democratization and Islam," *Middle East Journal* 45 (Summer 1991): 439.

24. Lewis, "Islam and Liberal Democracy," 97.

25. See, for example, Morton Zuckerman, "Beware of Religious Stalinist," *U.S. News and World Report,* March 22, 1993, 80.

26. Said Arjomand, "Unity and Diversity in Islamic Fundamentalism," in Marty and Appleby, eds., *Fundamentalisms Comprehended*, 188.

27. Ibid., 190.

28. Esposito and Voll, *Islam and Democracy*, 195-96.

29. Daniel Bell, *The End of Ideology*, rev. ed. (Cambridge, Mass.: Harvard University Press, 1988), 400.

30. See, for example, R. Steven Humphrey, "The Contemporary Resurgence in the Context of Modern Islam," in Ali E. Hillal Dessouki, ed., *Islamic Resurgence in the Arab World* (New York: Praeger, 1982), 67-82; Said Arjomand, "The Emergence of Islamic Political Ideologies," in James Beckford and Thomas Luckmann, eds., *The Changing Face of Religion* (London: Sage Publications, 1989), 109-23.

31. Lawrence, *Defenders of God*, 83.

32. Bell, *The End of Ideology*, 400.

33. Philip E. Converse, "The Nature of Belief Systems in Mass Publics," in David Apter, ed., *Ideology and Discontent* (New York: Free Press, 1964), 207.

34. Ibid., 208.

35. Erik Erikson, *Young Man Luther: A Study in Psychoanalysis and History* (London: 1958), 20.

36. Ibid., 69.

37. Cf., for example, Khurshid Ahmad, "Islamic Ideology," *Chirāgh-i-Rāh* (December 1960): 32.

38. Ibid.

39. Bell, *The End of Ideology*, 400.

40. Mawlana Abul Ala Mawdudi's speech at the University of Punjab, December 1965, published under the title *Islāmī Nazm-i-Maʿīshat ke Usūl awr Maqāsid* (Lahore: Islamic Publishers Ltd., 1969), 28.

41. *Socialism Kufr Hay: Akābir Ulamā kā Muttafiqa Faysla* (Karachi: Nazim Dawat al-Haq, 1970).

42. John O. Voll, *Islam: Continuity and Change in the Modern World*, 2nd ed. (Syracuse, N.Y.: Syracuse University Press, 1994), 387.

43. Ibid., 387.

44. Ibid., 387–88.

45. Ibid., 389.

46. Ibid., 389.

47. Ernest Gellner, "Fundamentalism as a Comprehensive System: Soviet Marxism and Islamic Fundamentalism Compared," in Marty and Appleby, eds., *Fundamentalisms Comprehended*, 283.

48. Ibid., 284.

49. Ibid.

50. Ibid.

51. Ibid.

52. Lawrence, *Defenders of God*, 2.

53. Gabriel A. Almond, Emmanuel Sivan, and R. Scott Appleby, "Fundamentalism: Genus and Species," in Marty and Appleby, eds., *Fundamentalisms Comprehended*, 402.

54. See, for example, Rhys H. Williams, "Movement Dynamics and Social Change: Transforming Fundamentalist Ideology and Organizations," in Martin E. Marty and Scott R. Appleby, eds., *Accounting for Fundamentalisms* (Chicago: University of Chicago Press, 1994), 785–89; Gabriel A. Almond, Emmanuel Sivan, and R. Scott Appleby, "Fundamentalism: Genus and Species," in Marty and Appleby, eds., *Fundamentalisms Comprehended*, 403–5.

55. Gabriel A. Almond, Emmanuel Sivan, and R. Scott Appleby, "Explaining Fundamentalisms," in Marty and Appleby, eds., *Fundamentalisms Comprehended*, 441.

56. Lawrence, *Defenders of God,* 83.

57. Daniel Lerner, *The Passing of Traditional Society* (London: Collier-Macmillan, Ltd., 1958), 45.

58. Ernest Gellner, "Fundamentalism as a Comprehensive System: Soviet Marxism and Islamic Fundamentalism Compared," in Marty and Appleby, eds., *Fundamentalisms Comprehended,* 278.

59. Ernest Gellner, *Postmodernism, Reason and Religion* (London: Routledge, 1992), 18.

Bibliography

I. SOURCE MATERIAL

A. BOOKS AND ARTICLES

Ahmad, Khurshid. *Islamic Resurgence: Challenges, Directions and Future Perspectives: A Roundtable with Prof. Khurshid Ahmad.* Ed. Ibrahim M. Abu-Rabi. Islamabad: Institute of Policy Studies; [Tampa, Fla.]: World and Islam Studies Enterprise, 1995.

———, ed. *Studies in Islamic Economics.* Ann Arbor, Mich.: New Era Publications, 1980.

Ahmad, Shaikh Iftikhar. "Islām, Sarmāyadārī, Yā Socialism." *Nusrat* (October 1966).

Ahmad, Syed Moizuddin. "The Quest for Identity." In Waheeduz Zaman, ed., *The Quest for Identity.* Islamabad: Islamabad University Press, 1974.

Ahmed, Ishtiaq. *The Concept of an Islamic State in Pakistan: An Analysis of Ideological Controversies.* Pakistan ed. Lahore: Vanguard, 1991.

Akhtar, Muhammad Shafi. *"Hamārā Thaqāfatī Wirtha."* In Waheeduz Zaman, ed., *The Quest for Identity.* Islamabad: Islamabad University Press, 1974.

Al-Husayni, Mukhtar Ahmad. *Tadhkirah Jamīyyat-i-Ulamā-i-Islam, Pakistan.* Lahore: Maktabah Talim-i-Hayat, n.d.

Ali, Shawkat. *Jamhūriyyat kā Wāhid Rāsta.* Lahore: National Awami Party, n.d.

Allana, Ghulam Ali, ed. and comp. *Pakistan Movement: Historic Documents.* Karachi: Paradise Subscription Agency, 1st ed., 1967; 2nd ed., 1968.

Ansari, Muhammad Zafar Ahmad. *Our Constitutional Problem: The Ideological Factor.* Karachi: Afaq Publications, December 23–28, 1955.

Arberry, A. J. *Aspects of Islamic Civilization: The Muslim World Depicted through Its Literature.* Ann Arbor: University of Michigan Press, 1967.

Asad, Muhammad. *Principles of State and Government in Islam.* N.p., n.d.

Azad, Muhammad Ismail. "Islāmī Socialism awr A. K. Sumar." *Nusrat,* March 8, 1970.

———. "Jamaat-i-Islami kā Tāza Dastūr." *Nusrat,* March 25, 1970.

Aziz, K. *The Historical Background of Pakistan, 1857–1947.* An Annotated Digest of Source Material. Karachi: Pakistan Institute of International Affairs, 1970.

Badayuni, Mawlana Abdul Hamid. *Ishtrākiyyat awr Zirāatī Musāwāt.* Karachi: Muhammad Abid al-Qadiri, Nazim Dar al-Tasnif, 1949.

Barelvi, Mahmud. *Islamic Ideology and Its Impact on Our Times.* Karachi: N.p., 1967.

"Basic Principles of an Islamic State." Translated in William Theodore de Bary, ed., *Sources of Indian Tradition.* 2:309–12. New York: Columbia University Press, 1958.

Bhutto, Zulfiqar Ali. *Islāmī Socialism awr Pakistan.* Lahore: Baligh-ud-Din Javaid, April 1969.

Bugti, Faqir M. "Islām kā Maāshī Nizām." *Nusrat* (October 1966).

Bureau of National Reconstruction, East Pakistan. *Our Thoughts: A Collection of Articles Read at the Seminars Held at Different Places of the Province.* Dacca: Bureau of National Reconstruction, n.d.

———. *Pakistani Nationhood: A Collection of Papers Read at the National Seminar, 1961.* Dacca: Bureau of National Reconstruction, 1962.

Bureau of National Reconstruction, West Pakistan. *National Reconstruction: A Brief Report of the B.N.R. 1965–66.* Lahore: Bureau of National Reconstruction, 1965–66.

Chapra, M. Umer. *Islam and the Economic Challenge.* Leicester, U.K.: Islamic Foundation; Herndon, Va.: International Institute of Islamic Thought, 1992.

Chaudhry, Muhammad Sharif. *Taxation in Islam and Modern Taxes.* Lahore: Impact Publication International, 1992.

Choudhari, G. W. *Constitution of Pakistan, Documents and Speeches.* Dacca: Green Book House, 1967.

Choudhury, Masudul Alam. *Contributions to Islamic Economic Theory: A Study in Social Economics.* Houndmills, Hampshire, U.K.: Macmillan, 1986.

———. *The Principles of Islamic Political Economy: A Methodological Enquiry.* New York: St. Martin's Press, 1992.

Chronology of Important Events during Six Years of the Revolutionary Government in Pakistan, 1958–1964. Karachi: Pakistan Publications, 1961.

Court of Inquiry Constituted under Punjab Act III of the Inquiry into Punjab Disturbances of 1953. *Munir Report.* Lahore: Government of Punjab, 1954.

Dar, Bashir Ahmad. *Why Pakistan?* Lahore: New Era Publications, 1946.

De Bary, William Theodore, ed. *Sources of Indian Tradition.* 2 vols. New York: Columbia University Press, 1958.

Dobbin, Christine E. *Basic Documents in the Development of Modern India and Pakistan, 1835–1947.* London: D. van Nostrand, 1970.

Fahim Khan, M. *Essays in Islamic Economics.* Leicester, U.K.: Islamic Foundation, 1995.

Faruqi, Ijaz. *Pakistan: A Crisis in the Renaissance of Islam.* Lahore: Sang-e-Meel Publication, 1991.

Faruqi, Muhammad Tahir, and Khatir Ghaznavi. *Pakistan men Urdu: Urdu Zabān wa Adab kā Pakistanī Dawr, 1944–1964.* Peshawar: University Book Agency, 1965.

Faruqi, Mujtaba. *Islam, Socialism kiyā Hay? Qur'ān awr Hadīth kī Rawshnī men.* Karachi: Educational Press, 1970.

——. *Socialism ke Khilāf 113 Ulamā ke Fatwe kā Jawāb.* Karachi: Millet Press, June 1970.

Faruqi, Ziya-al-Hasan. *The Deoband School and the Demand for Pakistan.* Lahore: Sh. Muhammad Ashraf, 1964.

Fatimi, Qudratullah. "The Territorial Basis of the Two Nation Theory." In Waheeduz Zaman, ed., *The Quest for Identity.* Islamabad: Islamabad University Press, 1974.

Ferdinand, Klaus, and Mehdi Mozaffari, eds. *Isl█: State and Society.* London: Curzon Press; Riverdale, Md.: Riverdale Co., █88.

Ghayasuddin, M., ed. *The Impact of Nationalism█n the Muslim World.* London: Open Press, Al-Hoda Publishers, 1986.

Government of West Pakistan. *Census of Pakistan 1961.* Vol. 4: *Pakistan, Non-Agricultural Lahore.* Vol. 5: *East Pakistan.* Vol. 6: *West Pakistan (2 parts).* Karachi: Manager of Publications, Government of Pakistan, 1964.

——. *The Constitution of the Islamic Republic of Pakistan.* Pakistan: Ministry of Law, March 2, 1956.

——. *Report of the Commission on National Education.* Pakistan: Ministry of Education, January–August 1959.

——. *Report of the Seminar on Greater National Integration.* Held under the auspices of the Bureau of National Reconstruction. Lahore: Government Printing, 1963.

——. *Statistical Pocketbook of Pakistan.* Karachi: Manager of Publications, 1969.

——. *Twenty Years of Pakistan in Statistics.* Karachi: Manager of Publications, Government of Pakistan, 1968.

Haim, Sylvia G., ed. *Arab Nationalism: An Anthology.* Berkeley: University of California Press, 1962.

Hakim, Khalifa Abdul. *Islam and Communism.* 4th impression. Lahore: Institute of Islamic Culture, 1951.

——. *Islamic Ideology.* 3rd rev. ed. Lahore: Institute of Islamic Culture, 1951.

Hanna, Sami, and George H. Gardener. *Arab Socialism: A Documentary Survey.* Utah: University of Utah Press, 1970.

Hasan-uz-zaman, S. M. *Economic Functions of an Islamic State: The Early Experience.* Leicester: Islamic Foundation, 1990.

Hashim, Abul. *As I See It.* Dacca: Islamic Academy, 1965.

——. *Integration of Pakistan.* Dacca: Sayyid Mujibullah, n.d.

Hashimi, Yusuf Abbas. "The Quest for Identity." In Waheeduz Zaman, ed., *The Quest for Identity.* Islamabad: Islamabad University Press, 1974.

Husayn, Yusuf, ed. *Selected Documents from the Aligarh Archives.* New York: Asia Publishing House, 1967.

Hussain, Dr. Mahmud. "Welcoming Address." In *Pakistani Nationhood: A Collection of Papers Read at the National Seminar, at Dacca, in 1961.* Dacca: Bureau of National Reconstruction, [1962].

Ikram, Shaikh Muhammad. *Mawj-i-Kawthar.* Lahore: Ferozesons Ltd., 1954.

Iqbal, Afzal. *Islamisation of Pakistan.* Lahore: Vanguard Books, 1986.

Iqbal, Javid. *The Ideology of Pakistan and Its Implementation.* Lahore: Sh. Ghulam Ali and Sons, 1959.

Iqbal, Muhammad. *Mysteries of Selflessness.* Trans. A. J. Arberry. London: John Murray, 1953.

———. *Poems from Iqbal.* Trans. V. G. Kiernan. London: Murray, 1955.

———. *The Reconstruction of Religious Thought in Islam.* Lahore: Sh. Muhammad Ashraf, 1962.

———. *Speeches and Statements of Iqbal.* Comp. Shamloo. 2nd ed. Lahore: N.p., 1948.

Iqbal, Munawar, ed. *Distributive Justice and Need Fulfillment in an Islamic Economy.* Rev. ed. Islamabad: International Institute of Islamic Economics, International Islamic University; Leicester, U.K.: Islamic Foundation, 1988.

Irfan, Arif. *Ulamā ke Liye Lamha-i-Fikr.* Lahore: Dar al-Fikr, n.d.

Islāmī Manshūr. Lahore: Kul Pakistan Jamiyyat Ulama-i-Islam, [1970].

Ismail, Muhammad. *Critical Analysis of Capitalism: Socialism and Islamic Economic Order.* Lahore: Oriental Publications, 1989.

Jeffrey, Arthur, ed. *Reader on Islam.* Passages from Standard Arabic Writings Illustrative of the Beliefs and Practices of Muslims. The Hague: Mouton and Co., 1960.

Jinnah, M. A. "Presidential Address." March 1940. In G. Allana, ed., *Pakistan Movement: Historic Documents.* Karachi: Paradise Subscription Agency, 1968.

Jinnah, Quaid-i-Azam Muhammad Ali. *Speeches as Governor General of Pakistan, 1947–1948.* Karachi: Pakistan Publications, 1950.

Kabir, Hafizullah. *Outlines of Islamic Ideology.* East Pakistan: Noakhali Puthigar, 1963.

Kamali, M. H. *Principles of Islamic Jurisprudence.* Rev. ed. Cambridge: Islamic Text Society, 1991.

Kandhalwi, Muhammad Idris. *Dastūr-i-Islam.* Lahore: Talimi Press, 1968.

Karpat, Kemal H., ed. *Political and Social Thought in the Contemporary Middle East.* New York: Praeger Publishers, 1968.

Khaliquzzaman, Ch. *Pathway to Pakistan.* Lahore: N.p., 1961.

Khan, Javed Ahmad, ed. *Islamic Economics and Finance: A Bibliography.* London and New York: Mansell Publishing, 1995.

Khan, Liaqat Ali. *Pakistan: The Heart of Asia.* Speeches in the United States and Canada. Cambridge, Mass., 1950.

Khan, Mehr Muhammad Nawaz. *Islamic and Other Economic Systems.* Lahore: Islamic Book Service, 1989.

Khan, Muhammad Akram. *An Introduction to Islamic Economics.* Islamabad: International Institute of Islamic Thought and Institute of Islamic Studies, 1994.

Khan, Muhammad Ayub. *Friends Not Masters.* Karachi: Oxford University Press, 1967.

———. *Ideology and Objectives.* Rawalpindi: Ferozesons Ltd., 1968.

Kritzeck, James. *Modern Islamic Literature from 1800 to the Present.* New York: Holt, Rinehart and Winston, 1970.

Landen, Robert G. *The Emergence of the Modern Middle East.* Selected readings. New York: Van Nostrand Reinhold Co., 1970.

Mahmood, Sohail. *The Concept of an Islamic State.* Lahore: Progressive Publishers, 1989.

Mahmud, Mawlana Mufti, and Mawlana Ghulam Ghaus Hazarvi. *Assembliyon ke andar Alimāna awr Mujāhidāna Taqrīren.* Lahore: Daftar Jamiyyat-i-Ulamā-i-Islam, n.d.

Matters of Moment: Fourteen Essays on Literature, Culture and the Nation. Dacca: Bureau of National Reconstruction, [1962].

Maudoodi, Syed Abul Ala. *Islamic State: Political Writings of Maulana Sayyid Abul Ala Maudoodi.* Comp. and trans. Mazheruddin Siddiqi. Karachi: Islamic Research Academy, 1986.

Mawdudi, Abul Ala. "Pakistan men Islāmī Qānūn kī Amalī Tadābīr." *Chirāgh-i-Rāh Islāmī* (Qānūn number, 1958).

———. *Tahrīk-i-Islam kī Akhlāqī Bunyāden.* 5th ed. 1954. Translated in Aziz Ahmad and Gustave E. von Grunebaum, eds., *Muslim Self-Statement in India and Pakistan.* Wiesbaden: Otto Harrowitz, 1970.

Mawdudi, Sayyid Abul Ala. *Guidelines in the Conflict of Ideologies.* Trans. Kaukab Siddiqi. N.p., n.d.

———. *Islām awr Jadīd Maāshī Nazariyyāt.* Lahore: Islamic Publishers, Ltd., December 1959.

———. *Islamic Law and Constitution.* Ed. Khurshid Ahmad. Karachi and Lahore: Islamic Publications, 1955.

———. *Islāmī Nazm-i-Maʿīshat ke Usūl awr Maqāsid.* Lahore: Islamic Publishers Ltd., n.d.

———. *Islām kā Iqtisādī Nizām.* Karachi: Idara Matbuat Mudafat, n.d.

———. *Islām kā Maʿāshī Nasb al-Ayn.* Karachi: Jamaat-i-Islami, n.d.

———. *Islām kā Siyāsī Nazariyya.* N.p., n.d.

———. *al-Jihād fi'l-Islām.* 2nd ed. 1948. Translated in Aziz Ahmad and Gustave E. von Grunebaum, eds., *Muslim Self-Statement in India and Pakistan.* Wiesbaden: Otto Harrowitz, 1970.

———. *Masala Milkiyyat-i-Zamīn.* Lahore: Islamic Publishers Ltd., 1950.

———. *Sarmāyadārī, Socialism, awr Islam.* Karachi: Idara Matbuat Mudafat, n.d.

———. *Tahrīk-i-Azādi-Hind awr Musalmān.* Lahore: Islamic Publishers Ltd., 1964.

McNeill, William H., and M. R. Waldman, eds. *The Islamic World.* New York: Oxford University Press, 1973.

Moten, A. Rashid. *Political Science: An Islamic Perspective.* Houndmills, Hampshire, U.K.: Macmillan Press; New York: St. Martin's Press, 1996.

Mujahid, Shariful. "Basis of Pakistani Nationhood." In *Pakistani Nationhood: A Collection of Papers Read at the National Seminar, at Dacca, in 1961.* Dacca: Bureau of National Reconstruction, [1962].

Munawar Iqbal, ed. *Distributive Justice and Need Fulfillment in an Islamic Economy.* Islamabad: International Institute of Islamic Economics. International Islamic University, [1986].

Mutamar al-Alam-al-Islami. *Islam: Some Economic Aspects.* Comp. the Secretariat. Karachi: Umma Publishing House, n.d.

———. *Studies on Commonwealth of Muslim Countries.* Karachi: Umma Publishing House, n.d.

Naqvi, Syed Nawab Haider. *Islam, Economics, and Society.* London and New York: Kegan Paul International, 1994.

Naseef, Abdullah Omar, ed. *Today's Problems, Tomorrow's Solutions: The Future Structure of Muslim Societies.* London and New York: Mansell, 1988.

Nomani, Farhad, and Ali Rahnema. *Islamic Economic Systems.* London: Zed Books, 1994.

Numani, Muhammad Manzur. *Qur'ān Āp Se Kiyā Kehtā Hay?* Lucknow: Kutub Khana al-Qur'ān, 1960.

Parwez, Ghulam Ahmad. *Islam: A Challenge to Religion.* Lahore: N.p., 1968.

People's Party. *Islām awr Socialism.* N.p.: People's Party, n.d.

Phillips, C. S., ed. *The Evolution of India and Pakistan, 1858–1947.* London: Oxford University Press, 1962.

Pirzada, S. Sharifuddin. *Foundations of Pakistan: All India Muslim League Documents, 1906–1947.* Karachi: National Publishing House, 1969–70.

Qadri, Abdul Hamid. *Ishtirākiyyat awr Zirāatī Musāwāt.* Karachi: Dar al-Tasnif, n.d.

The Qur'ān. Karachi: Taj Company, Ltd., n.d.

Qureshi, I. H. *Pakistan: An Islamic Democracy.* Karachi: 1951.

———, et al. *The Problem of National Character.* Lahore: 1961.

Qutb, Muhammad. *Islam and Socialism.* Karachi: New Era Publications, n.d.

Rahman, Fazlur. "Economic Principles of Islam." *Islamic Studies* (March 1969).

———. "Implementation of the Islamic Concept of State in the Pakistani Milieu." *Islamic Studies* (September 1967).

———. *Islamic Methodology in History.* Karachi: Central Institute of Islamic Research, 1965.

———. "Some Reflections on the Reconstruction of Muslim Society in Pakistan." *Islamic Studies* (June 1967).

Rahman, Shaikh Mujibur. *6-Point Formula: Our Right to Live.* Dacca: Tajuddin Ahmad, Secretary, East Pakistan Awami League, March 23, 1966.

Rahmat Ali, Chaudhary. *What Does the Pakistan National Movement Stand For?* Cambridge: Cambridge University Press, 1942.

Ramey, Muhammad Hanif. *Iqbal awr Socialism.* Lahore: Jadid Press, 1970.

———. "Islāmī Socialism." *Nusrat* (September–October 1966).

Rashid, Ghulam Dastgir. *Islāmī Ishtirākiyyat.* Lahore: Al-Bayan, n.d., 8.

Rivlin, Benjamin, and Joseph S. Szyliowicz, eds. *The Contemporary Middle East: Tradition and Innovation.* New York: Random House, 1965.

Sandalwi, Muhammad Ishaq. *Tajdīd-i-Sabāiyyat.* Lahore: Matbuat Jamiyyat-i-Ulamā-i-Islam, n.d.

Sarker, Abdul Bari. *The Concept of Islamic Socialism.* Sylhet: Shahjalal Press, 1964.

Schroeder, Eric, trans. *Muhammad's People.* Portland, Me.: Bond Wheelright Co., 1955.

Shafi, Mufti Muhammad. "Bahth wa Nazar: Islāmī Qānūn awr Tamīr-i-Nau." *Chirāgh-i-Rāh* (July–August 1958): 270–73.

———. *Basic Principles of the Qur'ānic Constitution of the State.* Karachi: Dar al-Ulum, 1953.

———. *Congress awr Muslim League ke Mutaalliq Shar'ī Faysla.* N.p., n.d.

———. *Dār al-Ulūm.* Karachi: Dar al-Ulum, 1962.

———. *Distribution of Wealth in Islam.* Trans. Muhammad Hasan Askari and Karrar Husain. 7th ed. Karachi: Ashraf Publications, 1988.

———. *Islām kā Nizām-i-Taqsīm-i-Dawlat.* East Pakistan: Anjuman Ishaat-i-Islam, n.d.

———. *Mas'ala-i-Sūd.* Karachi, 1961.

———. *Rights of Non-Muslims under Islamic Law: A Supplement to the Qur'ānic Constitution of the State.* Karachi: Dar al-Ulum, n.d.

Shelley, Mizanur Rahman. *How to Build Pakistan into a Well-Knit Nation.* Dacca: Bureau of National Reconstruction, n.d.

Sherwani, Latif A., ed. *Pakistan Resolution to Pakistan.* Karachi: National Publishing House, 1969.

Sialkoti, Hakim Mahmud. *Mawdudi awr Jamhūriyyat.* Sialkot: Idara-i-Maarif-i-Islamiyya, May 1966.

Siddiqi, Kaukab. *Islam and Muslims in China.* Karachi: New Era Publications, [1968].

———. *Socialism and Democracy.* Karachi: New Era Publications, 1969.

———. *Socialism: The Peasant and the Land.* Karachi: New Era Publications, [1968].

Siddiqi, Naim. *Islām awr Shakhsī Milkiyyat.* Karachi: Maktaba Chiragh-i-Rah, October 1953.

Siddiqi, Shujaatullah. *Islam versus Democracy: Vis-à-vis Pakistan.* Karachi: Royal Book Co., 1992.

Siddiqui, Allama Allauddin. "Islam and National Outlook in Pakistan." In *Report on Seminar on the Greater National Integration.* Lahore: Government of West Pakistan, 1963.

Sigmund, Paul E., ed. *Ideologies of the Developing Nations.* New York: Praeger, 1967.

Socialism Kufr Hay: Akābir Ulamā kā Muttafiqa Faysla. Karachi: Nazim, Dawlat al-Haq, 1970.

Sultana, Abida. *Ahmadiyyat kiyā Hay awr Ahmadiyyūn ko Aqalliyyat Kiyūn Qarār Diyā Jāe?* [Lahore: N.p., 1974.]

Turabi, Hasan. *Islam, Democracy, the State and the West: A Round Table with*

Dr. Hasan Turabi, May 10, 1992. Ed. Arthur L. Lowrie. Tampa, Fla.: World and Islam Studies Enterprise, 1993.

Uthmani, Mawlana Shabbir Ahmad. *Hamarā Pakistan: Khutba-i-Sadārat, Muslim League Conference, Merath.* Lahore: Hashimi Book Depot, [1946].

———. *Mukalāma al-Sadarayn.* Lahore: Hashimi Book Depot, [1945].

———. *Payghām.* Lahore: Hashimi Book Depot, [1946].

Uthmani, Shaikh al-Islam Allama Shabbir Ahmad. *Payghām.* Lahore: Hashimi Book Depot, [1945].

Vahid, S. A., ed. *Thoughts and Reflections of Iqbal: A Collection of Miscellaneous Writings, Speeches and Press Statements of Iqbal.* Lahore: Sh. Muhammad Ashraf, 1964.

Waliallah, Shah. "Iqd al-Jīd fī Ahkām al-Ijtihād w' al-Taqlīd." Trans. M. Daud Rahbar in *Muslim World* (October 1955).

Williams, John Alden, ed. *Themes of Islamic Civilization.* Berkeley: University of California Press, 1971.

Zaman, Hassan, comp., and Syed Sajjad Husain, ed. *Pakistan: An Anthology.* Dacca: Society for Pakistani Studies, 1964.

Zaman, Mukhtar, ed. *Banking and Finance, Islamic Concept.* Karachi: International Association of Islamic Banks, 1993.

Zaman, Rafi-uz. *Pakistan Year Book, 1971.* Karachi: National Publishing House, 1971.

Zaman, Waheeduz, ed. *The Quest for Identity.* Islamabad: University of Islamabad Press, 1974.

B. JOURNALS, MAGAZINES, AND NEWSPAPERS

Asia (weekly), Lahore

Chatān (weekly), Lahore

Chirāgh-i-Rāh (monthly), Karachi

Concept of Pakistan (monthly), Dacca

Dawn (daily), Karachi

Hurriyyat (daily), Karachi

Islamic Studies (quarterly), Islamabad

Jang (daily), Karachi

Mashriq (daily), Lahore

Nusrat (weekly), Lahore

Pakistan Observer (daily), Dacca

Pakistan Times (daily), Lahore

Voice of Islam (monthly), Karachi

II. COMMENTARIES ON PAKISTAN AND ISLAM:
POLITICS, NATIONALISM, MODERNIZATION

Abecassis, David. *Identity, Islam, and Human Development in Rural Bangladesh.* Dhaka, Bangladesh: University Press, 1990.

Ahmed, Akbar S. *Pakistan Society: Islam, Ethnicity, and Leadership in South Asia.* Karachi and New York: Oxford University Press, 1986.

———. *Postmodernism and Islam: Predicament and Promise.* London: Routledge, 1992.

———. *Resistance and Control in Pakistan.* London and New York: Routledge, 1991.

Ahmed, Rafiuddin. *The Bengal Muslims, 1871–1906: A Quest for Identity.* 2nd ed. Delhi and New York: Oxford University Press, 1988.

Al-Azmeh, Aziz. *Islams and Modernities.* London: Verso, 1993.

Almond, Gabriel A., Emmanuel Sivan, and R. Scott Appleby. "Examining the Cases." In Martin E. Marty and Scott R. Appleby, eds., *Fundamentalisms Comprehended.* 445–82. Chicago: University of Chicago Press, 1995.

———. "Explaining Fundamentalisms." In Martin E. Marty and Scott R. Appleby, eds., *Fundamentalisms Comprehended.* 425–44. Chicago: University of Chicago Press, 1995.

———. "Fundamentalism: Genus and Species." In Martin E. Marty and Scott R. Appleby, eds., *Fundamentalisms Comprehended.* 399–424. Chicago: University of Chicago Press, 1995.

———. "Politics, Ethnicity, and Fundamentalism." In Martin E. Marty and Scott R. Appleby, eds., *Fundamentalisms Comprehended.* 483–504. Chicago: University of Chicago Press, 1995.

Anderson, Benedict. *Imagined Communities: Reflections on the Origins and Spread of Nationalism.* Rev. ed. London: Verso, 1983; repr., 1991.

Appleby, Scott. *Religious Fundamentalisms and Global Conflict.* Ithaca, N.Y.: Foreign Policy Association, 1994.

Apter, David E., ed. *Ideology and Discontent.* New York: Free Press, 1964.

Arjomand, Said Amir. "The Emergence of Islamic Political Ideologies." In James Beckford and Thomas Luckmann, eds., *The Changing Face of Religion.* 109–23. London: Sage Publications, 1989.

———. *The Turban for the Crown: The Islamic Revolution in Iran.* New York: Oxford University Press, 1988.

———. "Unity and Diversity in Islamic Fundamentalism." In Martin E. Marty and Scott R. Appleby, eds., *Fundamentalisms Comprehended.* 179–98. Chicago: University of Chicago Press, 1995.

Ayubi, Nazih. *Political Islam: Religion and Politics in the Arab World.* London: Routledge, 1991.

Bannerman, Patrick. *Islam in Perspective: A Guide to Islamic Society, Politics and Law.* London and New York: Routledge, 1988.

Banu, Razia Akter. *Islam in Bangladesh.* Leiden and New York: Brill, 1992.

Banuazizi, Ali, and Myron Weiner, eds. *The State, Religion, and Ethnic Politics: Afghanistan, Iran, and Pakistan.* Syracuse, N.Y.: Syracuse University Press, 1986.

Bell, Daniel. *The End of Ideology.* Rev. ed. Cambridge, Mass.: Harvard University Press, 1988.

Bina, Cyrus, and Hamid Zangeneh, eds. *Modern Capitalism and Islamic Ideology in Iran*. New York: St. Martin's Press, 1992.

Binder, Leonard. *Islamic Liberalism: A Critique of Development Ideologies*. Chicago: University of Chicago Press, 1988.

———. *Religion and Politics in Pakistan*. Berkeley: University of California Press, 1963.

Bindra, S. S. *Politics of Islamisation, with Special Reference to Pakistan*. New Delhi: Deep and Deep Publications, 1990.

Bruce, Steve, ed. *Religion and Modernization*. New York: Oxford University Press, 1992.

Bulliet, Richard W. *Islam: The View from the Edge*. New York: Columbia University Press, 1994.

———, ed. *Under Siege: Islam and Democracy: Proceedings of a Conference Held at Columbia University, June 18-19, 1993*. New York: Middle East Institute, Columbia University, 1994.

Burgat, Francois, and William Dowell. *The Islamic Movement in North Africa*. Austin: Center for Middle Eastern Studies, University of Texas at Austin, 1993.

Burke III, Edmund, and Ira M. Lapidus, eds. *Islam, Politics, and Social Movements*. Berkeley: University of California Press, 1988.

Butterworth, Charles E. "Political Islam: The Origins." *Annals of the American Academy of Political and Social Science* 524 (November 1992): 26-37.

Butterworth, Charles E., and William Zartman, eds. *Political Islam*. Newbury Park, Calif.: Sage Publications, 1992.

Choudhury, Masudul Alam, and Uzir Abdul Malik. *The Foundations of Islamic Political Economy*. New York: St. Martin's Press, 1992.

Choueiri, Yousef. *Islamic Fundamentalism*. Boston: Twayne Publishers, 1990.

Converse, Philip E. "The Nature of Belief Systems in Mass Publics." In David Apter, ed., *Ideology and Discontent*. New York: Free Press, 1964.

Dabashi, Hamid. "'Islamic Ideology': The Perils and Promises of a Neologism." In Hooshang Amirahmadi and Manoucher Parvin, eds., *Post-Revolutionary Iran*. 11-22. Boulder, Colo.: Westview Press, 1988.

Dessouki, Ali E. H., ed. *Islamic Resurgence in the Arab World*. New York: Praeger, 1982.

Deutsch, Karl W. *Nationalism and Social Communication*. 2nd ed. Cambridge, Mass.: MIT Press, 1966.

Eaton, Richard M. *The Rise of Islam and the Bengal Frontier, 1204-1760*. Berkeley: University of California Press, 1993.

Eisenstadt, S. N. "Fundamentalism, Phenomenology, and Comparative Dimensions." In Martin E. Marty and Scott R. Appleby, eds., *Fundamentalisms Comprehended*. 259-76. Chicago: University of Chicago Press, 1995.

Erikson, Erik. *Young Man Luther: A Study in Psychoanalysis and History*. London: 1958.

Esposito, John L. *Islam and Politics*. 3rd ed. Syracuse, N.Y.: Syracuse University Press, 1991.

———. *The Islamic Threat: Myth or Reality.* 2nd ed. New York: Oxford University Press, 1995.

———. "Political Islam: Beyond the Green Menace." *Current History* 20 (January 1994): 19–24.

———. "Tradition and Modernization in Islam." In Charles Wei-hsun Fu and Gerhard E. Spiegler, eds., *Movements and Issues in World Religions.* 89–106. Westport, Conn.: Greenwood Press, 1987.

Esposito, John L., and James P. Piscatori. "Democratization and Islam." *Middle East Journal* 45 (Summer 1991): 427–40.

Esposito, John L., and John O. Voll. *Islam and Democracy.* New York: Oxford University Press, 1996.

Ferdinand, Klaus, and Mehdi Mozaffari, eds. *Islam: State and Society.* London: Curzon Press; Riverdale, Md.: Riverdale Co., 1988.

Fuller, Graham E. *Islamic Fundamentalism in Pakistan: Its Character and Prospects.* Santa Monica, Calif.: RAND, 1991.

———. *Islamic Fundamentalism in the Northern Tier Countries: An Integrative View.* Santa Monica, Calif.: RAND, 1991.

Fuller, Graham E., and Ian O. Lesser. *A Sense of Siege: The Geopolitics of Islam and the West.* Boulder, Colo.: Westview Press, 1995.

Garvey, John. "Introduction: Fundamentalism and Politics." In Martin E. Marty and Scott Appleby, eds., *Fundamentalisms and the State: Remaking Polities, Economies, and Militance.* Chicago: University of Chicago Press, 1993.

Gellner, Ernest. "Fundamentalism as a Comprehensive System: Soviet Marxism and Islamic Fundamentalism Compared." In Martin E. Marty and Scott R. Appleby, eds., *Fundamentalisms Comprehended.* 277–87. Chicago: University of Chicago Press, 1995.

———. *Nations and Nationalism.* Ithaca, N.Y.: Cornell University Press, 1989.

———. *Postmodernism, Reason and Religion.* London: Routledge, 1992.

Gibb, H. A. R. *Studies on the Civilization of Islam.* Boston: Beacon Press, 1962.

Guazzone, Laura, ed. *The Islamist Dilemma: The Political Role of Islamist Movements in the Contemporary Arab World.* Reading, Berkshire, U.K.: Ithaca Press, 1995.

Haddad, Yvonne, and John Esposito, eds. *The Islamic Revival since 1988: A Critical Survey and Bibliography.* Westport, Conn.: Greenwood Press, 1997.

Haddad, Yvonne, John Voll, and John Esposito, eds. *The Contemporary Islamic Revival: A Critical Survey and Bibliography.* New York: Greenwood Press, 1991.

Halliday, Fred. *Islam and the Myth of Confrontation: Religion and Politics in the Middle East.* London: I. B. Tauris, 1996.

Halpern, Manfred. *The Politics of Social Change in the Middle East and North Africa.* Princeton, N.J.: Princeton University Press, 1963.

Humphreys, R. Stephen. "The Contemporary Resurgence in the Context of Modern Islam." In Ali E. H. Dessouki, ed., *Islamic Resurgence in the Arab World.* 67–81. New York: Praeger, 1982.

Hunter, Shireen T., ed. *The Politics of Islamic Revivalism: Diversity and Unity.* Bloomington: Indiana University Press, 1988.

Ibrahim, Mahmood. *Merchant Capital and Islam.* Austin: University of Texas Press, 1990.

Jomo, K. S., ed. *Islamic Economic Alternatives: Critical Perspectives and New Directions.* Houndmills, Hampshire, U.K.: Macmillan Academic and Professional, 1992.

Juergensmeyer, Mark. "Antifundamentalism." In Martin E. Marty and Scott R. Appleby, eds., *Fundamentalisms Comprehended.* 353–66. Chicago: University of Chicago Press, 1995.

———. *The New Cold War? Religious Nationalism Confronts the Secular State.* Berkeley: University of California Press, 1993.

Kaplan, Lawrence, ed. *Fundamentalism in Comparative Perspective.* Amherst: University of Massachusetts Press, 1992.

Keddie, Nikki R. *Iran and the Muslim World: Resistance and Revolution.* New York: New York University Press, 1995.

Kepel, Gilles. *The Revenge of God.* University Park: Pennsylvania State University Press, 1994.

Kimmens, Andrew C., ed. *Islamic Politics and the Modern World.* New York: H. W. Wilson Co., 1991.

Kramer, Martin. "Islam vs. Democracy." *Commentary* 95 (January 1993): 35–42.

Kuran, Timur. "The Discontents of Islamic Economic Morality." *American Economists Review* 86 (May 1996).

———. "The Economic Impact of Islamic Fundamentalism." In Martin E. Marty and Scott R. Appleby, eds., *Fundamentalisms and the State: Remaking Polities, Economies, and Militance.* 302–41. Chicago: University of Chicago Press, 1993.

———. "Islamic Economics and the Islamic Subeconomy." *Journal of Economic Perspectives* 9, no. 4 (Fall 1995).

Landau, Jacob. *The Politics of Pan-Islam: Ideology and Organization.* New York: Oxford University Press, 1990.

Lapidus, Ira M. "The Golden Age: The Political Concepts of Islam." *Annals of the American Academy of Political and Social Science* 524 (November 1992): 13–25.

Lawrence, Bruce. *Defenders of God.* San Francisco: Harper and Row, 1989.

Lerner, Daniel. *The Passing of Traditional Society.* London: Collier-Macmillan, Ltd., 1958.

Lewis, Bernard. *Emergence of Modern Turkey.* New York: Oxford University Press, 1965.

———. "Islam and Liberal Democracy." *Atlantic Monthly* (February 1993): 89–98.

———. *Middle East and the West.* London: Weidenfeld and Nicholson, 1964.

———. "Muslims, Christians, and Jews: The Dream of Coexistence." *New York Review of Books,* March 26, 1992, 49–50.

———. *The Political Language of Islam.* Chicago: University of Chicago Press, 1988.

Malik, Hafeez, ed. *Muslim Nationalism in India and Pakistan.* Washington, D.C.: Public Affairs Press, 1963.

Mannan, Muhammad Abdul. *Economic Development and Social Peace in Islam: An Analytical Study of the Process of Economic Development in the Muslim Community of Today (with an Account of Real-life Experiments in Bangladesh).* London: Ta Ha Publishers; Dhaka: Bangladesh Social Peace Foundation, 1990.

——. *Islamic Economics: Theory and Practice.* Boulder, Colo.: Westview Press, 1987.

Mannheim, Karl. *Man and Society in an Age of Reconstruction.* New York: Harcourt Brace, 1951.

Marty, Martin E. "Fundamentals of Fundamentalism." In Lawrence Kaplan, ed., *Fundamentalism in Comparative Perspective.* 15–23. Amherst: University of Massachusetts Press, 1992.

Marty, Martin E., and Scott R. Appleby, eds. *Accounting for Fundamentalisms: The Dynamic Character of Movements.* Chicago: University of Chicago Press, 1994.

——. *Fundamentalisms and Society: Reclaiming the Sciences, the Family, and Education.* Chicago: University of Chicago Press, 1993.

——. *Fundamentalisms and the State: Remaking Polities, Economies, and Militance.* Chicago: University of Chicago Press, 1993.

——. *Fundamentalisms Comprehended.* Chicago: University of Chicago Press, 1995.

——. *Fundamentalisms Observed.* Chicago: University of Chicago Press, 1991.

Mehdi, Rubya. *The Islamization of the Law in Pakistan.* Surrey: Curzon Press, 1994.

Mernissi, Fatima. *Islam and Democracy: Fear of the Modern World.* Trans. Mary Jo Lakeland. Reading, Mass.: Addison Wesley, 1992.

Mikhail, Hanna. *Politics and Revelation: Mawardi and After.* Edinburgh: Edinburgh University Press, 1995.

Moore, Clement H. "Islamic Banks: Financial and Political Intermediation in Arab Countries." *Orient* 29 (1988).

Munson, Henry. *Islam and Revolution in the Middle East.* New Haven, Conn.: Yale University Press, 1988.

Mutalib, Hussin, and Taj ul-Islam Hashmi, eds. *Islam, Muslims, and the Modern State: Case-Studies of Muslims in Thirteen Countries.* Houndmills, Hampshire, U.K.: Macmillan Press; New York: St. Martin's Press, 1994.

Naim, Abdullah A. *Toward an Islamic Reformation: Civil Liberties, Human Rights and International Law.* Syracuse, N.Y.: Syracuse University Press, 1990.

Nasr, Seyyed Hossein. *Traditional Islam and the Modern World.* London: Kegan Paul International, 1990.

Nasr, Seyyed Vali Reza. *The Vanguard of the Islamic Revolution: The Jama'at-i Islami of Pakistan.* Berkeley: University of California Press, 1994.

Nehme, Michel G. "Saudi Development Plans between Capitalist and Islamic Values." *Middle Eastern Studies* 30 (July 1994).

Noman, Omar. *The Political Economy of Pakistan 1947–85.* London and New York: KPI, 1988.

Perlmutter, Amos. "Wishful Thinking about Islamic Fundamentalism." *Washington Post,* 22 January 1992.

Piscatori, James P. "Accounting for Islamic Fundamentalisms." In Martin E. Marty and Scott R. Appleby, eds., *Accounting for Fundamentalisms.* 361–73. Chicago: University of Chicago Press, 1994.

———. *Islam in a World of Nation-States.* Cambridge and New York: Cambridge University Press, 1986.

Roff, William R., ed. *Islam and the Political Economy of Meaning: Comparative Studies of Muslim Discourse.* Berkeley: University of California Press, 1987.

Rosenthal, Franz. *The Muslim Concept of Freedom.* Leiden: 1960.

Rosenthal, J. *Islam in the Modern National State.* Cambridge: Cambridge University Press, 1965.

Roy, Olivier. *The Failure of Political Islam.* Trans. Carol Volk. Cambridge, Mass.: Harvard University Press, 1994.

Ruedy, John, ed. *Islamism and Secularism in North Africa.* New York: St. Martin's Press; Washington, D.C.: Center for Contemporary Arab Studies, Georgetown University, 1994.

Saeed, Javaid. *Islam and Modernization: A Comparative Analysis of Pakistan, Egypt, and Turkey.* Westport, Conn.: Praeger, 1994.

Sayeed, Khalid Bin. *Western Dominance and Political Islam: Challenge and Response.* Albany: State University of New York Press, 1995.

Schacht, Joseph. *An Introduction to Islamic Law.* Oxford: Oxford University Press, 1988.

Shaikh, Farzana, ed. *Islam and Islamic Groups: A Worldwide Reference Guide.* Harlow, Essex, U.K.: Longman Group UK, 1992.

Shils, Edward. "Ideology." In *Encyclopedia of Social Sciences,* vol. 7:68.

Sisk, Timothy D. *Islam and Democracy: Religion, Politics, and Power in the Middle East.* Washington, D.C.: United States Institute of Peace, 1992.

Sivan, Emmanuel. "The Enclave Culture." In Martin E. Marty and Scott R. Appleby, eds., *Fundamentalisms Comprehended.* 11–70. Chicago: University of Chicago Press, 1995.

———. "The Islamic Resurgence: Civil Society Strikes Back." In Lawrence Kaplan, ed., *Fundamentalism in Comparative Perspective.* 96–108. Amherst: University of Massachusetts Press, 1992.

Smith, Donald Eugene. *India as a Secular State.* Princeton, N.J.: Princeton University Press, 1967.

Smith, Wilfred. *Modern Islam in India.* Repr. of 1946 ed. Lahore: Shaikh Muhammad Ashraf, 1963.

Snyder, Louis L. "Introduction." In *Encyclopedia of Nationalism.* Saint Paul, Minn.: Paragon House Publishers, 1990.

——, ed. *The Dynamics of Nationalism: Readings in Its Meaning and Development.* Princeton, N.J.: D. van Nostrand-Reinhold, 1964.

Taylor, Alan R. *The Islamic Question in Middle East Politics.* Boulder, Colo.: Westview Press, 1988.

Titus, Murray T. *Islam in India and Pakistan.* Karachi: Royal Book Co. Repr., 1990.

Tritton, A. S. *The Caliphs and Their Non-Muslim Subjects.* London: F. Cass, 1950.

Veer, Peter Van Der. *Religious Nationalism: Hindus and Muslims in India.* Berkeley: University of California Press, 1994.

Voll, John O. "Fundamentalism in the Sunni Arab World." In Martin E. Marty and Scott R. Appleby, eds., *Fundamentalisms Observed.* 345–402. Chicago: University of Chicago Press, 1991.

——. *Islam: Continuity and Change in the Modern World.* 2nd ed. Syracuse, N.Y.: Syracuse University Press, 1994.

von Grunebaum, Gustave E. *Medieval Islam.* 2nd ed. Chicago: University of Chicago Press, 1954; repr., Westport, Conn.: Greenwood Publishing Company, 1983.

——. *Modern Islam.* New York: Vintage Books, 1962; repr., Westport, Conn.: Greenwood Publishing Company, 1983.

Watt, Montgomery. *Islamic Fundamentalism and Modernity.* London: Routledge, 1988.

Weinbaum, Marvin. *Pakistan and Afghanistan: Resistance to Reconstruction.* Boulder, Colo.: Westview Press, 1994.

Weiner, Myron, and Ali Banuazizi. *The Politics of Social Transformation in Afghanistan, Iran and Pakistan.* Syracuse, N.Y.: Syracuse University Press, 1994.

Weiss, Anita, ed. *Islamic Reassertion in Pakistan.* Syracuse, N.Y.: Syracuse University Press, 1986.

Williams, Rhys H. "Movement Dynamics and Social Change: Transforming Fundamentalist Ideology and Organizations." In Martin E. Marty and Scott R. Appleby, eds., *Accounting for Fundamentalisms.* 785–834. Chicago: University of Chicago Press, 1994.

Wright, Robin B. *Sacred Rage: The Wrath of Militant Islam.* Robin Wright. Rev. ed. New York: Simon and Schuster, 1986.

Zakaria, Rafiq. *The Struggle within Islam: The Conflict between Religion and Politics.* London: Penguin, 1989.

Zartman, I. William. "Democracy and Islam: The Cultural Dialectic." *Annals of the American Academy of Political and Social Science* 524 (November 1992): 181–91.

Zuckerman, Morton. "Beware of Religious Stalinist." *U.S. News and World Report,* March 22, 1993, 80.

Index

Lightning Source UK Ltd.
Milton Keynes UK
UKHW010038100619
344035UK00001B/181/P